W9-BJU-101

Autism ... What Does It Mean to Me?

A workbook for self-awareness and self-advocacy, with life lessons for young people on the autism spectrum

Structured teaching ideas for home and school

Catherine Faherty

Foreword by Dr Gary Mesibov, former director of Division TEACCH, University of North Carolina

Autism ... What Does It Mean to Me?

All marketing and publishing rights guaranteed to and reserved by:

FUTURE HORIZONS INC.

721 W. Abram Street

Arlington, TX 76013

(800) 489-0727

(817) 277-0727

(817) 277-2270 (fax)

E-mail: *info@fhautism.com*

www.fhautism.com

©2014 Catherine Faherty

Cover and interior design, John Yacio III and Catherine Faherty

All rights reserved.

Printed in the United States of America.

No part of this product may be reproduced in any manner whatsoever without written permission of Future Horizons, Inc, except in the case of brief quotations embodied in reviews.

ISBN: 9781935274919

Dedicated to the autistic community, whose time has come.

"We should acknowledge differences; we should greet differences, until difference makes no difference anymore."

—Adela A. Allen

Contents

Chapter 3: Ways of Thinking 67

Chapter 4: Talent and Creative Expression 115

Chapter 5: People 135

Chapter 6: Understanding 165

Chapter 9: School 259

Chapter 10: Friends

Chapter 11: Feeling Upset 385

Chapter 12: Happiness—A Feeling of Well-Being .. 425

Foreword

It was a personal thrill for me to introduce the first edition of this wonderful book by Catherine Faherty, and I feel privileged to be invited to introduce the revision. As I predicted, the first edition was a great success, thanks to Catherine's creativity, intelligence, keen observational skills, remarkable clinical ability, and her knack for understanding what it's like to have an autism spectrum disorder (ASD). Catherine brings the same skill set and depth of understanding to this revision, and this second edition is even better than the first.

Since the first edition was published in 2000, Catherine has received feedback from all over the world, from readers who have used ideas from the first edition of this book to improve their work with children with ASD. Catherine is a marvelous listener and is totally nondefensive and open to suggestions and new ideas, and this revision includes many ideas based on feedback from others. In addition, Catherine continues her active involvement in the field, and this revision also reflects many changes that have occurred in the field and in her personal work since the original book was published.

The book is a superb combination of the format that was so successful in the first addition, plus some excellent new material. One of the important changes in this book is the workbook section that accompanies most of the chapters. This is designed to make the book more accessible to older children, teenagers, and adults with ASD. This meets an important need in the field that has grown substantially in the past decade, with more and younger children with ASD growing up and many older people receiving a diagnosis of ASD as adults and wanting to learn more about what it means and to understand themselves better. These new workbook sections meet the needs of the older group very effectively.

Another change to the book that reflects the differences between today and a decade ago is the greater recognition that people with ASD are more aware of their shortcomings than professionals had perceived previously, and this greater awareness has led to an increase in depression among this group. Teachers, parents, and others who work with these youngsters have had trouble addressing this depression, as have the youngsters with ASD themselves. The section of this revision on happiness will provide many terrific ideas and suggestions for those working with this population. It is well designed for the needs and skills of people with ASD who are seeking a better and more positive life experience.

Another change in the field, which is a good thing in many ways, is that there is much more information about ASD than ever before. The downside of this development is that the information is often confusing and is not always consistent or clear. Catherine's ability to present a clear, accurate, sensible, and understandable approach to what ASD is, how to understand it, and how to help those with ASD will be of great benefit to those with on the spectrum, as well as to their family members, communities, teachers, and anyone else who comes into contact with them.

For those who have read the first book, I am sure you will appreciate how this revision reminds you of Catherine's amazing insights and sensitivity to people on the spectrum. I'm sure you will find this edition to be inspiring and invigorating, in the same way the first book was for you. You will also find enough new ideas and suggestions to help you move ahead in your important work. For those of you who are being exposed to Catherine's ideas for the first time, I think you will find the same excitement that so many readers of the first edition found as they learned about her many creative insights and strategies and her unique way of understanding, accepting, and helping people with ASD to grow. Most of the readers of this book fully realize that some people dwell on the differences that often make it harder for those with ASD to fit in to our society as it operates today, and although Catherine does not ignore this aspect, her primary emphasis is on how to understand and accept the differences and celebrate the diversity that those on the spectrum bring to our society. This approach is quite uplifting and leads to many practical and important insights and ways to be more effective in helping them to live fuller, richer, and happier lives.

Gary B. Mesibov, PhD

Professor Emeritus, University of North Carolina at Chapel Hill

Preface

Margaret Mead wrote the following: "If we are to achieve a richer culture, we must recognize the whole gamut of human potentialities, and so weave a less arbitrary social fabric, one in which each diverse gift will find a fitting place."

"A fitting place" for each. What a wonderful and essential gift for a child, to have the knowledge while growing up that each of us has a place where we fit! Each of us, in all our diversity, is the perfect expression of a unique self.

From my years of knowing and working with people who did not receive a diagnosis until adulthood, I learned of the painful breach that grows inside children with autism during early childhood. What if you did not see yourself reflected in the world around you? Children with autism have the added plight of having differences that are "invisible" on the outside. Most kids with autism look like their typically developing peers, so behavioral and social differences are not easily or obviously explained to the mainstream community by something like a visible "handicap." I have witnessed miraculous relief when these adults finally got real answers—when they realized that it was being autistic that was the pervasive missing link in their lifelong yearning for self-understanding—and that it doesn't mean something is "wrong."

At the time I wrote the first edition of this book, in the late 1990s, I suggested that autism is a way of being, and I gave readers an autism-friendly way to explore what this means. At that time, it was considered a novel—even radical—idea to tell a child about his or her diagnosis. The parents of these children never imagined they would be in the position of parenting a child who turned out to be so different from what they expected. And, how do you explain something to your own child, whom you don't even understand yourself—especially as you struggle with your own conflicting emotions? Most often, the subject was simply avoided. That's where this book fit in.

I wanted to offer young people and those who care about them a way to understand themselves (and each another) in a calm, nonjudgmental, factual, and reassuring manner. Many positive reviews from teachers, parents, and children, along with the workbook's popularity, suggest that it is serving its purpose! Now, 14 years later, I have examined and evaluated every single page— omitting, revising, and expanding most of the chapters. I am pleased to present new workbook pages that target older children, teenagers, and interested adults. And, I am delighted to finally offer a brand new chapter on happiness.

I admit that another purpose in writing this book initially as a simple guide for children was to create something easily accessible for parents, teachers, grandparents, aunts, uncles, cousins, neighbors, landlords, priests, rabbis, swimming instructors, summer camp counselors, librarians, and others to use to educate the community about autism in simple, clear language. These days, with the media onslaught of theories on causes and cures, I feel it is vital to present both autistic and typically developing members of society with this book. It represents a sensible, calm, and personal approach, based on acknowledgment, acceptance, and celebration of diversity.

How is this book organized?

Take a few moments to look at the Table of Contents. You will see there are 12 chapters. Chapter 1 introduces the term *autism* and explains the ways you and the reader will be writing in the workbook. The subsequent chapters each focus on an important aspect of life (ie, communication, understanding, and friends).

Most chapters are divided into three parts. The first section is referred to as "the Workbook," which is usually followed by supplementary workbook pages, titled, "Especially for Older Readers." The final section of each chapter is titled, "For Parents, Teachers, and Therapists." Individual topics are listed by page number for easy reference in the Table of Contents.

Prior to beginning the book with your child, preview it on your own, so you know what to expect.

The Workbook

The workbook pages are for you and your child to read together and fill in, mark, or circle the relevant information. Suggestions about this process for parents are included in chapter 1 on pages 24-28. Most chapters feature a section written specifically for older children and teenagers, although the content is relevant for adults, as well. The workbook pages are found easily by the dark labels on the outer edge of each workbook page.

The workbook presents ordinary circumstances of everyday life, sometimes pointing out typical behaviors of autistic children and their typically developing peers. It suggests in simple terms how and why the reader's experience may sometimes differ from others' experiences. With the help of a parent, teacher, or friend, the young reader is encouraged to add personal details, individualizing the information on the pages. In this way, the workbook will come to more accurately represent each reader's uniqueness.

On some of the workbook pages, the young reader may be introduced to ideas or strategies that require the cooperation of his family or school personnel. The information in the workbook is for parents, teachers, and therapists, too! In most cases, details about the strategies are provided in the corresponding sections for parents, teachers, and therapists in the last part of each chapter.

For Parents, Teachers, and Therapists

The last part of each chapter has been written specifically for parents, teachers, therapists, and other significant adults in a child's life. This part supplements the workbook pages with related concepts, ideas, and practical suggestions for home, school, and community.

Some of the ideas, such as schedules, work systems, visual cues, and the social level assessment, are examples of widely used TEACCH (Treatment and Education of Autistic and related Communication-handicapped Children) structured teaching strategies that I and the other therapists, teachers, directors, and parents in the TEACCH program have developed and adapted for individual children and adults during the course of the TEACCH program's existence. Other ideas are the inspired work of prominent colleagues in the field of autism (credit is given when these are presented); while my own ideas and creativity, based on my extensive experience, fill the pages of this book.

Who wrote the workbook, anyway?

In the text of the workbook pages, you will notice frequent use of the first-person pronoun "I." My intent is not to pretend that I am an autistic person. In fact, in earlier versions I had written before the book was published, I wrote the workbook pages in the usual expected style, using the second-person pronouns "you" and "your," where appropriate. However, several children and adults said that when they read the word "you," they weren't sure if it meant them, or if it meant ME, the literal interpretation of YOU! Consequently, I made the decision to write the workbook in the first person, using "I" instead of the pronoun "you." My intent in writing in the first-person point of view is to provide clarity for the reader.

Keys to keep in mind when using the ideas in this book

The first step is to try to see life through your child's eyes. Strive to give meaning to the environment and the everyday activities he encounters from his perspective. The most effective strategies are always those that you individualize for your child.

Provide Meaning

Use strategies that are visual and easy for him to understand. Provide a sense of order, familiarity, and clarity. Take your cue from your child's strengths and interests. Make things meaningful from his point of view.

When an event or a situation has meaning, anxiety and all sorts of undesirable behaviors frequently fall away. Most important, learning is free to take place when a child's activities and the environment around him make sense. Most people, young and old, autistic and typically developing, are happier when things make sense. We are at peace when our lives have meaning.

Individualize the Strategies

When visually structured strategies are tried, there is almost always an immediate, positive effect. However, the most exciting, ongoing results occur when the basic strategies are fine-tuned to fit the individual.

Obviously, I do not know your child. Though you might find an idea in this book that will work exactly as described, it is more likely that you will need to make it fit your child and his particular circumstance. Try it, observe what happens, adapt accordingly, try it again, see how it works, adapt again, try it again, and so on. The "right" strategies and the "right" adaptations become apparent as you proceed. Your child will show you what works and what needs changing through his successes and his frustrations.

Every child, family, and classroom is unique. The process of assessment, structuring, reassessment, and adaptation, referred to by TEACCH as *restructuring*, allows for the merging of your experience with, intuition about, and knowledge of your child with objective observations.

There is no single recipe that works for everyone. Real effectiveness of the structured teaching strategies presented in this book depends on our ability to individualize the strategies for one person.

Chapter 1
Introduction

Workbook

I Might Have Questions

This book can help me understand myself better. Learning about autism may help me understand myself better.

I will (circle) the questions that I have:

▶ What does autism mean?

▶ Is there something wrong with me?

▶ Am I the only one like this?

▶ Isn't everyone like me?

▶ Are there other people like me?

▶ Whom should I tell about this?

I might not have any questions. That is OK. But, if I have more questions, I can write them on the next page, or I can have someone write them for me, or I can type them on my tablet or computer.

If I have more questions, I can write them here. This book may help answer my questions.

I might not have questions now, but if I have some later, I can turn to this page and write them here.

1. _____ ?

2. _____ ?

3. _____ ?

4. _____ ?

5. _____ ?

6. _____ ?

7. _____ ?

8. _____ ?

9. _____ ?

10. _____ ?

11. _____ ?

12. _____ ?

Reading This Book

I may read this book with my parent, teacher, therapist, or other adult. I will start by reading this book with:

- ♦ my parent

- ♦ my teacher

- ♦ someone else: _____

📖 Later, I can read it by myself. There might be certain pages I like. Sometimes my parent, teacher, or therapist might want to read a page with me again.

Other people might like to read this book, too. I might show this book to one or more of these people:

- ♦ my grandparent

- ♦ my aunt and/or uncle

- ♦ my brother or sister

- ♦ my cousin

- ♦ my friend

- ♦ my teacher and/or therapist

- ♦ someone else: _____

This Is a Workbook

This is a workbook. It is OK to write on the pages. There are places to mark things, blank lines to write on, and things to circle.

Every page has a number at the bottom. After reading a page, I may think about what I read. If there is something I want to remember, or if the page is important to me, I can draw a circle around the page number on the dotted line, like this:

When I have finished reading this book, all of the page numbers that are circled will mark the pages that are important to me.

These pages may help other people understand me better.

Writing in This Book

Some pages in this book have things to read and mark. There might be blank lines to write on or sentences to mark with a pen or pencil.

> The directions usually say:
>
> **I will** circle **or** highlight **what is true for me.**
>
> Or, sometimes the directions might say:
>
> **I will mark what is true for me.**

In this book, **mark** means to **highlight** or circle.

We can **mark** the pages of this book with a colored highlighter pen ...

highlighting through the words like this.

or, we can **mark** with a regular pen or pencil, like this ...

circling or drawing a line around the words

Practice Marking What Is True

Different things are true for different people. Every person who has a workbook like this might mark different things.

This page is for me to practice filling in the blank lines and marking what is true for me. I will only mark or write things that are true for me. If the statement is not true for me, I will not mark it.

I will circle or highlight what is true for me. 🖊

▶ I am a boy.

▶ I am a girl.

▶ I am one million years old.

▶ I am ten years old.

▶ I am _____ years old.

▶ I live in North Carolina.

▶ I live in the USA. I live in the state of.

▶ I do not live in the USA. I live in .

▶ I like to eat pizza.

▶ I do not like to swim.

▶ I like to swim.

▶ I do not have a sister.

▶ I have a sister.

▶ The name of a person who lives with me is _____ .

▶ Sometimes I have fun doing this: _____ _____ _____ .

Practice Page

My parent, teacher, or therapist can prepare this practice page by writing sentences on the blank lines. Some are true for me, and some are not true for me.

I will circle or highlight what is true for me. 🖊

▶ I like to read.

▶ I do not like to read.

▶ I have a sister.

▶ I have a brother.

▶ I am the oldest child in my family.

▶ I am the youngest child in my family.

▶ _____

▶ _____

▶ _____

▶ _____

▶ _____

▶ _____

▶ _____

▶ _____

▶ _____

▶ _____

▶ _____

Introducing Me

My name is _____ .

My birthday is _____ .

Today's date is _____ .

I will draw a picture (or tape a photo) of myself here.

Strengths and Talents

Everyone has strengths and talents. My strengths and talents are things that I can do well and enjoy doing.

I will circle **or** highlight **what is true for me.** ✐

My strengths or talents are:

▶ Reading

▶ Spelling

▶ Alphabetizing

▶ Handwriting or doing calligraphy

▶ Speaking foreign languages

▶ Drawing or painting

▶ Using computers

▶ Doing addition or subtraction

▶ Doing multiplication or division

▶ Finding things that match

▶ Remembering facts

▶ Putting things in numerical order

▶ Playing a musical instrument

▶ Knowing facts about:

   _____

▶ Singing with perfect pitch

▶ Seeing/noticing patterns

▶ Remembering how things look

▶ Writing stories or poetry

▶ Doing photography

▶ Sports

▶ Cooking or baking

▶ Cleaning

▶ Straightening up

▶ Putting things in order

▶ Doing drama

▶ Doing mechanical projects

▶ Constructing things

▶ Understanding animals

▶ Sewing, knitting, or weaving

▶ Doing algebra

▶ Other: _____

▶ Other: _____

Autism Is Another Thing about Me

Another thing about me is that I am autistic. Or, I might say I am a person with autism.

In this book, we use the word *autism*, but other words for autism are:

▶ Autism spectrum disorder, or ASD

▶ Autism spectrum difference*

▶ "On the spectrum" or just "spectrum"

▶ Asperger's syndrome or just "Asperger's"

▶ High-functioning autism

▶ Pervasive developmental disorder, or PDD

▶ Pervasive developmental disorder—not otherwise specified, or PDD-NOS

▶ Another term: _____

On the list above, my parent will circle **or** highlight **the terms that have been used with me.** ✏

---

* The author informally prefers to say that ASD stands for "autism spectrum difference" instead of "autism spectrum disorder." She feels that a helpful way to understand autism is that it is a difference—one way of being—rather than a disorder.

What Is Autism?

Autism is invisible. No one can see autism. It is one of the things that make me who I am. This book will explain what is different and unique about autism.

Autism has to do with my brain. The brain is like a computer, which is always on and keeps people living and learning. Brains with autism sometimes work differently than non-autistic brains.

Having an autistic brain is like having a computer with an Autism Operating System (AOS), while most other people have a Plain Operating System (POS).*

Autism makes me experience the world in a certain way. Sometimes it's the same as other people, but sometimes I experience the world very differently.

Autism is a way of thinking and being.

Older readers may want to read about neurodiversity on page 18.

---

* The Autism Operating System analogy was created by Ellen Tanis, the mother of a boy with Asperger's syndrome. She suggested to her son that perhaps he had an ASOS (Asperger's Syndrome Operating System), while other people have a POS (Plain Operating System). Ms Tanis's delightful essay was published on page 15 of the Fall 1996 issue of "The Morning News," a publication by Carol Gray that is now out of print. Thank you to Ellen for giving permission to include this here.

Why Autism?

No one really knows why some people are not autistic and some people are autistic. But, here are some facts:

- Autism is not an illness or a disease, and it does not mean I am wrong or bad.

- Sometimes it appears to be genetic. This means that sometimes parents, cousins, uncles, aunts, brothers, sisters, or other family members might be autistic, too.

- At the time of this writing, for every 88 people in the world, there is one autistic person. (Go to page 436 to estimate how many autistic people are in your city, state, or country.)

There are many different ways of being in the world. Autism is one way of thinking and being.

Introduction

Was I Born with Autism?

My parent and I can fill in the spaces below. ✎

When I was born, my parent(s) did not know about autism and me. No one knows if a newborn baby is autistic.

My parent(s) first thought that there might be something different about me when I was _____ years old, but they still did not know about autism. They loved me very much, and they did not understand why I …

_____

_____

_____

_____

My parent(s) found out about autism when I was _____ years old. Then they understood me better. They kept on loving me very much.

Now, I know about me being autistic. I am _____ years old. My parent(s) gave me this book to help me understand myself better. They want me to know that I am perfect being me!

Older readers may want to read about neurodiversity on page 18.

Especially for Older Readers

The previous topics in this chapter are relevant when individually selected for older children, teenagers, and—in some cases—adults. Supplementary information *specifically* for older readers is provided on the following pages.

This section provides an introduction to self-knowledge, the concept of neurodiversity, and self-identifying language related to autism. It provides opportunities for self-reflection and self-advocacy about what is personally meaningful.

> If this is the first time you are thinking a lot about autism, then you may want to skip this section and return to it when you have read more of this book.

Chapter 1

Self-Knowledge

As people grow from childhood to adolescence to adulthood, they naturally learn more about themselves. The result of "getting to know yourself" is called self-knowledge. This process continues throughout life.

People learn about their strengths, skills, and talents. They learn about their challenges. They may notice how they react in different situations. They may observe how they feel and what they think. They may learn how to communicate clearly and how to understand others better.

They may learn how to live a good life, even when there are difficulties and challenges. They may learn to ask for help and offer help to others. They may discover their unique purpose in life. The process of self-knowledge continues throughout a person's entire life.

I may <u>underline</u> the sentences that interest me in the paragraphs above. Below, I will circle or highlight what is true for me. ✐

- ▶ I would like to learn more about myself.

- ▶ I would like to understand myself better.

- ▶ I would like other people to understand me better.

- ▶ I would like to understand other people better.

- ▶ I may be interested in the topic of self-knowledge.

- ▶ I am not very interested in learning about myself.

- ▶ Other: _____.

Autism and Self-Knowledge

Self-knowledge for people who have discovered autism includes learning about the autism spectrum. One good way to learn more is by reading blogs and books written by autistic authors. Another way is reading books (like this one) by non-autistic authors who work in partnership with autistic people.

Many people on the spectrum find that it helps them learn more about themselves by meeting, connecting, and communicating with other autistic people. This can be done in person or online.

I will (circle) or highlight what is true for me. 🖉

- I would like to know more about autism and/or Asperger's syndrome.

I will <u>underline</u> the ways that I would like to get more information: 🖉

- ▶ Read books by autistic authors.
- ▶ Read blogs by autistic bloggers.
- ▶ Go to Internet sites like ASAN (*autisticadvocacy.org*).
- ▶ Meet other autistic people in person.
- ▶ Meet other autistic people online.
- ▶ Watch videos.

- ▶ Keep reading this book.
- ▶ Another way: _____
  _____ .

- ▶ I don't want to learn more about autism now, but maybe later.

- ▶ I am not interested in autism now, but I do want to know more about myself.

- ▶ Other: _____
  _____
  _____ .

Chapter 1

Neurodiversity

All people have their own brain, which keeps them living, growing, thinking, and learning. Each brain is different and unique. That's one of the reasons why people are different from each other. Some people use the term *neurodiversity* to describe this fact.

The word *neurodiversity* is made up of two smaller words: *neuro* and *diversity*. The term *neuro* refers to the functioning of the brain and the nervous system, which is controlled by the brain. The term *diversity* is related to the fact that there is variety among humans, and, with all our differences, we are all members of the human race.

The idea of *neurodiversity* is to promote acceptance and the understanding that each child and adult is an individual, with differences in how they think, learn, grow, and live … and that we are all are equals in society. This book promotes the idea of neurodiversity because it helps readers understand more about themselves and that it is perfectly okay (and wonderful) to be who they are! This book helps people learn to appreciate and celebrate the ways that the reader—and all people—are different and unique.

I will (circle) or highlight what is true for me. 🖉

▶ I want to feel okay about my brain.

▶ I want to feel okay about autism.

▶ Sometimes I like the way my brain works.

▶ Sometimes I don't like the way my brain works.

▶ Neurodiversity is a new idea for me.

▶ I don't understand what *neurodiversity* means.

▶ The idea of neurodiversity is good.

▶ What does it mean to celebrate being different and unique?

▶ I want to talk with someone or write about neurodiversity.

▶ I want to talk with _____ (person) about this.

▶ I don't know whom to talk with about this.

▶ Other: _____.

The Wording for Me and Autism: "Identity First"

The words we choose to use help us communicate what is true for us. Combinations of words are referred to as *wording*. Some children and adults prefer a certain *wording* when they talk or write about themselves and autism. Some people like to hear and to use the word *autistic*.

They feel that being autistic is important to who they are. It is how they think and communicate and how they understand the world and other people. They may enjoy learning about autism. They may like reading about and being with other autistic people. They want others to know that they are proud of being who they are—an autistic person. They choose to say (and like to hear) the wording on this list:

▶ He is autistic.

▶ He is an autistic boy (or man).

▶ She is autistic.

▶ She is an autistic girl (or woman).

▶ I am autistic.

▶ I am an autistic person (or girl, boy, woman, or man).

▶ I am an Aspie.

▶ Aspies are awesome!

▶ Autistic people are awesome!

If I like any of those sentences above, I will circle or highlight the ones I like to hear, or say, or write. I will <u>underline</u> the ones that describe me. 🖉

This wording is referred to as *identity first,* because the first, most important word has to do with an autistic identity. Children, teens, and adults who like "identity first" wording feel that autism cannot be separated from who they are.

There is more information about wording on the next page.

More about the Wording for Me and Autism: "Person First"

Some people believe that autism is a part of who they are, but that *it is not necessarily an important part of who they are.* They may think of autism as separate from their real selves. They may not want people to think of them as autistic or as an Aspie. They prefer hearing and saying statements such as the ones in the list below. Notice that the word "with" separates the person from the autism, ASD, or Asperger's syndrome.

▶ She (or he) is a person with autism.

▶ She (or he) is a person with ASD.

▶ She (or he) is a person with Asperger's.

▶ I am a person with autism.

▶ I am a person with ASD.

▶ I am a person with Asperger's.

▶ People with autism are awesome!

▶ People with Asperger's are awesome!

If I prefer any of those sentences above, I will circle the ones I like to hear, or say, or write. I will underline the ones that describe me. 🖊

The wording on this list is referred to as *person first* because the words "person with" come before the word "autism." People who like this wording may feel that autism isn't really important or that it is something separate from their real selves.

There is more information about wording on the next page.

The Wording Doesn't Matter to Me

Some people don't care about the wording. It doesn't matter to them if someone says, "She is autistic" or "She is a person with autism." It doesn't matter to them if someone says, "He is autistic" or "He is a person with autism."

Or, they may not understand the difference between the types of wording: "Identity first" or "Person first."

I will circle or highlight what is true for me. 🖉

▶ It doesn't matter to me which wording is used to describe me.

▶ I don't care.

▶ I really don't understand the differences in the wording.

▶ I want more time to think about this.

▶ I want to understand the difference.

▶ I don't know which wording I like best.

▶ I like some of the wording on the lists on pages 20 and 21.

▶ I don't care about the wording on the lists on pages 20 and 21.

▶ I don't know which wording I like, but I might decide in the future.

▶ I want to read about this again later, on another day.

▶ I want to talk about this with someone I trust.

▶ I want to talk about this with a parent or teacher or therapist.

▶ I want to communicate in writing about this with (name)

_____.

▶ I don't want to decide which wording I like best.

▶ I am awesome … no matter what wording is used for me!

▶ This is confusing.

▶ It's really not important to me right now.

▶ Other: _____.

For Parents, Teachers, and Therapists

An introductory message from an autistic adult:

> As a person with autism that went undiagnosed until age 46, I have watched with gratitude as the body of knowledge concerning autism has grown in recent years. Not only are there many more books describing autism from an academic, medical, or parental perspective, but there are also an increasing number of autistic people who are adding their own views, experiences, and insights to the available literature. This book offers another approach to furthering the understanding of autism—that of encouraging autistic children to learn more about themselves and guiding them through a journey of self-discovery. The workbook is a valuable resource for autistic children's awareness and understanding of their natures, as well as a boost for their self-esteem. Such a book could have been very helpful to me and my family when I was a child.
>
> ***With best wishes,***
> **Dave Spicer,**
> **Asheville, North Carolina**

The introductory workbook acknowledged that the reader has heard about "autism" or a related diagnostic term. It set the tone for the workbook and helped the adult helper assess the child's ability to accurately describe himself by marking what is true. Older readers were introduced to the concept of self-knowledge, diversity, and the language of "identity first" versus "person first."

Ideas in This Chapter:

☑ Marking what is true

☑ The workbook requires your partnership and guidance

☑ What if the young reader wants to mark all the options or won't mark any of them?

☑ Have the reader underline with a strip of paper to help focus

☑ Pick and choose which pages to read

☑ How to tell?

☑ Language: "person first" and "identity first"

Marking what is true

Many children may not be able to identify, from a list of qualities, opinions, or descriptions, the things that apply to themselves. On the other hand, there are children and adolescents who, with teaching, practice, repetition, and encouragement, will easily participate in marking and filling in accurate and insightful information.

Keep a pen, pencil, or highlighter available to use for the workbook pages.

The workbook requires your partnership and guidance

This workbook is intended to be completed with guidance, if needed. Because of the wide range of abilities and skills in workbook users, the level and amount of support and direction that is needed will vary from person to person. In addition, much of the information presented on the workbook pages is meant for support people, as well.

What if the young reader wants to mark all the options or won't mark any of them?

To help determine whether a reader can accurately mark what is true, the first workbook chapter contains concrete instructions and practice pages. Use these pages as an assessment and teaching tool. You can refer back to them as needed, during the reading of the book. Some children may still routinely and indiscriminately continue to mark all the options as they progress through the book. Or, they may revert to marking all the options when they come across information they do not comprehend. Some children insist upon marking what they perceive as the correct answers, whether or not they are really true. If your child has difficulty marking what is really true for him, you can try one or more of these suggestions:

☑ **You can highlight ahead of time.**

Before reading the book with your child, go through the lists with a highlighter and highlight the items you know to be absolutely true about him. Then, as you read the book together, he can circle what is highlighted. *If you do this, be very careful to only highlight what you are absolutely sure of.* Even if you are leaving some options blank that may be true (but you aren't positive), it is better to leave them blank than to "put words in his mouth" that may not really be true for him.

☑ **Let him leave all the choices blank.**

Even if this book is read without marking anything, there is still enough critical information on any one page for a reader to benefit. Perhaps, as your child matures, he may develop his ability to self-reflect. Later on, he can mark what is true.

☑ Let him mark all the options, if he insists.

The important thing is that he is interested in the book. You can read the book together again later. Before the second reading, you can mark what you know to be true about your child. If he has circled, you can mark with a highlighter. If he has highlighted, you can circle. During the second reading, he will notice what you have marked.

Keep in mind that you should only mark what you are absolutely sure of.

☑ Use the blank line, next to "Other:_____ ."

At the bottom of most of the lists, a line labeled "other" has been left blank. Use this line in a way that is most helpful for your child. You can fill in what you know to be true, or it can be left blank. Your child might suggest what you should write, or he might write it himself. Then, it can be circled or highlighted, in the same way as the others. If there is no blank line, but there is something that is true for your child that was not listed, you can simply draw a blank line, write what is true, and then circle or highlight it.

☑ Talk about the lists under "what is true for me."

Start a dialogue and help your child understand if and how the relevant information on the lists might apply to him. Depending on your child's tolerance for talking with you about the issues and his own ability to self-reflect, you may want to use some of the items on the lists to initiate a discussion by talking or typing. Of course, for you, talking about the items may come naturally. It may not be so natural or easy for your child. If the discussion is upsetting to him, or if he resists at all, it would probably be better to let the book speak for itself. Do not push for a "meaningful discussion" if it is upsetting or confusing to your child, no matter how important it might be from your point of view. In some cases, it might be best if you let him explore the book in his own way, on his own terms. You might also try one of the previous suggestions above. Later on, you can try having a conversation by typing, as suggested in chapters 6 and 8.

Have the reader underline with a strip of paper to help focus

There is a lot of visual information on the workbook pages. Most of the lists contain a number of options to read, think about, choose from, and mark. If I had insisted on making the workbook as visually clear as possible for all children, then I would have had to modify the pages in ways that might have stretched this book to be 30 times longer than it is! Not having done that, I suggest instead that you try this method—cut a wide strip of paper and keep it with the book.

When reading, use the strip of paper to underline what your child is reading, so it covers the rest of the text, as demonstrated here:

For some children, it helps if previous lines are also covered up. If your child is distracted by the lines of text he has already read, then you can get a larger piece of paper and cut a "window" in it. The window should be as long as a line of text and as thick as a few lines.

As demonstrated here, the window highlights what is currently being read. When it is time to read the next group of lines, move the window down.

Pick and choose which pages to read

Some pages may not describe your child. Other pages will probably contain concepts beyond your child's current level of comprehension. There may be pages that give an accurate description of a particular aspect of your child's unique personality or behavior, even though he might not be able to understand what is written. In these cases, you should allow or encourage your child to skip the page, while you make a mental note to yourself to "earmark" it for his teachers' or other family members' enlightenment.

How to tell?

Back in the 1980s and 1990s, a highly controversial topic of debate amongst parents and professionals was how to answer the question, "Should we tell our child that she has autism?" Today, most people agree that such self-knowledge is essential. Autistic adults who didn't discover they had autism until later in life speak clearly about how it would have been different—better—if they had known and if the people around them had known, when they were children.

A perfect supplement to this book is an article, available as a free download from my Web site, titled, "10 Guidelines for Telling Your Child about ASD." It gives practical advice, along with an easy activity you can do at home with your family. Go to *catherinefaherty.com* and click on "Publications" and then "Articles."

Language: "person first" and "identity first"

At the time of this writing, person-first language is considered by many parents and professionals to be the preferred and/or respectful way to refer to children and adults. The phrases "child with autism" or "person with autism" are examples of person-first language. Some school systems require that this terminology be used on the students' legal paperwork for Individualized Education Programs and related documents.

However, many autistic self-advocates—adults and teenagers who speak for themselves—refer to themselves as an "autistic person." They may feel strongly about the importance of using identity-first language. If you want to understand the significance between person-first and identity-first language beyond the information provided in the workbook pages, please read the following essays by Jim Sinclair and Lydia Brown.

The first essay explaining the difference was written by Jim Sinclair and can be found on several Internet sites. Try *autismmythbusters.com* and then search for "identity-first language."

You may also want to read Lydia Brown's very thorough essay at *autisticadvocacy.org/identity-first-language*. At the end of Lydia's essay, she includes an extensive collection of links to other articles that explain both viewpoints, as well as links to articles that consider both views as valid or report no preference.

I have tried to use both types of terms in the text of this book, but I admit you may encounter more identity-first wording (autistic person) than person-first terms (person with autism). My commitment is to listen carefully and respect what I hear people saying when they speak for themselves. Up to now, I have heard and read more self-advocates describing themselves as an autistic person rather than a person with autism. I will keep listening, and I encourage you to, as well.

Chapter 2
The Sensory Experience

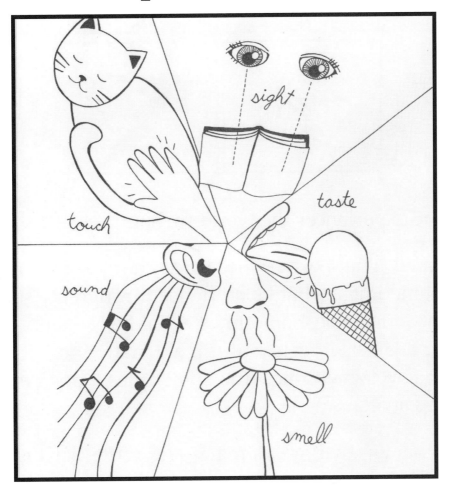

Workbook

The Five Senses

Usually, people say there are five senses.* They are:

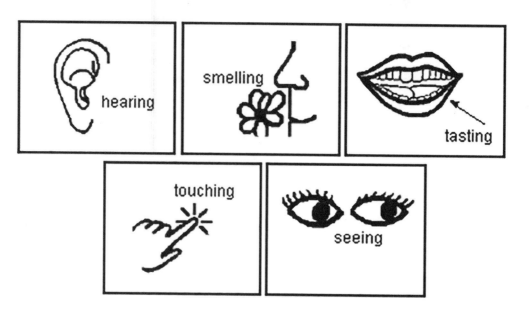

Everyone experiences the world through senses.

Sometimes, what I experience through my senses feels good. Sometimes, what I experience through my senses feels uncomfortable. Sometimes, what I experience through my senses feels painful. No matter how it feels, it may be overwhelming. And sometimes, I don't feel anything at all.

In this chapter, I will read, mark, and write what is true for me about my senses.

---

*   Picture Communication Symbols © 1981-2014 Mayer-Johnson Company, are used with permission of the Mayer-Johnson Company.

The Sensory Experience

Loud or Sudden Sounds

Hearing is how people are aware of sounds in the world. Some loud or sudden sounds are listed below. Many people aren't bothered by some of these sounds, but some people don't like these sounds.

I will circle or highlight the noises that bother me. ✏

▶ Vacuum cleaner

▶ Blender turned on

▶ Telephone ringing

▶ School intercom

▶ Lawn mower

▶ People talking at the same time

▶ Babies crying

▶ Dogs barking

▶ Car horns and sirens

▶ Machines or motors starting up

▶ People coughing or laughing or yelling

▶ Bird calls and other nature sounds

▶ Ocean surf

▶ Thunder, rainstorms

▶ Other: _____

There may be sounds at home and at school and in other places that hurt or bother me. I might become anxious or angry. I might yell or cry. Some children might cover their ears or run away.

Sometimes loud or sudden noises make me do this or feel this way:

_____

_____ .

"Quiet" Sounds Others Don't Notice

There are some sounds I notice that other people do not hear, or they do not pay attention to them. People call them *quiet sounds*. My experience of these sounds may be different. Examples are:

- Insects

- Fluorescent lights, fans, refrigerators, computers

- Airplanes or engines far away

- Radio or TV sounds in other rooms

- Background musical tracks in movies

- People talking or working in other rooms

- People breathing or turning the pages of a book

- People chewing or scratching

Most people may not pay attention to these kinds of sounds, because they seem quiet or unimportant to them. They might ignore these sounds. Many autistic people cannot ignore some of these sounds. Some of these sounds bother me. They change how I feel.

Sometimes these sounds make me anxious, angry, or another emotion:

_____

_____

Touching

Touching is what I feel when things make contact with my skin. Sometimes touch feels good, and sometimes touch bothers me. It might hurt or feel uncomfortable. Many people with autism are bothered by certain kinds of touch. Or, they might like to feel a certain kind of touch a lot.

I will ~~cross out~~ what I do not like, and I will circle what I do like. Some things may be crossed out and circled! ✏️

- Shirts and sleeves
- Seams or tags
- Zippers or waistbands
- Socks, seams at the toes
- Shorts and long pants
- Underwear
- Slips, dresses, skirts
- Hats, caps, stocking caps
- Headbands, scarves, hoods
- Silk, denim, cotton, flannel
- Velvet, wool, rayon, polyester
- Necklaces and other jewelry
- Someone kissing me
- Taking a shower
- Taking a bath

- Swimming
- Brushing my hair
- Shampooing my hair
- Cutting my hair
- People hugging me
- People bumping me
- Being tapped on the shoulder
- Soft, light touch
- Someone tickling me
- Firm, deep touch or massage
- Someone holding my hand
- Doctors or nurses touching me
- Unexpected touch
- Other: _____

_____

Odors

Smelling is how people are aware of the world through their noses. Smells are called "odors." Some odors are stronger than others.

Many people notice the odor of roses, or the air after it rains, or freshly baked bread. They might say these things smell good. Other times they notice rotten food odors or a poopy diaper. They say those things smell bad. But usually people do not pay much attention to most mild odors.

Many people with autism notice odors, even if other people don't notice them. If I notice an odor, it may be difficult for me to think about something else.

I will circle or highlight what is true for me. ✏

▶ I pay attention to odors, a lot.

▶ I usually want to smell things I see or touch.

▶ I like to smell people's hair or their skin.

▶ The odor of perfume or some deodorants bothers me.

▶ If an odor is strong, I can't think about anything else.

▶ Other: _____ .

▶ I like these odors: _____

_____ .

▶ I do not like these odors: _____

_____ .

Seeing

Seeing is what people do with their eyes. Many people with autism see things that other people might not notice. Some people enjoy watching certain things.

I will (circle) or highlight what is true for me. 🖉

I like:

▶ Watching things that are spinning (like ceiling fans)

▶ Looking at things that are stacked or lined up

▶ Watching things that are flipping (like pages of a book)

▶ Watching things that move around randomly

▶ Sudden, unexpected movement

▶ Looking at things from out of the corner of my eye

▶ Holding my fingers and hands in different positions

▶ Staring at my favorite things, for a long time

▶ Looking at things that have a certain shape or color

▶ Looking at bright lights

▶ Cloudy, overcast days

▶ Bright sunlight

▶ Darkness or nighttime without the lights turned on

▶ Other: _____
_____
_____

Some autistic people get confused or anxious when there are too many things to see at the same time. Or, some people might get anxious when things around them are moving. On the list above, I will cross out the things I do NOT like seeing.

Tasting

Tasting is what I do when I eat or drink something. Everyone has favorite foods and foods that they don't like to taste.

In addition to taste, some people pay attention to the color of food or how it feels in their mouths. Some young children want to drink liquids, instead of chewing solid food. Some might like tasting things that aren't food. They might put paper or toys or other things in their mouths. Some people might want to eat the same thing for every meal, every day. If that is true, parents may say that the child is a picky eater.

I will mark the things that are important to me about food. ✏

▶ The texture of food—how it feels in my mouth.

▶ The flavor of food—how it tastes.

▶ The color of the food.

▶ I want the same food every day.

▶ I like different foods and trying new things.

▶ Other: _____.

When a parent or teacher or therapist says, "Just taste it," or "Just try it," or "Just take a little bite," it means I just have to take one bite and then chew and swallow it. When that swallow is finished, I do not have to take another bite of that food during that meal, unless I want to. I can decide, after one taste.

Physical Pain

Physical pain is what people feel when a part of their body is hurt or injured or sick. The word "physical" refers to the physical body.

The purpose of physical pain is to remind the injured person to stop what they are doing so they do not continue to get hurt, and to get help. But some autistic people might not know if their body is hurt or when they are sick. They might not know when they need help. They might be so focused on something that they do not think about the physical pain. Sometimes people with autism feel pain, a lot. They might be very sensitive.

Examples of things that can cause pain are:

- Touching a hot burner on the stove

- Falling down

- Dropping something heavy on your foot

- Eating food that is too hot

- Closing a door on your fingers

- Getting cut and bleeding

- Touching water that is too hot or too cold

- Getting a sore throat or a fever

- Getting a headache or stomachache

- Having bare hands in cold weather

I will circle or highlight what is true for me. 🖉

▶ I rarely notice pain. I might be injured and not notice.

▶ I am very sensitive to pain. It's easy for me to feel hurt.

▶ When I am focused on something, I don't notice anything else.

▶ I like cold.

▶ I like heat.

▶ I like to feel pain.

▶ I usually don't feel pain.

▶ I like to feel this kind of pain: _____.

▶ Other: _____.

The Sensory Experience

Stimming: How I Do It

Stimming is short way of saying "self-stimulation." Everyone stims sometimes, but autistic people may stim more often than non-autistic people. Stimming may feel good. It may help me focus, or relax, or something else.

I will circle or highlight how I stim. 🖉

▶ Flapping my hands

▶ Jumping up and down

▶ Rocking my body

▶ Spinning my body around

▶ Spinning toys or other objects

▶ Tapping my fingers or drumming on something

▶ Pacing back and forth

▶ Repeating sounds

▶ Breathing quickly and hard

▶ Wiggling or holding fingers in different positions

▶ Flicking my fingers and hands

▶ Playing with my hair

▶ Looking at certain things (more on page 37)

▶ Other: _____

Some stimming may hurt me. In that case, it is called *self-injurious behavior*. Information about self-injurious behavior can be found later in this chapter.

Stimming: Why I Do It

Stimming serves an important purpose, especially for children with autism. I may not always know why I stim, but this list contains some possible reasons for stimming, as explained by some autistic adults.

I will circle or highlight what may be true for me. ✎

I sometimes stim when:

- ▶ I am excited, happy, joyful, or another good feeling.

- ▶ I am anxious, worried, scared, or other emotion.

- ▶ I am angry, sad, disappointed, or other emotion.

- ▶ Stimming makes me feel better.

- ▶ There are too many sounds or sights around me.

- ▶ I am tired.

- ▶ I am thinking about something or processing.

- ▶ I have a lot of energy to get out.

- ▶ I am feeling sick.

- ▶ I am feeling pain somewhere in my body.

- ▶ I want to calm down.

- ▶ I want to feel better.

- ▶ I am having fun.

- ▶ I am bored.

- ▶ I stim when _____.

- ▶ Sometimes I stim because: _____
  _____.

- ▶ I don't know why I stim.

- ▶ Other: _____
  _____.

Understanding Stimming

Most non-autistic children my age do not stim as much as I do. They don't flap their hands or rock or spin around very often or stim in other ways, like me. But, stimming is natural to me. Other people are sometimes surprised or bothered when they see me stim. It may bother them because it makes me look different from what they expect. Maybe they worry that others will make fun of me. Or, they could be uncomfortable or embarrassed by seeing me do something unexpected and different. This is why they may tell me to stop.

Sometimes, parents or teachers say, "Quiet hands!" when I am flapping my hands or stimming with my hands another way. But, I may be a person whose hands are flappy!

However, when other children and adults learn more about autism and stimming, it might not bother them so much. They might realize that stimming is not a bad thing. They might notice that they stim, too! They may play with their hair, chew on the inside of their cheeks, tap their fingers on the table, or _____

_____

(my parent or teacher may fill this in).

> It may be fun if sometimes my teacher or my parent announces, "It's time for a stimming break, everyone!" Then, the whole class or the whole family jumps up and flaps, spins, or stims, just like me!

Chapter 2

Especially for Older Readers

The previous topics in this chapter are relevant when individually selected for older children, teenagers, and—in some cases—adults. Supplementary information specifically for older readers is provided on the following pages.

This section provides information and opportunities for self-awareness and subsequent communication related to sensory stimulation, such as tics; overwhelming experiences, such as emotional pain and emotional empathy; and self-injurious behavior.

Parents, teachers, and therapists can simplify these topics to use with younger children, if needed.

Tics

Tics are other types of body movements. Tics are different than stimming. Tics happen unexpectedly. They usually occur during times of heightened anxiety. Tics do not feel good, the way it may feel good to stim. Examples of tics are:

- A part of the body will suddenly move quickly.

- The body will shudder or jolt or tense.

- An arm might suddenly "jump up."

- A muscle in a part of the body will tense or squeeze.

- Other: _____ .

Some tics might also occur by saying or yelling sounds or words suddenly and unexpectedly, without the person intending to say it. The person might:

- Whisper something

- Talk in a different voice

- Say real words unexpectedly

- Say made-up words that might sound like a foreign language

- Repeat the same words over and over

- Say impolite words, like swearing or cursing words

- Yell or shout any of these things (above)

- Laugh or yell out loud, unexpectedly

Tics are unexpected to everyone! Tics surprise the person who tics and other people nearby. Sometimes, tics seem funny and make other people laugh. Sometimes, tics are frightening and scare people. Tics may be confusing and make people anxious. Everyone needs to learn more about tics if someone in their family, classroom, or workplace has tics.

Some autistic children and adults have tics. They may have Tourette syndrome. Some non-autistic children and adults have Tourette syndrome, too.

I will highlight or <u>underline</u> the sentences in this section about tics that are true for me.

Emotional Pain

The topic of physical pain was covered earlier in chapter 2. There is another type of pain, called *emotional pain*. Emotional pain is what people feel "inside" themselves when they feel certain, strong emotions that are uncomfortable or scary. Emotional pain has names, such as sadness, fear, depression, anger, anxiety, worry, or another uncomfortable or painful emotion. Emotional pain can be a combination of two or more emotions. Often, emotional pain occurs with physical pain.

Sometimes the body gives clues when a person has emotional pain, like a stomachache, or sweating, or a feeling of nervousness, or another sensation in the body. But a person may not notice the clues in his or her body. It may be difficult to understand emotional pain.

Emotional pain is a part of life. Everyone feels emotional pain sometimes. Children and adults can learn what they can do to live more calmly or more happily, even when there is emotional pain in life.

I will circle or highlight what is true for me. 🖉

▶ Sometimes, I feel emotional pain (emotions such as sadness, anger, or worry).

▶ I don't know if I feel emotional pain.

▶ Sometimes, I feel a little bit of emotional pain.

▶ Sometimes, I feel a lot of emotional pain.

▶ I want more information about emotional pain.

I will highlight the sentences in the paragraphs that are interesting to me. 🖉

Chapter 2

I will highlight the sentences in the paragraphs that I want to learn more about. 🖊

I have something to say or questions to ask: _____

_____

Other: _____ .

Emotional Empathy

Some people, especially many autistic people, may be "extremely sensitive." They might be able to feel strong emotions from other people in their environment. Examples of strong emotions could be feelings of emotional pain (see page 47) and also feelings of other strong emotions, such as joy, happiness, or glee. Feeling the emotions that other people are feeling is called *emotional empathy*.

Sometimes, when I feel what others are feeling, I feel it inside of me, too. It comes in fast, and I may become overwhelmed. I may not know what to do.

I will circle or highlight what is true for me. 🖉

▶ When someone else feels very sad, I usually feel sad, too.

▶ When someone else feels very happy, I usually feel happy, too.

▶ When someone else feels
   I usually feel the same way, too.

▶ Often, I feel the emotions of other people.

▶ Usually, I don't feel the emotions of other people.

▶ I might feel like I am "losing myself" in these feelings.

▶ I usually don't feel the emotions of other people.

▶ Sometimes, I feel overwhelmed with feelings.

▶ Sometimes, feelings come in so fast, I can't think.

▶ When feelings come in so strongly, I don't know what to do.

▶ When someone is upset, I am upset, too.

▶ It might be difficult to think or talk at times like this.

The Sensory Experience

▶ I don't know what to do at times like this.

▶ I've never felt other people's emotions.

▶ It doesn't bother me to feel other people's emotions.

▶ Other: _____ .

Self-Injurious Behavior (SIB)

Physical pain, emotional pain, and other overwhelming sensory stimulation may sometimes cause people to hurt themselves. This may happen especially with some autistic children, teens, and adults. They might hit or bite themselves or bang their heads on a wall or the floor. They might scratch their faces or arms or another part of their body—not because of an insect bite, but to hurt themselves. They might do other things that injure their bodies. Hurting yourself is referred to as *SIB*, which is an abbreviation for self-injurious behavior.

It can be difficult for an autistic person to explain why they do SIBs. It is difficult for other people to understand SIBs, too. When other people (parents, teachers, therapists, friends, and loved ones) see the autistic person hurting themselves, they become worried, scared, upset, and/or sad. They often try to make the person stop the SIB. Sometimes they might try to restrain the person to forcibly stop the SIB.

Afterward, they might try to figure out what caused the SIB and try to help the person make changes in their life to keep them safe from harm. Sometimes, doctors prescribe medications that help the person feel calmer, to stop SIB from happening. But still, SIB remains difficult for everyone to understand, including the person doing it.

Some autistic people say that the SIB helps them get through a time of physical pain, emotional pain, or other overwhelming stimulation. Even though their body is getting hurt, it might feel better in the moment than the other physical or emotional pain they feel. Some people say that SIB helps them calm down. It may be helpful if they work together with an understanding doctor, family member, or support person to find other ways to help feel better and calmer and to prevent frequent SIB.

I will (circle) or highlight what is true for me. 🖉

▶ Sometimes I hit or bite or bang or scratch myself. (Which?)

▶ I hurt myself, but I do it when no one is around.

▶ I usually don't try to hurt myself, except once in a while.

▶ I never try to hurt myself.

▶ I used to try to hurt myself, but not anymore.

▶ I usually want to do SIB when I am confused about something.

▶ I usually want to do SIB when I am worried about something.

▶ I usually want to do SIB when I am angry about something.

▶ I usually want to do SIB when I am excited about something.

▶ I usually want to do SIB when I am overwhelmed, when too much is going on.

▶ I want to stop doing SIB.

▶ I want to stop doing SIB, but I don't know how.

▶ I usually want to do SIB when _____

_____ .

▶ I don't know what makes me want to do SIB.

▶ I want to figure out what makes me want to do SIB.

▶ I want help figuring out what makes me want to do SIB.

▶ I want to continue SIB, and I don't want to stop it.

▶ I am not sure if I want to stop SIB.

▶ I want someone to restrain me, to forcibly stop me, when I do SIB.

- ▶ I like to be restrained.

- ▶ I have hurt someone, not on purpose, when they restrained me.

- ▶ I am sorry I hurt someone when they restrained me.

- ▶ I do not want someone to restrain me when I do SIB.

- ▶ I want to be left alone when I do SIB.

- ▶ I want to be kept safe when I do SIB (with pillows, etc), but not be restrained.

- ▶ I want the room to be quiet when I do SIB.

- ▶ I want the room to be dark when I do SIB.

- ▶ I don't want to hear talking when I do SIB.

- ▶ When I do SIB, please show me a picture to remind me of what helps me calm down.

- ▶ When I do SIB, please show me a picture of something I like, to help me calm down.

- ▶ During SIB, these things will help me get calmer: (write down ideas)

_____

_____

_____

- ▶ I want to communicate more about SIB with someone I trust.

- ▶ Other: _____ .

- ▶ Other: _____ .

 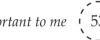

For Parents, Teachers, and Therapists

Everything through the senses seems to come through unfiltered. The finest little detail of something is there, whether I want to pay attention to it or not. There's all this information coming in all of the time. Noticing little motions on the side of my field of vision, seeing great levels of details on something I'm not really looking at, hearing lots of things all at once, noticing the feel of my clothes …

From what I understand, ordinarily most folks don't pay that much attention to all that … as though it doesn't really reach their conscious awareness. But those filters are not there for me. I'm getting all of this data all the time, whether I want it or not.

You've seen the acts in circuses when somebody with a bunch of long thin sticks and a bunch of plates holds them up and spins them, and they run around, seeing how many they can get going all at once? Dealing with everything in life, not just sensory stuff, is like having a bunch of plates going all at once. And when the sensory stuff comes in unfiltered, that means there are even more plates to take care of.

I've noticed that if I'm under stress, I'll have problems with sensory stuff that is ordinarily OK for me, like a sudden noise I usually would not respond to. If I'm really stressed, I'd have to wince or cringe. Or a touch that ordinarily would be OK, if I'm real stressed, I'll pull away from it.

So my responses to sensory things are not constant, not the same way all the time. It's just that there is a lot of information, and sometimes I can deal with it, and sometimes I can't.

—Dave Spicer

Ideas in This Chapter:

☑ The quiet area

☑ Reducing visual stimulation

☑ Managing auditory stimulation

☑ Handling tactile stimulation

☑ Odors

☑ Oral stimulation

☑ Eating

☑ Visual preferences and distractions

☑ Stimming

☑ Sensory integration evaluation

☑ Physical pain

☑ Emotional empathy

☑ Tics

☑ Self-injurious behavior

The quiet area

Provide regularly scheduled time and a place in which your young person may retreat, relax, and recover from sensory overload. Designate a room, or a special area of a room, away from the hustle and bustle. Refer to it as *the quiet area*. Respect the quiet area. It is a sanctuary. Schedule an adequate number of quiet-area times during the day. As your child grows, teach him to go to the quiet area before overwhelm takes over.

Outside, a playhouse, tree house, or special place in the yard might appeal to some children. One family created a quiet area for their child in a camper, parked in the backyard of their home. One man explained that as a child, he used to climb trees. As a high-school student, he would sneak into the dark vent system at school. Later, in college, he would sit on rooftops. He discovered at an early age that most people didn't look up, so when he went "up," he was almost always guaranteed a reprieve from the sensory and social demands he found so overwhelming.

Reducing visual stimulation

Many autistic adults say that night is their favorite time. The peace and quiet, the reduced visual stimulation, the fact that most people are asleep, all combine to create a wonderfully peaceful time in which to read, work, walk, or just sit. One woman told me that she becomes alert and energized when the sun goes down.

Experiment with a darkened room or one with soft lighting that may prevent or help your child recover from overstimulation. A cleared out room or empty space may be more relaxing for some children and adults than a cluttered room. Many individuals have discovered that wearing sunglasses and hats with brims help when outdoors.

Managing auditory stimulation

Respect each individual's auditory experiences. Experiment with wearing earplugs or headphones. Carpeting and drapery in rooms help to absorb sounds. Some people like to use white-noise machines in their bedrooms. Prepare your child for noises that can be predicted. For example, let him know ahead of time when the lawn mower or the chainsaw will be running, and help him make a plan for those times (where to go, what to do). At school, explain to the principal why you are asking the school personnel to let your child know when there will be a fire drill. Make a plan for these times, too. Generally, listening to favorite music or books on tape may help to soothe and distract your child from other, less appealing sounds.

Handling tactile stimulation

Allow your child to choose which clothing to wear to prevent unnecessary discomfort, distraction, or distress. Some adults have learned to buy two or three duplicates of the same outfits. This way, there is less variation in how the clothing feels from day to day, as well as fewer choices your child must face first thing in the morning when getting dressed!

Identify which types of physical touch are soothing, calming, or comforting. Respect the needs, preferences, and discomfort of each individual. Schedule time for deep-pressure massage, if indicated. One woman said that even though it can be uncomfortable for her to receive a therapeutic massage, she benefits greatly from giving them. The repetitive movement and the deep pressure against the palms of her hands is calming and relaxing. Another woman benefits by wearing compression arm warmers—the type worn by cyclists. Weighted lap pads, blankets, and other products offer steady pressure. Squishy balls and other sensory toys are readily available for "fidgeting." A family pet—dog, cat, rabbit, or guinea pig—may be perfect for your child, although the decision to find an animal friend for your child must be made carefully. Companion animals are not necessarily appropriate for all people (and, all people are not necessarily good friends for animals!). More information about animal companions can be found in chapter 10.

Odors

Many autistic children and adults are especially sensitive to odors like deodorant, perfume, and hand lotion. Some scents might cause discomfort, distraction, or anxiety. Some children become very active and "hyper" when they smell certain scents. Become aware of what odors might be aversive to your child. On the other hand, there may be certain scents that are especially soothing. Some families might want to explore the possible benefits of "aromatherapy"—the therapeutic uses of oil essences.

Oral stimulation

Allowing a student to chew gum in school may provide the oral stimulation needed, rather than fighting (a losing battle) with chewed necklines or shirtsleeves. If oral stimulation is a need, explore the many products now available, such as chewy wristbands, bracelets, and necklaces.

Eating

Your child, like many other children with autism, may be a picky eater. There are some children who eat only crunchy foods, or smooth foods, or foods of a certain color, or a certain brand of a particular food. Your child may have a sensitivity to the texture of the food. One adult says that if left alone, he will eat the same thing every day for long periods of time, especially when he is experiencing a lot of stress. He explains that for him,

> "… there is so much sensory stimulation in daily life that cannot be avoided, that eating the same thing for all my meals is one way of controlling the overwhelming amount of sensory input I have to deal with."

He goes on to explain that when he is more relaxed and less anxious, he is more able to enjoy a broader variety of food. Keep this in mind as you try to help your child expand his food preferences! Avoid working on it during times when your child may be experiencing more stress than usual.

Your child may be one who eats a variety of food, so this is not an issue. Or, you may struggle with refusals to taste new things on a day-to-day basis. Introduce only one new food at a time, instead of a variety of different foods every day. Make this one new food available for "trying" and introduce this same food over a period of time, according to the daily schedule or weekly calendar. As he grows more familiar with this one new food, he may be willing to try it and eventually learn to enjoy it. Vary the meal or snack when it is introduced, if possible, so he won't develop a routine of rejection every time he sits down for dinner. Depending on your child's interests, you may want to make it fun by making it theatrical, complete with regional accents and historical or scientific facts about the food!

Some parents and teachers have been successful in expanding their child's limited diet by using the routine of the work system (chapter 9). If your child is well versed in following a work system at school or at home, then using the same strategy at mealtime may work nicely. Once your child has learned the routine of following a work system, then you can use the same strategy to help him learn to "take a bite" or "eat one spoonful" by showing him a sequence of food on the table. Place small bites of food, each on their own spoon or small plate, next to each other in a line from left to right. Alternate the new food with a favorite food. In this way, it is absolutely clear to him what to expect, because he can see exactly how much of the new food he is to eat. He can also see what comes next, after he is finished with the new food. Start with only one bite of a new food, followed by his favorite food, eventually expanding the sequence after he gets used to this routine. The familiar routine of the work system may help to "override" previously established food routines.

Special diets designed by nutritionists, such as gluten-free and/or casein-free diets, are currently popular treatment approaches. An abundance of information and support is available in books and publications, as well as online.

Visual preferences and distractions

Introduce and teach activities or hobbies that appeal to your child's compelling sensory needs or visual preferences, like spinning, flipping pages, or lining things up. He will be more apt to pay attention to activities and will enjoy learning new things when you make it appealing. Hobbies that satisfy sensory and visual interests might reduce unusual repetitive behaviors, as well as increase leisure skills. Examples are doing Spin Art, playing board games with spinners, playing "Flippin' Flap Jacks," solitaire, rummy, dominoes,

Concentration, memory card games, and other games that require lining things up and putting them in order. Look for board games that can be adapted for solitary use or simplified for younger children for social play. Other ideas include doing paint-by-number, needlepoint, beading, rug hooking, knitting, crocheting, and other crafts. The list is unlimited. Take a trip to your local craft store for ideas.

The structured teaching approach includes conducting a careful assessment of the physical environment and, along with it, making careful observation of the things that may be distracting—especially visual and auditory distractions. Chapter 9 offers suggestions to help students focus in a classroom environment.

Stimming

This is an area that calls for deeper respect and understanding on the part of typically developing family members, friends, and professionals. For the longest time, "self-stimulatory behavior" was (and still is) deemed inappropriate and targeted for "extinction" by some autism treatment programs. The prevailing theory early on was that if you allow it to occur even a little bit, it will increase in frequency. Subsequent research, however, and our clinical experience at TEACCH, pointed to just the opposite. If you allow students to engage in self-stimulatory activities on a regular basis, at specific times and in specific places, it actually decreases the total amount of self-stimulation. It seems that this self-stimulatory behavior meets a need, and, when that need is met, the children become calmer and have less of a need for this behavior overall. In my 30 years of

experience with TEACCH, we did not focus on forced elimination of flapping, rocking, and other such stims unless they were harmful to the person or others, and this helped our students improve their classroom experiences.

My understanding is that stimming is an outward response related to particular neurologic processing. Stimming is a natural behavior that is often enjoyable and/or beneficial to the person who is stimming. Just imagine what it may feel like to be a child whose "normal" body movements are labeled inappropriate, wrong, bad, or deviant, and must be stopped immediately. In some cases, punishment is part of the "treatment." The demand of "Quiet hands!" teaches the child that her hands—and their natural movements—are wrong. The strategy of repeatedly prompting a child to stop stimming (either through implication, announcement, or demand) often results in the child's conclusion that enjoying the moment, or helping herself to handle the moment, or just moving in her own natural way, is so bad, so wrong, that it must be stopped immediately. For the child, some treatment strategies may be experienced as being an act of aggression, leaving her feeling vulnerable and unprotected. Read the book *Loud Hands: Autistic People, Speaking*, published in 2012 by the Autistic Self Advocacy Network, to better understand a perspective that may be very different from your own experience of typical development.

It is true that much of the time, stimming results in the person appearing "different" than what is expected. Okay. What a beautiful reminder to educate others about difference and diversity—about understanding and respect. And … what if a teacher announced to the entire class that it's time to take a jump-up and flapping break? What might that communicate to the original "stimmer" AND to non-autistic classmates? Wouldn't it be just plain fun to have some regularly scheduled flapping times—not just for the autistic student, but for everyone? Think about it. Try it. And then write to me about it at *catherine@catherinefaherty.com*.

Introducing physical activities and equipment to provide sensations that may serve purposes similar to stimming is a positive strategy. Having rocking chair time or bouncing on a mini-trampoline are examples. According to the natural preferences and needs of your child, include times for swinging, rocking, running, using Sit 'n Spins, riding scooter boards, jumping on a trampoline, and playing on other equipment suggested by occupational and physical therapists. Provide locations and times on his schedule for stim times and places. And, remember my earlier suggestion of classroom-wide (or entire family) stim breaks!

Additional suggestions about physical activity and exercise in your child's daily schedule are offered in chapters 11 and 12.

Sensory integration evaluation

Evaluation, consultation, and an individualized treatment program by an occupational therapist experienced in Sensory Processing Disorder and therapy with a sensory-integration focus is often indicated. There are many resources, books, and online information to research. School programs and developmental pediatric clinics in many countries offer sensory-integration services, sometimes in combination with speech therapy.

Physical pain

Typically developing family members, teachers, and therapists make automatic assumptions about what happens and what we do when we are injured or feeling sick. However, it is not as easy as it might seem for your child or student to identify or communicate about injuries or symptoms of illness. For specific, detailed, and concrete autism-friendly information, complete with Communication Forms to use about injuries and illness, how to know when it has happened, what to do about it, how to get help, and more, I refer you to my book, *Understanding Death and Illness and What They Teach about Life: An Interactive Guide for Individuals with Autism or Asperger's and Their Loved Ones*, published by Future Horizons in 2009.

Emotional empathy

Unlike what many professionals and the media in general have thought in the past about the emotional experience of autistic family members, friends, students, or clients, most autistic people are extremely sensitive—and consequently overwhelmed—by the emotions of others in their environment. Their experience of overwhelm helps explain what is interpreted as "uncaring" responses. The sections in this chapter's workbook pages for older children, teenagers, and adults provide a place to start exploring this topic together.

Tics

If your child has frequent vocal or motor tics (involuntary sounds, words, or movements) that are increasing or causing problems, you may want to consult a psychiatrist who is familiar with both autism and Tourette syndrome. Symptoms of Tourette syndrome may be triggered by anxiety. For more information about Tourette syndrome, visit the Tourette Syndrome Association at *tsa-usa.org*.

Self-injurious behavior

An introduction to self-awareness and self-expression concerning self-injurious behavior (SIB) is found in this chapter's workbook section for older children, teens, and adults. SIB is not an easy topic to talk about; it is frightening to watch your loved one hurt himself. The workbook pages are designed to make it as easy as possible for your child (or client) to identify his experience and express himself. Take time to really listen to what he is communicating about SIB. Remember that most of the strategies contained throughout this entire book—in almost every chapter—suggest structuring the environment, supporting authentic communication, providing ways for the person to make sense of life, and understanding sensory sensitivity and offering protection. All of these strategies could help ease the buildup of anxiety that may result in SIB. If SIBs continue, find professionals who will truly listen to what the individual has to communicate, who will respect and be willing to use whatever communication strategies are easiest and most natural for the individual during these discussions. Find psychiatrists who are experienced in medications and autism, and, again, who will really listen to the thoughts, questions, and feedback of the individual during medication trials and beyond. Developing an ongoing, solid relationship with a trusted physician over time is another important relationship to nurture in the life of your child or teenager.

Chapter 3
Ways of Thinking

Workbook

Ways of Thinking

Focused Interests

Everyone has interests—things they like. One of the important things about autism is that it helps me focus on my interests. I usually feel good when I am focused on my special interests. I might have just one focused interest, or I might have more than one.

My current focused interests are:

_____

_____

_____

I will mark the ways I like to enjoy my interests.

- ▶ I like to think about my focused interests.

- ▶ I like to read about my focused interests.

- ▶ I like to talk about my focused interests.

- ▶ I like to draw pictures about my focused interests.

- ▶ I like to write about my focused interests.

- ▶ I like to make things related to my focused interests.

- ▶ Other: _____.

Some people have the same focused interests for a long time—many years—or for their whole lives! Sometimes, focused interests change after a few months or years. On the next page is a list of some of my focused interests over the past few years.

These are some of my focused interests in my life, so far:

1. _____

2. _____

3. _____

4. _____

5. _____

6. _____

7. _____

8. _____

(Add more numbers if needed.)

Ways of Thinking

Details

Sometimes, people say I have a good memory for details.

Many autistic children and adults have excellent memories for details. Details can be colors, letters, numbers, shapes, places, statistics, names, signs, smells, sounds, dates, times, phone numbers, and other things. Some of the details I notice are things other people don't think are important, so they might not notice or remember them.

I usually remember details that are interesting to me or related to my focused interests. The types of details I notice and remember are:

_____

_____

_____

_____

_____

Most autistic children and adults are good at noticing and remembering certain types of details.

Ways to Learn

Sometimes learning comes easily and quickly, and sometimes learning takes more time. This is true for all children, teenagers, and adults. People learn best in different ways—each in their own way.

I will circle or highlight what is true for me. ✎

My best ways to learn are by ...

▶ Watching other people before I try something new.

▶ Getting information from photos or pictures.

▶ Reading about it.

▶ Listening to people tell me about it.

▶ Thinking about how it fits into my focused interest.

▶ Talking to others about what I am learning.

▶ Writing about what I am learning.

▶ Making things related to what I am learning.

▶ Staying focused on it, so I do not have to do other things.

▶ Experimenting and figuring things out by myself.

▶ Asking people questions.

▶ Having people type the answers so I can read them, because it's better than listening to someone tell me about it.

▶ Listening to someone talk, because it's better for me to listen than to read what they type.

▶ Learning some other way ... I like learning when: _____

_____

_____ .

Perfection

Many people on the autism spectrum like things to be perfect or want to always be first. Doing things perfectly, or making them look perfect, or being first, is okay, but sometimes it can cause problems.

I will circle or highlight what is true for me. ✏

> ▶ I want to be the first one finished with my work.
> ▶ I want my work to look a certain way, so I keep correcting it until it looks perfect.
> ▶ I erase many times.
> ▶ I do not want to see any mistakes on my work.
> ▶ If it doesn't look right, I give up and get angry or anxious.
> ▶ Other: _____.

Everything cannot always be perfect. I am not wrong or bad if other people are first or if there are mistakes on my work. Everyone makes mistakes—even the smartest people in the world. Good ideas to try are:

- Let it be OK if someone else finishes first. I may finish second, third, or later.

- Correct the mistakes I know how to correct.

- Ask someone for help with the mistakes I don't understand.

- Continue with the activity or assignment.

- I do not need to start over from the beginning.

- Other: _____.

Perfection versus Doing Your Best

Does "doing your best" mean having to be perfect?

The answer is "no." Doing your best does not mean having to be perfect. All humans make mistakes sometimes, even when they are doing their best. No one does everything perfectly correctly all the time.

When someone says "Do your best," it is meant as a reminder to work carefully and to try to keep my attention on what I am doing. A person can do his or her best and still make mistakes. It is okay to make mistakes. In fact, making mistakes is a necessary part of learning!

The instruction "Do your best" includes learning what to do after making a mistake. My parent or teacher and I may choose to read pages 87-88, about the purpose of mistakes and what to do after making a mistake.

I will circle , highlight, or write what is true for me. 🖉

- ▶ Teachers, parents, and others tell me to "Do your best."

- ▶ I think I make too many mistakes.

- ▶ I get upset or anxious or angry when I make mistakes.

- ▶ I want my work to be perfect.

- ▶ It is okay if my work is not always perfect.

- ▶ I want to feel okay, even when I make mistakes.

- ▶ Other: _____ .

Ways of Thinking

Routines and Familiarity

Most people like routines and familiarity. A routine is when I do the same things in the same ways. Familiarity means being used to something because of seeing or doing it previously. Familiar things are not new.

Routines feel especially good to me because I know what to expect. I like to know what is going to happen and when it will happen. Routines help things feel familiar.

I like these things to stay the same:

_____

_____

_____

_____

Sometimes things change. Unexpected things happen in life. Sometimes people know ahead of time that things will change. It helps me to know when a change is going to happen.

Sometimes people don't know that there is going to be a change until it is happening.

Changes

Sometimes, I am focused on something and I don't want to stop. Or, something may be familiar, and I don't want it to change.

But, someone might say it is time to do something else, or "things have changed." Sometimes, there is a surprise.

Many people like surprises. Surprises are when things change unexpectedly, and we do not know exactly how they will change. Some people enjoy surprises and think surprises are fun, but many autistic people enjoy it more when they know what to expect or when things stay the same.

When things change or are new or different, I might wonder if they will ever be the same again.

When things change, I might feel happy, anxious, confused, sad, frustrated, angry, or _____ .

I do not have to write on all the lines, only what is true for me.

Some changes that bother me are:

_____

_____

_____

_____

Ways of Thinking

_____

_____

_____

Some changes that I enjoy are:

_____

_____

_____

_____

_____

A Schedule Can Help Me Be Flexible

Everything cannot always stay the same. *Being flexible* means that when things change, I try to go along with the change without getting too upset. People who are flexible may still enjoy things, even when they change. Following a schedule can help me be flexible.

A schedule is a list of what is going to happen today. There should be a schedule for each day, because all of every day isn't the same! Looking at the schedule:

- I know which things will be the same as usual today, and which things are going to be different.

- I can see if a surprise is going to happen, because it is written on the schedule for the day!

- I can see what is going to happen first and what is going to happen later.

- I know that I will not be stuck doing something I don't like, because I can see that it will end and that something else will happen next.

- I can see when it is going to be time for my focused interests.

- I am involved and have some control. I'll mark the things on my schedule, one by one, each time I check it.

Ways of Thinking

Last-Minute Changes

Sometimes, things have to change unexpectedly. It might happen right away, or it might happen soon. An unexpected change may be a last-minute change.

If there are last-minute changes, my parent, teacher, friend, or I may get my schedule and cross out what was supposed to happen. Then we will write (or draw) on my schedule what new thing will happen.

Even if the change is going to happen immediately, it can still be written (or drawn) on my schedule, so I can see this important information with my eyes. It is easier for me to understand and handle changes when I can see what is going to happen.

If I do not have a schedule, then someone can help me cope with a last-minute change by writing me a note about it.

The last-minute change might be easier to deal with if I read about it. Then I can keep the note with me and check it again, whenever I want.

Examples of schedules used in a variety of situations can be found at the end of this chapter in the section, "For Parents, Teachers, and Therapists," on pages 109-114.

Especially for Older Readers

Many of the previous topics in this chapter for children are relevant when individually selected for older children, teenagers, and even adults. Relevant supplementary information *specifically* for older readers is provided on the following pages.

This section provides information and opportunities for self-awareness and subsequent communication related to ways of thinking, such as issues regarding attention: single-mindedness, multitasking, and getting distracted. It also introduces *organizational strategies* to support complications in executive-functioning skills. It covers topics related to uncertainty, perfection, mistakes, and doing one's best.

Parents, teachers, and therapists can simplify these topics to use with younger children, if needed.

Chapter 3

Attention and Single-Mindedness

A person's attention is usually what he or she is watching, looking at, listening to, thinking about, and/or doing. Another word for attention is "focus" or "concentration."

For some people, especially many children and adults with autism, it is natural to stay focused on *one thing at a time*. Another way of describing this is *single-mindedness*.

This is when a person's attention is concentrated on a single thing, idea, thought, or activity. It's easy for him to focus on the same thing for a long time. If it's his focused interest, it might feel good. It may be difficult for the person to stop focusing on that one thing and "shift attention" to another thing.

I will circle or highlight what is true for me. 🖉

▶ It feels good to focus on one thing at a time.

▶ Single-mindedness comes naturally to me.

▶ I like being "single-minded."

▶ I like to "shift my attention" to new things.

▶ It feels good to shift my attention from one thing to another.

▶ It is easy to stop thinking about something when I am focused on it.

▶ It is difficult to stop thinking about it when I am focused.

▶ Sometimes, I get angry when I have to shift my attention to something else.

▶ People often tell me to "Pay attention."

▶ I wonder why other people tell me to "pay attention."

▶ It helps me when others say, "Pay attention."

▶ It doesn't help me when they say, "Pay attention."

▶ I like to think about many different things at the same time.

▶ I like to focus on one thing at a time.

▶ Other: _____ .

Attention and Multitasking

Although single-mindedness is natural for many autistic people, there are some people who naturally and easily pay attention to many things at the same time. This is when a person can think about many things at the same time, switching attention, back and forth, from one thing to another easily. Maybe the person has several projects going at the same time, and he routinely switches his attention from one to the other. This is called multitasking.

For some people, multitasking feels natural or good or fun. It is easy for them to multitask. For other people, multitasking is not very fun. They may be single-minded (see the previous page). Some people can do both, easily.

I will circle or highlight what is true for me. ✏

▶ I like to focus on one thing at a time.

▶ I like to focus on many things at the same time.

▶ I am naturally single-minded.

▶ Usually, I can easily and naturally multitask.

▶ I like to multitask.

▶ I like to stay focused on only one thing.

▶ Usually, I don't like to switch my attention from one thing to another.

▶ I prefer to focus on one thing at a time.

▶ If I could focus on one thing of my choice, I would do it for a long time!

▶ It is fun for me to switch my attention to new things, depending on what the new thing is.

▶ I can switch my attention, but I don't like to.

▶ I can switch my focus more easily to the next thing if I know ahead of time what the next thing is going to be.

▶ To me, switching attention to something else is a distraction.

▶ I want to stay focused on one thing, but I get distracted easily.

▶ Other: _____

Getting Distracted

Getting distracted feels like my attention "jumps around." I usually don't stay focused on one thing, even if I want to. It is similar to multitasking, except that it may not be enjoyable, and I can't get anything done.

Being distracted is when a person hears, sees, feels, thinks, or otherwise notices something *other than* what he wants or needs to do. Or, a person might get distracted by something he would rather do (like a focused interest), instead of what he needs to do. In this case, he might like being distracted, but it can cause problems if he is supposed to be doing something else. Getting distracted makes it difficult to stay focused on what needs to be done.

I will circle or highlight what is true for me. 🖉

▶ It is easy for me to stay focused on one thing.

▶ I wish I could stay focused on one thing without getting distracted by other things.

▶ I get distracted by sounds and noises.

▶ I get distracted by people talking.

▶ I get distracted by things I see.

▶ I get distracted by things I smell or feel.

▶ I get distracted by other people.

▶ I get distracted by my own inner feelings.

▶ I get distracted by my own thoughts.

▶ I get distracted by thinking about my focused interests.

▶ I am not sure what distracts me.

▶ Other people tell me often to "Pay attention."

▶ Telling me to "pay attention" usually doesn't help.

▶ Telling me to "pay attention" usually helps me.

▶ Getting distracted is frustrating.

▶ I usually don't get distracted.

▶ I wish I could work by myself, so I won't get distracted.

▶ I like to work while there are distractions around me.

▶ I take medication to help with this.

▶ I wish I could take medication to help with this.

▶ Other: _____ .

Getting Organized

When a person is organized, daily life may become a little easier. Many people in the world want to get more organized. Scientists think that there is something different about the brains of some people, including some autistic children, teenagers, and adults, which can make it difficult to get organized. (The function of the brain that most directly affects organizational skills is called *executive function*.)

If a person wants or needs to get more organized, the most important thing is to use organizational strategies. Each strategy needs to be designed to fit the person and the situation. Next it needs to be tried out, and then fine-tuned (changed a little bit) until the strategy fits the person and the situation. You'll know it's right when it works! The same strategy does not fit all people. Strategies work best when individualized for a specific person. Here are some examples of organizational strategies:

- Placing labels on drawers, doors, tubs, bins, and containers

- Sorting items into separate drawers, containers, folders, etc

- Using written schedules and checklists

- Using schedules and checklists with icons* or pictures*

- Using work systems**

- Placing reminder notes in helpful places

- Using auditory alerts or alarms

- Using calendars on the wall, phones, computers, or tablets

- Organizing the week so a specific day is reserved for specific activities

- Meeting with a support person to create the daily, weekly, and/or monthly schedule

- Meeting with a support person to review the daily, weekly, and/or weekly schedule

---

* Many highly intelligent people prefer to use icons instead of written words, so their visual processing can be streamlined. This is similar to using Japanese kanji or Chinese hanzi characters instead of spelling out each word.

** The information on schedules and work systems presented earlier in this chapter are excellent models for all ages and purposes.

What Does It Mean to "Learn from Your Mistakes"?

First, read about perfection and mistakes on page 72.

Now, there are three ways of thinking about mistakes.

1. "MISTAKES ARE BAD." (THIS IS NOT TRUE.) Some people, especially young children, might think mistakes mean that the person who made the mistake is wrong or bad. However, this is not true. Mistakes DO NOT mean a person is bad. Everyone makes mistakes sometimes. Young people make mistakes. Old people make mistakes. Intelligent people make mistakes. All humans make mistakes sometimes.

    There are better ways to think about mistakes. Here are two intelligent ways of understanding the importance of mistakes:

2. MISTAKES ARE MESSAGES. Mistakes are messages that show people what to learn next. They may be thought of as messages from the universe or from a wise person, a master, a wizard, or God. The message comes in the form of a mistake to get the person's attention! It shows the person exactly what needs to be learned next. Mistakes show an intelligent person what needs to be added to his or her knowledge.

3. MISTAKES ARE CLUES. Another way to think about mistakes is that they are clues for a detective. Detectives look for clues. Clues show them where to go or what to do next. A mistake is a clue for the person who made the mistake, as if the person is a detective! The clue shows him or her what to do next.

> So, mistakes are messages about what to add to my knowledge or clues about what to do next.

Ways of Thinking

The Seven-Step Plan: When Finding a Mistake

Here is the Seven-Step Plan to follow when a person discovers that he or she has made a mistake:

1. Stay calm. Take three slow, deep breaths.

2. Think, "Okay, this is a message for me to add something to my knowledge." (Read the previous page.)

3. Think, "Okay, this is a clue, showing me what to do next."

4. Try to understand the mistake and fix it. OR, if you cannot fix it by yourself, ask someone for help. Sometimes, the best person to ask for help is the person who noticed the mistake. Or, you could ask another trusted person for help.

5. Fix the mistake.

6. If necessary, return the work to the person who noticed the mistake.

7. Afterward, ask yourself, "What did I learn that can be added to my knowledge?" Think about the answer to this question, or tell the answer to someone you trust: "From this mistake, I learned that _____."

Uncertainty

There are unexpected events in life that no one can predict. Even the most intelligent people cannot always predict what is going to happen.

Life is uncertain. This means we cannot really be sure things will happen the way we think they will happen. It is natural for people to have desires and preferences. It is intelligent to make plans and schedules; however, uncertainty and change are still parts of life. No one, not even teachers, parents, doctors, or others, really knows for sure what is going to happen in the future. People have to remind themselves that "Change is a part of life."

Accepting that change is a part of life is an important realization that comes as people live and grow. They learn that even though there are changes, life continues on.

I will circle , highlight, or write what is true for me. 🖉

▶ I know that uncertainty and change are parts of life.

▶ I don't know what it means that "Change is a part of life."

I have ways to cope with uncertainty and change—and the anxiety that may result. **I will mark which of the following I sometimes do:**

▶ I use a daily schedule or checklist that shows what to expect during the day, including changes from the typical routine.

▶ I read information that has been written for me, explaining the change(s).

▶ I read a Social Story about the topic.

▶ If I want more information about what is going to happen, I ask someone to write a description and a reason for the change.

▶ I follow a daily relaxation routine.

▶ I go to a quiet area throughout the day.

▶ I practice meditation or sitting quietly.

▶ I exercise on a regular schedule.

▶ Other: _____ .

I don't do most of these things, but I will <u>underline</u> the things I'd like to try. ✎

For Parents and Teachers

"I would have liked it if I could have made better sense out of what was happening … if there was some kind of order or predictability that I could have relied on."

—Dave Spicer at 49, talking about his childhood

Ideas in This Chapter:

☑ The need for success

☑ Mistakes

☑ Assessment

☑ Daily informal assessment

☑ Inconsistency

☑ Visually structured teaching

☑ The schedule:

1. Why use a schedule?

2. How to individualize the schedule

3. How do I make a schedule?

4. How long a period of time should it cover?

5. Do I need to write the times on the schedule?

6. Keep it clear and easy to read

7. How can the schedule teach my child to be more flexible?

8. How can it help my child stay organized?

9. Checkboxes, check-lines, and crossing things out

10. How can the schedule help me deal with my child's restricted interests?

11. How can the schedule help neutralize arguments?

12. What if my child is not interested in using the schedule?

13. Incorporating the schedule as part of life

14. Is the goal for my child to write his own schedule?

15. To use or not to use?

The Need for Success

Most of us learn through trial and error. Life presents us with opportunities to learn through our mistakes, as well as through our successes. We remember what to do differently next time. We understand the connection between our behavior and its consequences. This process works so naturally that many current parenting manuals suggest discipline methods that promote the use of situations that allow children to learn through the consequences of their actions.

In contrast, learning by trial and error can feel so unpredictable and even frightening to children with autism that they become unwilling to try. Many parents have watched as their child avoids involvement in an activity until he or she feels confident that it will be done perfectly.

It has been observed that the need for success among many autistic children is immediate and total. Making mistakes may be so demoralizing that many don't risk trying until they are sure they can do something perfectly and flawlessly, without failing. They don't easily learn from mistakes; they may not see the connections, the process, and the relationship between making a mistake, almost succeeding, and reaching achievement.

To expect a child with autism to learn only through the natural events of trial and error is to risk raising a child whose self-image is sacrificed to a feeling of shame and harsh self-judgment. Children who focus on obvious polarities (good/bad, black/white, right/wrong) will naturally come to the conclusion that they are bad or wrong when they make a mistake. One adult says that as a child, he perceived life as "failure after failure," which to him served as proof that he was a failure.

Mistakes are an unavoidable part of life for all of us. Autistic individuals who live in an environment that is designed best for typically developing folks will of course automatically experience a higher degree of confusion, awkwardly timed responses, and often total misunderstanding.

Consequently, children with autism experience even more mistakes than the average child! The fact that they may not make connections between behavior and its consequences and that learning from mistakes is so evasive only makes these experiences more random, senseless, and unbearable.

If applicable, introduce the concept of "learning from your mistakes" and the "Seven-Step Plan: When Finding a Mistake" in the workbook pages for older children and teenagers. Help the person make sense of the inevitable experience of "mistakes."

Strategies that parents and teachers of children with autism rely on must embrace the principle of building on a solid foundation of mastered skills and competence. Daily observation and constant

assessment are essential. Teaching strategies that are designed to prevent failure and delight in accomplishment will ensure that learning is free to take place. Providing more information by explaining the true purpose of mistakes and helping the maturing young person understand this concept is essential.

Mistakes

As mentioned previously, information about mistakes for your older child or teenager was provided in the workbook pages. In addition, I offer free downloads of ideas for social games I have created to play at home or to modify for the classroom. These "games" are intended to make it easy and fun to actually practice making mistakes on purpose (one of the rules of the game) and to practice not being first, but being second, third, or later. My intention is that through structure, repetition, creativity, goofiness, and fun, the child will gradually let go of any unpleasant emotional attachment to making mistakes and having to be first. These games, as well as other games about personal space, arm's length, and friends, are offered as free downloads and can be found by going to *catherinefaherty.com* and clicking on "Publications" and then "Articles."

Assessment

Conducting an overall assessment of your child's skills and pattern of learning is necessary. Formal and informal assessment will reveal his unique pattern of strengths and weaknesses, talents, and interests. No single numerical score (and no single test) can accurately describe your child's development. Children with autism have "peaks and valleys" in their development. Nonverbal skills may be more developed than verbal skills, or verbal skills may be highly developed, while deficits may be seen in nonverbal skill areas. Within these two general areas, development is often scattered. Adaptive functioning scores (how the child does in the real, everyday world) are typically much lower than his or her cognitive (thinking) skills.

Your child's particular pattern of development, strengths and needs, style of learning, attention style, organizational skills, and focused interests must be taken into account when planning his educational program.

Daily Informal Assessment

Your careful observations from day to day and from activity to activity constitute some of the most valuable assessment information about your child or student. What triggers anxiety? Anger? Withdrawal? What captures his interest? When is he the calmest? What strategies help him get the most organized? Involved? Engaged? Inspired?

Your detailed observations can be used when developing teaching strategies and individualizing his educational program.

Inconsistency

Many parents have said that the only thing consistent about their child is the fact that he is inconsistent! Having "peaks and valleys" of development and difficulty generalizing what is learned in one situation to another situation is the norm. Being able to do one thing, on one day, does not ensure he will be able to do it again tomorrow. It is tempting to judge such inconsistent behavior with statements like, "He is just being manipulative," or "He can do it if he wants to."

It is important to remember that in most cases, when a child with autism cannot do something or is not doing it, it usually means there is something about the activity that doesn't make sense to him—even if he was successful at it yesterday. Small changes in the external environment, such as a different teacher, a different location, different materials, or too much stimulation, can make a major difference. Variations in his internal state, such as feeling tired, sick, anxious, or distracted, can cause dramatic variation.

Remember that inconsistency is a part of his style of learning. Accepting this at face value, instead of jumping to conclusions about

Ways of Thinking

his motives, will help teachers and parents look at his skills and development in a fresh light.

Observe what is. Using teaching methods that offer consistency in his external environment can be a place to start.

Visually Structured Teaching

To maximize your child's learning potential, any methods for teaching new skills and managing behavior must be tailored to the way your child learns. Most children with autism respond positively to visually structured teaching methods. Even when a child is very verbal and has advanced skills, structured teaching techniques are reassuring and help organization, focus, and sequencing and therefore increase independence from prompts. For those children who may have weak visual processing skills, such as children with nonverbal learning disabilities, structured teaching adds at least an organizational element and can promote independent skills. One of the most powerful and effective visually structured teaching strategies is the individualized daily schedule.

The Schedule

An effective visual strategy to provide predictability while teaching flexibility is to have an individualized daily schedule. This strategy for students with autism was initially developed by the pioneers in TEACCH in the 1970s and has been widely used by the TEACCH program ever since. Most

current educational programs over the years have adopted its use in various forms. Visual schedules help children and adults anticipate and prepare for activities throughout the day. Transitions and changes become easier, expectations are clearer, and the person using the schedule becomes more organized. The proper use of schedules actually teaches flexibility. Schedules are used at school, at home, and anywhere else.

Typically, children and adults who can read and write are given a schedule that has been written or typed. However, the use of icons or pictures, sometimes paired with the written information (or not), is often more effective! One adult, a mathematician with a genius-level IQ, explained that he more quickly understands and processes a schedule that displays icons instead of written words. He compared it to Japanese kanji or Chinese hanzi (symbolic picture characters).

Please note that when referring to "the schedule," it does not mean the actual activities themselves, nor to an exact, predetermined sequence of daily activities. "The schedule" refers simply to the visual strategy that clarifies which activities or events will occur and the sequence in which they will occur. It is not the same every day. Examples of schedules can be found on pages 109-114.

1.   Why use a schedule?

When used consistently, the schedule is a valuable strategy that often results in positive short- and long-term changes. Using an individual schedule:

- Capitalizes on visual strengths
- Promotes independence

- Rations time for focused interests

- Teaches flexibility

- Helps build necessary vocational skills

- Helps redirect a tendency toward argumentativeness into more cooperation

2.   How to individualize the schedule

As with all successful teaching methods, the benefit lies with the teacher's, therapist's, or parent's ability to individualize the schedule for this one child. Perhaps even more essential to the teaching of autistic children as opposed to typically developing children is the concept that gearing the strategy to the individual may determine success or failure.

The rest of this chapter offers significant issues to be considered when individualizing a schedule for your child.

3.   How do I make a schedule?

A written schedule is comparable to a typical calendar or appointment book. It must be easily accessible. Use a note pad, stenographers' notebook, spiral notebook, or clipboard. If appropriate, the current day's school schedule may be clipped onto the front of a loose-leaf binder.

Write the child's schedule at the beginning of the day, listing the activities and events in sequence. Include favorite activities, as well as the things he resists doing. Be specific enough so he can see small or big changes from the usual routine. Add relevant details to avoid confusion. Be literal.

Schedules with icons or pictures should present the activities in sequence. Attach each picture to a strip of cardboard with Velcro.

4. How long a period of time should it cover?

After using the schedule with your child for a while, carefully observe the optimum number of items on the list that he can handle at one time. For some children, seeing all of the day's events at the same time is too distracting or stressful. If this is the case, write only the sequence of events for the morning. At noon, start a fresh schedule by listing the afternoon's activities in sequence.

On the other hand, there are some children who may become distressed if they can't see the entire day's plan from beginning to end. These children might function with greater ease when shown a full day's schedule all at once.

Some parents use a schedule at home just to get through the "rough spots"—for example, a certain time period that causes their child the most distress or frustration. This may help immensely on weekends, in particular, when the nature of the day may be unstructured or when there's a possibility of frequent last-minute changes in plans.

5. Do I need to write the times on the schedule?

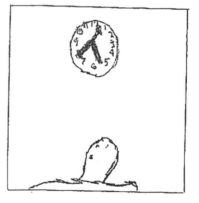

Include the actual "clock time" if it is helpful and not distressing to your child when things don't happen exactly (literally) on time. Usually showing the sequence of events, without the times, works well enough. A single schedule frequently has a combination of entries; some are defined by a specific time, and others are not.

Many children have learned the meaning of "approximately" through the consistent use of the schedule with "approximate times." Use of visual cues, such as color-coding a 20-minute range of time on a picture of a clock face, can help clarify the meaning of "approximate."

6. Keep it clear and easy to read

The visual information should be simple, clear, and concise. Use words, icons, or pictures your child can understand as effortlessly as possible. Use what he will recognize most easily on his "worst days," when he is the most anxious. One- or two-word entries, or short phrases, are all that is needed. If using icons or pictures, you may want to label each picture with its written word.

Make sure the list is visually clear, keeping it orderly and leaving enough space between the lines to clarify the separate entries.

Depending on your child's response to the schedule, you might need to highlight or underline key words, drawing attention to the most important information.

7. How can the schedule teach my child to be more flexible?

When changes need to occur or additions need to be made after the schedule has already been given to the child, you can revise the schedule "on the spot." Explain the change clearly and simply in a matter-of-fact tone of voice, while you cross out and/or add the change on the schedule. Keep in mind that you want to simultaneously pair verbal information (talking) with visual information (writing on the schedule), so this new information can be processed most easily. In some cases, you may simply show the new information without talking (more on this later).

If using pictures, simply rearrange, delete, or add the new information, adjusting the sequence as needed. It is usually best to do this while your child is watching and while you explain calmly that there is a "change."

As your child becomes more familiar with using a schedule, he will adapt to changes more easily. After all, they are accounted for on the schedule!

8. How can it help my child stay organized?

Make sure your child has easy access to a pen or pencil, so he can mark the schedule at each transition. Sometimes, keeping the schedule on a clipboard and hanging a pencil or pen on a clipboard with a string or attaching the pencil to a spot of Velcro is most convenient. Teach the child to check off or cross out each entry as the day progresses. This clarifies the passage of time and keeps him organized. It also promotes independence by giving him an active role in staying on track.

If using pictures, your child can be in charge of taking the picture off and putting it in a "finished" envelope.

9. Checkboxes, check-lines, and crossing things out

Providing blank boxes on the schedule clarifies and defines the act of "checking the schedule." Seeing the empty boxes will remind him that there are specific things to do, and he will get to mark the boxes with checks as he moves through the day. Placing a short line in the margin next to each entry is another way to structure a place to mark the schedule. Other children learn to cross a line through each entry as they begin or complete the activity.

Those of us who use "to-do" lists typically cross items out after each errand is completed. However, when teaching your child to mark his schedule, another option that may work more effectively is to check off or cross out each activity before beginning. This way, after an activity is completed, he can look back on the schedule and instantly notice the next unmarked entry on the list. This unmarked entry clearly shows "what is next" on the schedule and reminds him what to do to get started—he needs to check the box and then begin by doing what it says.

10. How can the schedule help me deal with my child's focused interests?

Some children want to talk about one subject or do one thing exclusively. The structure of the schedule can help them participate in other activities, while it "rations" time for the favorite subject, respecting their focused interest. They can see that they can engage in their focused interest—and exactly when they can engage in their focused interest—because it is on the schedule one or more times, as part of the day's plan.

When your child insists on talking about a favorite theme beyond what is an appropriate length of time or frequency, simply refer to the schedule and point out when he can talk about his special interest during the day.

If time allotted for the focused interest or favorite theme has not been written on the schedule at all, or not frequently enough, you should add it in, on the spot, following the same procedure for making a last-minute change or addition to the schedule. (See the heading, "How can the schedule teach my child to be more flexible?" on pages 100-101.) Allotting time for favorite subjects shows respect for what is important to this individual child.

11. How can the schedule help neutralize arguments?

Some children and their parents or teachers have developed a verbal routine of unproductive back-and-forth questions and explanations.

Despite your most well-intentioned desires to "not get sucked in," you may find yourself arguing or trying unsuccessfully to  explain why something is or is not happening.

The schedule can help change even the most firmly established patterns of arguing in a way that is nonthreatening to both child and adult. The schedule allows the adult to be directive without appearing confrontational from the child's point of view. The child's attention is drawn to the fact that "the schedule says …" rather than to the adult who is telling him what to do or to a familiar pattern of words that the adult usually uses. The fact that you are presenting information in a visual—and not strictly verbal—manner creates a greater ease with which the child can receive, process, understand, and accept new information. *In addition, make sure the schedule includes things that your child looks forward to; the schedule should not exclusively be a list of dreaded chores and responsibilities!*

To help break a well-established argumentative routine, the adult can try quietly handing the schedule and pencil to the child, without making eye contact. Keep your focus on the schedule itself. Refrain from talking or responding verbally to your child's objections, but simply behave calmly, as if you assume the child will do what the schedule tells him to do. It may be that your explanations or threats (so predictable to your child) trigger his arguments and set the old routine in motion. Use a matter-of-fact, calm tone of voice. Look at the schedule, hand it to your child or place it near him, and say simply, "The schedule says that …"

For most children, stress will dramatically decrease if no one tries to talk or explain the issue. Try staying quiet, referring him to the schedule, and then perhaps walking away, giving him space. Do not respond if he rips up the paper. Just wait. In most cases, a child will still do what is says, even if he rips it up!

Dealing with difficult behavior is addressed in more detail in chapter 11.

12. What if my child is not interested in using the schedule?

Sometimes, older children and teenagers who have not been introduced to using a schedule or who have not developed the routine of using one will resist using it. Even a younger child might need extra motivation. Consider these ideas:

Appeal to his special interest by drawing a border or adding an illustration (eg, a picture of a train or a map of the U.S.A.) that relates to his interest. You might try writing the schedule in a special "theme" notebook that relates to his focused interest or give him a special pencil or pen to be used only for checking the schedule.

For example, if he is especially interested in flags of other countries, attach a miniature flag of his favorite country to the end of a pencil. The pencil is kept with the schedule and is used only for the purpose of checking the schedule.

Some children are motivated by a bonus system. Each time he checks and follows his schedule, he earns a point. A certain number of points is good for a cash refund, a video rental, or another activity that is particularly meaningful to your child. If this isn't meaningful or helpful, discontinue its use.

Have the school principal or someone else in an official role, especially someone he particularly likes, show him his or her appointment book or day planner. Visit an office supply store and have your child choose an "official" appointment book or day planner.

There might be something about how the schedule looks that makes it visually unappealing or confusing to your child. Try simplifying it. Use one or two words for each entry. Leave enough space between the lines. Emphasize important information by highlighting or color-coding.

Go high tech! The daily schedule can be created on a mobile device, tablet, or computer. This technology continues to expand. At the time of this writing, apps for schedules have been developed with autistic teenagers and adults in mind.

13.   Incorporating the schedule as part of life

The schedule can serve many purposes, now and in the future. Use it daily, refer to it often, consult it when there are questions or issues, change it to reflect each day's uniqueness, and include it in everyday conversation to illustrate the things you are saying.

Refer to the schedule when there is discussion about what to do or when something will happen. Adapt your behavior or change the schedule accordingly. Help your child see it as a dynamic, valid, and trusted part of daily life. It will prove to be a valuable tool, now and in the future.

In North Carolina, we have observed that the adults with autism who are most successful in getting and keeping jobs are those who are proficient in following a schedule and using other organizational strategies. The time to teach, practice, and master these strategies is when the child is young and still in school.

14. Is the goal for my child to write his own schedule?

Not necessarily. The goal is to teach him to use a checklist to stay on track, stay organized, and function successfully in academic, social, and work situations. In adulthood, even if he cannot generate the list himself, owing to inherent organizational difficulties, he may still stay organized and work independently when he is given checklists written for him. In fact, it is an important vocational skill to be able to follow a supervisor's instructions.

15. To use or not to use?

Sometimes, parents or teachers feel that a daily written schedule is not needed during the school day because their child "goes with the flow" or usually "does what he is told." Or, after the schedule is used for a period of time, it is discarded because it "doesn't seem necessary."

In these cases, it is tempting to decide that using a schedule, along with other visual strategies recommended later in this book, is not really appropriate for your child. On one hand, this may appear to be true. In school, he may respond to verbal directions and seem to cope with transitions. He may be able to wait, without too many questions, until he has time to engage in his focused interests. Or, he may have memorized the routine of the school day and knows what is supposed to happen in the usual sequence. He might be easygoing, seemingly unconcerned, or unaware about upcoming events. He may get good grades and achieve academically in some subjects, "better than other students." After school, though, it may be a different story.

One first grader who was a "model student" would fall apart when he got home, wildly throwing whatever he could get his hands on.

A quiet sixth grader, after getting picked up by his mother at the end of the school day, would get into the car and immediately bang his head on the window.

Upon arriving home after school, a fourth grader in a program for the gifted and talented would run upstairs to his room, strip off his clothes, and refuse to talk to anyone for the rest of the evening.

A second grader who was impeccably polite at school would swear loudly and incessantly at home, calling his mother names.

It is not uncommon for autistic students to perform well in school, only to fall apart at home, as these examples illustrate. The amount of energy it takes for children with autism to function successfully in the overstimulating and demanding school environment may be inconceivable to those of us with typical development.

Structured teaching strategies, represented by the schedule in this chapter, offer predictability, familiarity, and clarity, resulting in an overall decreased level of anxiety. Along with the multiple uses already mentioned, "structure" is valued as a preventative behavioral management strategy because it helps children do the things they need to do more easily, requiring fewer times of nonrelenting effort and stress.

Six Examples of Schedules

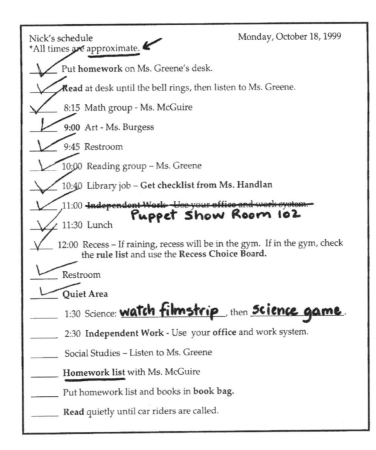

Nick's schedule
*All times are approximate.   Monday, October 18, 1999

___ Put **homework** on Ms. Greene's desk.

___ **Read** at desk until the bell rings, then listen to Ms. Greene.

___ 8:15 Math group - Ms. McGuire

___ 9:00 Art - Ms. Burgess

___ 9:45 Restroom

___ 10:00 Reading group – Ms. Greene

___ 10:40 Library job – **Get checklist from Ms. Handlan**

___ 11:00 ~~Independent Work - Use your office and work system.~~
     Puppet Show Room 102

___ 11:30 Lunch

___ 12:00 Recess – If raining, recess will be in the gym. If in the gym, check
     the **rule list** and use the **Recess Choice Board.**

___ Restroom

___ Quiet Area

___ 1:30 Science: **watch filmstrip**, then **science game**.

___ 2:30 **Independent Work** - Use your **office** and work system.

___ Social Studies – Listen to Ms. Greene

___ **Homework list** with Ms. McGuire

___ Put homework list and books in **book bag.**

___ **Read** quietly until car riders are called.

Schedule Example #1

Earlier this morning, Nick's teacher printed out today's schedule. The sequence and details vary from day to day. Certain words appear in bold to get his attention. Nick checks each line, one at a time, before starting the activity. He keeps his schedule on a clipboard in his desk.

Note that his teacher had to make a last-minute change at 11:00.

Ms Greene always follows the same procedure for science class, first presenting information to the entire class, followed by doing small-group activities. When science appears on Nick's schedule, she fills in the lines appropriately, so he knows what to expect. Information about school jobs and checklists appears on pages 267 and 272.

Ty's Afternoon Schedule   Sept. 21, 1999

☐ Relaxation ("Train Trip") with Ms. Craver

☐ Choose: Quiet Area or (Game Center)

☐ Social Studies

☐ Quiet Work in Office

☐ Mini-Tramp - set timer for 5 min.

☐ Job - straighten books in Reading Center

☐ Homework List with Ms. Craver

☐ Put Homework List + books in book bag

☐ Train Magazines at desk

☐ Bell - line up for Afterschool Program

Schedule Example #2

Ty's teacher writes his schedule by hand. Earlier in the day, she gave him his morning schedule, and now this one is for the afternoon. The sequence and details vary from day to day. Ty loves trains. He used train stickers to decorate the cover of a spiral notebook in which his "train schedule" is written. He is motivated to use his schedule and mark it as the day progresses by coloring in the "train cars," an adaptation of checkboxes designed just for him.

Note that his relaxation practice (which occurs right after lunch) is called "Train Trip." After the relaxation practice, Ty can choose to either continue to sit in the quiet area or join the other students for the busy after-lunch activities. This afternoon, Ty chose to go to the game center instead of staying in the quiet area.

Information about the quiet area can be found on page 280; relaxation on page 429; mini-trampoline on page 427; and school jobs on page 272.

Catie

After School - Monday

- Change Clothes
- Snack
- Alone Time
- 4:30 Feed Fish
- Show Mom Homework List
- Homework - follow checklist
- Dinner
- Vitamins
- Dishes to Sink
- Finish Homework, then Free Time
- Bath + P.J.s - follow checklist
- Check Calendar
- Quiet Time in bedroom
- 9:30 Lights Out
- "Good Night" ~ Kisses + Hugs ♡

Schedule Example #3

Sometimes, Catie can be very stressed after school. Her mother wrote this schedule by letting her begin the evening with solitary, less demanding activities: alone time, snack, and feeding the fish.

Catie loves fish. She is motivated by the little fish her mother draws on her schedule. There is a dot to the left of each line. This shows Catie where to put her pen to start drawing the line. She stops at the drawing of the little fish. In this way, Catie is motivated to accomplish and cross out each entry as she progresses through the evening.

Information can be found about alone time on page 280 and 321; homework on page 277 and 318; checklists on page 298; and the calendar on page 155.

July 3, 1999   Adam's Schedule
1. Breakfast
2. Wear shorts
3. Pack: Swim suit
        towel
        goggles
        Legos
4. Free Time: Ninendo or Legos
5. 10:30 Uncle Ron's house

6. Drive to Lake
7. Picnic Lunch
8. Fishing + Legos
9. Swim + Raft with Uncle Ron
        → Build Sand Castle!
10. McDonalds
11. Home
12. Bath
13. Bed

Schedule Example #4

Adam's mother wrote this schedule on both sides of an index card to help Adam prepare for an unusually busy and different day with the family.

Adam packed his swimming gear independently by checking the list under #3. He sees that there will be time for his favorite activities (Nintendo or Legos) after getting up and packing and before leaving for Uncle Ron's house.

When the family arrived at Uncle Ron's house, they discovered that he couldn't bring the raft because there was a hole in it. Uncle Ron suggested that they build a sand castle, instead. Adam watched his mother as she wrote the change on his schedule.

Adam can see what will happen when the outing is finished—McDonald's, home, bath, and bed.

When I get to camp:

☒ Put lunch in the cooler.

☒ Meet with **Amy** to go over the schedule for today. 👤

☒ **Quiet Area** – look over today's **schedule** by myself. 📋

☒ 9:30 Group Meeting – listen to **Scott** 🗣

☒ 9:45 Morning exercises – Listen and watch 👤 _Carolyn_

☒ 10:00 Outdoor activity: _Obstacle Course_

☒ 10:45 Snack. When finished, choose (Quiet Area) or Music Center

☒ 11:15 Arts and Crafts: ✂ _Paper mache masks_

☒ 11:45 Bathroom. **Wash my hands.**

☒ 12:00 Lunch: 🍴 _eat at red table_

☒ 12:30 Free Time – Choose: (Uno) or Drawing

☒ 1:00 (Not raining = POOL) or **Raining = Indoor Games**
Choose: _balls or scooter boards_

☒ 2:00 Bathroom

☐ 2:15 Snack. When finished, choose: Quiet Area or _Game Center_

☐ 2:45 **Get ready** for home: _Get shell frame_

☐ 3:00 Ride the yellow van home. 🚌

Schedule Example #5

Molly's summer day-camp counselor uses duplicates of the same form for the schedule every day, although the details change from day to day. Amy, the counselor, fills in the details of Molly's schedule before they meet at the beginning of the day. Molly is less anxious when she knows what to expect at camp.

Molly draws an "X" in each box as the day unfolds. Significant words for Molly have been bolded. Other words can be highlighted with a marker, when needed. Note that at 1:00, the issue of rain has been addressed in a clear manner.

There are times when Molly makes a choice. Choices have been indicated clearly on the schedule to clarify and ease her anxiety. Amy and Molly routinely circle her choices when they preview the schedule at the beginning of the day. Information about free time and rules can be found on pages 273-275.

Ways of Thinking

> CHRISTOPHER   NOV. 4, 1999
>
> 1. DADDY - PICK UP CHRIS AT 2:30
> 2. GO TO DR. LOVE'S OFFICE
> 3. WAITING ROOM - READ COMIC BOOKS
> 4. DR. LOVE - ANSWER QUESTIONS
> 5. "CARD + MAGIC" STORE - CHOOSE 1
>   NEW THING
> 6. MS. FRALEY'S HOUSE -
>   PLAY AT KITCHEN TABLE OR YARD
>
> 7. Home

Schedule Example #6

Christopher's father wrote a schedule this afternoon to help Christopher handle the stress and uncertainty of leaving school early and going to the doctor. In addition, Christopher's father planned to stop in at a friend's house before going home.

Christopher can see that they are going to his favorite store after the appointment. Christopher knows what he can expect to do in the waiting room, as well as what he can do at Ms Fraley's house.

Chapter 4
Talent and Creative Expression

Workbook

Music

Many people like to listen to music. Some people can express themselves more easily when they make music than when they use words.

Some children and adults have perfect pitch and a natural ability to sing or play a musical instrument. They might have very sensitive hearing.

I will circle or highlight what is true for me. 🖉

▶ I do not like to sing or to play an instrument. If I marked this, then I do not have to read any more on this page.

▶ I like to sing.

▶ I like to play a musical instrument (or many instruments). I play the _____.

▶ I like to make music or sing when I am by myself.

▶ I like playing alone, but it is OK if others listen to me.

▶ I would like to play an instrument or sing with other people in a chorus, a band, or an orchestra. (Circle which ones.)

▶ I would like to take music lessons or singing lessons.

▶ I would like to learn how to _____

_____.

▶ I enjoy listening to music. I like (kinds of music): _____

_____.

Talent and Creative Expression

Drama

Drama is an art form that many people enjoy. Some people like to go see movies, plays, and musicals.

Actors must pretend they are someone else. Some autistic people enjoy acting. They might be skilled at observing and copying how people move and how they sound. They like to pretend they are different characters.

I will circle or highlight what is true for me. ✏

▶ I am not interested in drama. If I marked this sentence, then I do not need to read any more on this page.

▶ I like to imitate the way people move and talk.

▶ I like to pretend I am someone else.

▶ Memorizing and remembering my lines is fun.

▶ I like to learn different ways to act.

▶ I like to dance.

▶ I would like to learn more about _____ .

▶ I enjoy attending plays, musicals, and/or ballets. My favorites are

_____

_____ .

Talent and Creative Expression

Drawing

The act of drawing and looking at drawings adds to the beauty and enjoyment of life.

Many autistic children and adults are quite skilled at drawing. Maybe they are good artists because they see the details and remember what they see. Maybe they are visual thinkers who automatically see pictures in their minds. Maybe it is more natural for them to express themselves by drawing, rather than using words.

I will circle or highlight what is true for me. ✏

- I do not like to draw. If I marked this sentence, then I am finished with this page.

- I like to draw.

- I like drawing with pencils or crayons. (Which?)

- I like drawing with pens or markers. (Which?)

- I like black and white, colors, or both. (Which?)

- I like using coloring books.

- I like drawing with computer programs.

- I like drawing comics.

- It's OK if people want to see my drawings.

- I don't want people to see my drawings.

- I would like to take a drawing class.

- I would like to learn how to _____.

- I enjoy looking at artwork by other artists. My favorite artists are

  _____

  _____

Talent and Creative Expression

Painting

Painting pictures and spending time looking at paintings add to the beauty and enjoyment of life.

Many autistic children and adults are quite skilled at painting pictures. Maybe they are good artists because they see details and remember what they see. Maybe they are visual thinkers who automatically see pictures in their minds. Maybe it is more natural for them to draw or paint than to express themselves in words.

I will (circle) or highlight what is true for me. ✏

▶ I do not like painting pictures. If I marked this sentence, then I am finished with this page.

▶ I like to paint pictures.

▶ I have favorite colors. They are: _____
_____ .

▶ I like watercolors, pastels, oil paints, acrylics. **(Circle which ones.)**

▶ I like coloring with crayons in coloring books.

▶ It's OK if people want to see my paintings.

▶ I don't want people to see my paintings.

▶ I would like to take a painting class.

▶ I would like to learn how to _____ .

▶ I enjoy looking at artwork by other artists. My favorite artists are:
_____
_____ .

Photography and Filmmaking

Photography and filmmaking are forms of art that require the use of cameras. There are many different types of cameras. Just like other art forms, there are many styles of photography and filmmaking. These are forms of art that require the artist to use his or her eyes; it is a visual form of art. Many autistic children and adults see things in interesting ways and have excellent visual skills.

I will circle or highlight what is true for me.

▶ I do not like to use cameras. If I marked this sentence, then I do not have to read any more on this page.

▶ I like to take pictures with a camera.

▶ I like to make videos or films with a camera.

▶ I want to do more still photography.

▶ I want to make videos.

▶ This is a way I can communicate my ideas.

▶ I like photography.

▶ I would like to take photos of _____.

▶ I would like to film videos of _____.

▶ I have never tried taking photos, but I want to try.

▶ I have never tried filming a video, but I want to try.

▶ I'd like to have time for photography on my schedule.

▶ Other: _____

_____.

Writing

Writing includes stories, essays, poetry, e-mail messages, blog posts, and other kinds of writing. Writing can help the writers and the people who read their writing think clearly, appreciate beauty in the world, laugh, cry, dream, and imagine new things.

Writing includes using pens, pencils, and/or keyboards. Some autistic children and adults enjoy words and have an advanced vocabulary. Some autistic people communicate more naturally and easily by writing on paper or with a keyboard, rather than talking.

I will circle or highlight what is true for me. 🖉

▶ I do not like to write on paper OR with a keyboard. If I marked this sentence, then I do not have to read any more on this page.

▶ I like to write. I like to write poetry, essays, comics, stories, letters, blog posts, or e-mail messages. (Circle which ones.)

▶ I prefer to keep my writing to myself. I do not like others to read what I have written.

▶ I like other people to read what I have written.

▶ It is easier for me to communicate by writing, rather than talking.

▶ I like to read aloud while other people listen to me.

▶ I would like to write about _____ .

▶ Other: _____
_____ .

Comics

Creating comics usually combines drawing and writing. Some children and adults are good at creating comics. Some comics are funny, but they don't have to be funny. Some comics are serious. Some comics simply express the artist's ideas. Autistic children and adults who like to draw and write comics find it to be a good way to express their ideas, experiences, concerns, and/or questions.

I will circle or highlight what is true for me. ✎

▶ I do not like to draw and write comics. If I marked this sentence, then I do not have to read any more on this page.

▶ I like to read comics.

▶ I like to draw and write comics.

▶ I want to show my comics to someone.

▶ I don't know whom to show my comics to.

▶ It is easier for me to communicate my ideas in comics, rather than talking.

▶ I would like to create comics about _____

_____ .

▶ I have never tried drawing comics, but I am interested in trying.

▶ Other: _____

_____ .

Making Things

Making things includes building, constructing, and assembling. It includes using materials like Legos, wood, metal, paper, plastic, cloth, clay, and other materials. It includes what is called "fabric art," such as sewing, embroidery, knitting, crocheting, and other needlework. It includes activities that are referred to as "crafts," such as using clay or other materials. It includes the use of specific tools. This talent may also be used for the drawing of designs, plans, and blueprints, before actually making something.

Many children and adults with autism are skilled and talented at one or more of these ways of making things.

I will circle or highlight what is true for me. 🖉

▶ I do not like to make things. If I marked this sentence, then I do not have to read any more on this page.

▶ I like to make things.

▶ My favorite tools are: _____ .

▶ My favorite colors are: _____ .

▶ My favorite materials are: _____ .

▶ In the first paragraph on this page, I will underline which things I like to do.

▶ I'd like to have time to "make things" on my daily schedule.

▶ Other: _____

_____ .

Talent and Creative Expression

Cooking

Some people enjoy cooking. They may be interested in cooking certain types of food. They may be interested in baking cookies, cakes, and pies. Many professional cooks regard the act of cooking to be a combination of art and science.

Some children and adults with autism are talented cooks.

I will circle or highlight what is true for me. 🖉

▶ I do not like to cook or bake. If I marked this sentence, then I do not have to read any more on this page.

▶ I like to cook.

▶ I like to bake.

▶ My favorite foods to cook or bake are _____
  _____ .

▶ My favorite ingredients to use when cooking are_____
  _____ .

▶ I don't know if I like to cook, but I'd like to try.

▶ I'd like to make dinner for my family.

▶ I'd like to make dinner and invite someone to share a meal.

▶ I'd like to try cooking this: _____
  _____ .

▶ Other: _____
  _____ .

Mechanical Projects

Many people with autism have good mechanical ability. They might like to figure out how things work. They might like to take things apart. They might like to put things together.

I will circle or highlight what is true for me. ✏

▶ I like taking things apart.

▶ I like seeing how things fit together.

▶ I like figuring out how things work.

▶ I like building and constructing things.

▶ I like planning and designing things to build.

▶ I am not interested in mechanical things.

▶ I would like to learn more about: (Circle)

- Cars

- Trains

- Heating systems

- Carpentry

- Construction

- Plumbing systems

- Electrical systems

- Electrical appliances

- Computers

▶ Other: _____

Computers, Tablets, and Other Technology

Working with technology requires specific abilities.

Many children and adults with autism are known for having excellent computer skills. Computers are literal, concrete, and predictable. A computer program follows its rules, exactly. Working with technology, like tablets, computers, and other technical developments, might come naturally and easily to some autistic people.

I will circle or highlight what is true for me. ✏

▶ I am not especially interested in technology. If I checked this, then I do not have to read any more on this page.

▶ I like playing computer games.

▶ I like to e-mail.

▶ I like to visit different Web sites on the Internet.

▶ I like drawing and graphic design.

▶ I like programming computers. (Programming is using the language of the computer to make it do things.)

▶ I like taking computers apart.

▶ I like building computers.

▶ I like other technology: _____.

▶ I would like to learn how to _____.

▶ Other: _____.

Many Other Ways

Being "creative" means to imagine and make things, to do things in unique ways, or to invent something different or new. There are many other ways of expressing yourself creatively. Other examples of creative expression are:

- Collage

- Quilting

- Appliqué

- Other fabric art: _____

- Sculpture

- Woodworking

- Designing and building bicycles

- Designing and building motorcycles

- Designing and building cars

- Architecture

- Arranging furniture in rooms of the house

- Other: _____

If I have a different talent or if I am skilled at something not mentioned in this chapter, I may write it here: ✐

_____ .

Especially for Older Readers

Older readers are invited to read an extensive and relevant chapter in another autism-friendly book, by the same author. I refer you to chapter 17, "Being Inspired—Role Models and Mentors," on pages 317-330 in the book, *Understanding Death and Illness and What They Teach about Life: An Interactive Guide for Individuals with ASD and Their Loved Ones*, published by Future Horizons in 2009. That chapter covers the importance of developing skills, talents, and interests and introduces the process of identifying role models and mentors.

For Parents, Teachers, and Therapists

Dave Spicer, who is quoted several times in this book, is a talented poet and essayist; however, his talent was not noticed or encouraged as a child. He recalls that even though his highest SAT scores were in the verbal sections, he was expected to study engineering in college. Dave only became aware of his own creativity with words later; one day, Dave says, a poem just "jumped out" of him.

I asked Dave to think about the questions below and to share his thoughts. Many thanks to Dave for pondering this subject and writing this section for parents and teachers.

Ideas in This Chapter:

☑ Why do you think creative expression is important?

☑ What are ways that parents might encourage their child's talent?

☑ Do you have any other insights about persons with autism and talent?

☑ What is your personal experience of developing your talent?

Why do you think creative expression is important?

> Creative expression can serve a number of purposes for an autistic person. It can be physically pleasurable, owing to the motor or sensory aspects of the activity. These could include the feel or smell of the materials being used, the colors, the sounds made by using them, and so on.

> It can be intellectually pleasurable, as the patterns, rhythm, and harmonies being externally manifested bring a greater sense of order and balance to one's thoughts.

It can offer practice at self-expression, at having one's thoughts and feelings take form in a way that affects the outside world. This is useful, since the very concept of being able to influence the outside world may be foreign.

Particularly with feelings, it can be a way of "doing something" with them and perhaps even "taming" them, so they feel less overwhelming.

It can be a means of communication. The activity can serve as a kind of bridge to connect one's internal state with the eternal world. Some autistic people may not realize that it is even possible for this to happen, so they may never expect to be understood. Others may expect everyone to know all their thoughts automatically, so they do not understand that thoughts have to be communicated at all. Using artistic expression as a way to practice communication can help people find the middle ground between these extremes.

It can be a way of interacting with society and contributing to it. The viewpoints of those "outside the mainstream" can offer information and perspectives that are not easily available from within it. Systems function much better with feedback, and the impressions of autistic folks, as expressed through art, can help provide this. One result of this feedback can be a broader understanding of the term "society," so that those outside the mainstream are recognized as still being part of it. This in turn brings greater richness through diversity.

What are ways that parents might encourage their child's talent?

A starting point can be the recognition of what is already taking place. It has been suggested that one's very life can be viewed as a canvas upon which one "paints" by living it; with this as a guide, examples of creative expression are likely already present. A child's special interests can offer situations for using artistic talent. How many different ways can the object (or objects) of interest be represented? What different situations can they be represented in? Could there be stories or songs about them? How about "documentaries" or advertising?

Do you have any other insights about persons with autism and talent?

The amount of enjoyment an autistic person gets from an activity may not be evident from his or her demeanor or behavior. Intense absorption may look like dispassionate detachment, and strong feelings of pleasure may be tightly contained within oneself to keep them manageable. Because of this, it may take considerable time to learn

what a child is actually interested in and enjoys. If a number of choices are made available, some might be ignored for a long time, then suddenly taken up with great enthusiasm. Conversely, a longtime favorite interest might be dropped suddenly, without explanation.

While a parent may very much want to learn why this happens, the child may well be unable to communicate or even understand the reasons. It may be quite frustrating to have a child who acts and speaks very precisely, explaining some of his or her preferences and actions in detail, and yet is unable to answer a direct question about others.

The area of creative expression does not appear to be entirely rational, which can cause difficulty for those who seek logical understanding of things. Drawings, songs, poems, and the like can seem to appear "out of nowhere" for no apparent reason. This may be disquieting to the person creating them, perhaps causing a blend of simultaneous enjoyment and apprehension. On the other hand, if the creation occurs in response to strong feelings, like frustration or anger, matters of intellectual appreciation may be completely set aside as the process becomes almost a visceral one.

What is your personal experience of developing your talent?

My own experience with creative expression is that of pent-up energy seeking an outlet. This energy is intensified by enjoying the creative expression of others. I do not feel that this energy can be created, but, rather, people can seek to become conduits for it. My challenges in this area do not involve trying to "become

more creative," but rather removing the barriers that keep what I have inside me from being expressed more freely.

I am grateful I do not have to completely understand the process of "creative expression" to be able to use it. As an autistic person, there are some aspects of life that, even though they escape my full understanding, I can still participate in and enjoy.

Chapter 5
People

Workbook

People

People

People are a part of life. There are people at home and people at school. There are children, teenagers, adults, and elderly people. There are people in stores, in cars, and on the street. Sometimes they are alone, and sometimes they are in groups.

People are different from objects. Objects are things like furniture, toys, and rocks. Objects usually stay the same, unless you do something to them. Some favorite objects in my life are:

1. _____

2. _____

3. _____

4. _____

5. _____

People change. I don't always know what will happen with people. Sometimes they talk loudly. Sometimes they talk softly. Sometimes they laugh. Sometimes they are quiet. The same person may look different from one day to the next. Voices change, faces and hair change, clothes change, and movements change.

I never know when a person will look or sound differently from before. People can be unpredictable and puzzling. Sometimes I like being with people, and sometimes I prefer being alone.

I get confused when people do or say these things:

_____

_____

_____

_____

_____

The People in My Family

Most children live with their families. Some children live with one parent. Some children live with two parents. Some children have stepparents. My parents' names are:

1. _____

2. _____

3. _____

4. _____

Some children have brothers and sisters. If I have brothers and/or sisters, their names are:

1. _____

2. _____

3. _____

4. _____

5. _____

6. _____

Sometimes grandparents, aunts, uncles, cousins, or friends live together in the same house. Sometimes children live in group homes, with people who are not in their families. If other people live with me, their names are:

1. _____

2. _____

3. _____

4. _____

5. _____

6. _____

More on People in My Family ...

Some children have two families. This happens when their parents are separated or divorced. Or, a child might have two or even three families if he or she lives with a foster family.

I will circle or highlight what is true for me. 🖉

▶ I have one family. We all live together in one home.

▶ I have two families, in two different homes.

▶ I have three families, in three different homes.

▶ My parents live together.

▶ My parents live in separate homes.

▶ My parents are divorced. They live in different homes.

▶ One of my parents has remarried.

▶ Both of my parents have remarried.

▶ I have a stepmother. She is my father's wife.

▶ I have a stepfather. He is my mother's husband.

▶ I have half-brothers or half-sisters.

▶ I have stepbrothers or stepsisters.

▶ Other: _____ .

"Remarried" means that my parent is now married to a new person.

This new person is my stepparent (stepmother or stepfather).

Half-brothers and half-sisters are siblings whose parents are my parent and my stepparent.

Stepbrothers and stepsisters are siblings who were born when my stepparent was married to someone else, before.

New or Different People at Home

Sometimes, people come to my home for a visit. Some visits are short, but others might last a few days or weeks. Sometimes a new person might live with us for a while. It may take time for me to get used to changes at home.

I will mark the events that have happened in my home. 🖉

- ▶ Having company or visitors

- ▶ Holidays when grandparents, aunts, uncles, or cousins visit

- ▶ Family parties, birthday parties

- ▶ Friends of brothers or sisters coming to play

- ▶ My friend or friends coming to play

- ▶ Men or women coming to clean, repair, build, or paint something

- ▶ One or both parents going out of town

- ▶ Having babysitters

- ▶ The arrival of a new baby

- ▶ Moving to a new house in a new neighborhood

- ▶ Parents moving to different houses

- ▶ Parents that are divorced

- ▶ My divorced parents getting married to someone else

- ▶ The arrival of a new stepparent

- ▶ Having new stepsisters or stepbrothers

- ▶ Other: _____
  _____
  _____

- ▶ Other: _____
  _____
  _____

My Family Tree

A family tree is a diagram of how family members are connected. It is called a *family tree* because it is like branches and stems growing out from a tree trunk. My family tree shows how I am connected to my family.

My parent and I can fill out the family tree on the next page by following these directions. We will check each box as we do what it says.

☐ Start at the bottom by writing my name on the line.

☐ Write in the names of my mother(s) and/or father(s). If I have stepparents, I will write their names too.

☐ Write in the names of my brothers and sisters on the dotted lines going down.

☐ Write the names of my grandparents at the top.

☐ Write the name of my aunts and uncles on the lines going down from my grandparents.

☐ If I want to include my cousins, then I need to draw lines coming out from their parents (my aunts and uncles).

☐ When finished, I can show it to someone in my family.

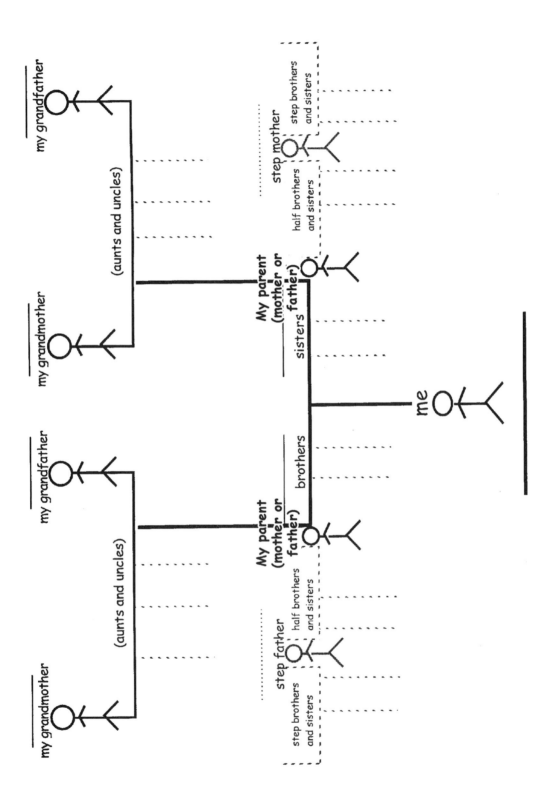

New or Different People at School

Sometimes, new or different people come into the classroom. Some children are happy to have new teachers and new students in the class. They think it is fun. Other children might become anxious, worried, scared, or angry when there are changes with people at school. It can be unfamiliar and different. At first, autistic children might not like these kinds of changes.

It may take more time for me to get used to new people at school.

I will mark what bothers me at school: ✏️

- ▶ Substitute teachers

- ▶ Student teacher

- ▶ New teacher or assistant

- ▶ Therapists coming to the classroom

- ▶ When the teacher moves my desk

- ▶ When other children's desks are moved

- ▶ My parents coming to my classroom

- ▶ Special visitors coming to the classroom

- ▶ Different children standing next to me in line

- ▶ Different children sitting next to me at lunch

- ▶ Different children playing on the playground

- ▶ A new student in my class

- ▶ Me going to a new class

- ▶ Other: _____
  _____
  _____

- ▶ Other: _____
  _____
  _____

Other Important People

There are other important people in my life. At school, the important adults are the ones I talk to every day. They might be teachers, assistants, therapists, the principal, office workers, cooks, and custodians. The names of the important adults for me at school are:

1. _____

2. _____

3. _____

4. _____

5. _____

There are children who are important to me at school. They might be friends or helpers. Their names are:

1. _____

2. _____

3. _____

4. _____

5. _____

There might be other important people in my life, too. They might be friends of my family, people at church or temple, people in the neighborhood, people at my parent's work, and people from other places. Other important people in my life are:

1. _____

2. _____

3. _____

4. _____

5. _____

Paying Attention to More Than One Person

Most children who have two parents have a relationship with both of their parents, and maybe relationships with other adults, like grandparents or aunts and uncles. In school, most students listen to and pay attention to more than one teacher.

Children with autism sometimes get confused when they have to pay attention to more than one person. Sometimes, it feels easier and more natural for a child with autism to pay attention to just one person at home. That is why some children might listen to one parent and ignore the other parent. If this is true, the other parent may feel left out.

I will mark what is true for me. ✏

▶ I usually pay attention to my mother and my father. I talk and listen to both of them.

▶ I usually just pay attention to only one of my parents. I mostly listen to my _____ .

▶ I live with one parent, or just one parent at a time.

▶ I pay attention to all of my teachers. I have   (number) teachers.

▶ I usually pay attention to only one of my teachers at school. I mostly listen to _____ (name).

▶ There are many adults who care about me, and I would like to have relationships with more of them. I would like to pay more attention to _____ (name).

▶ There are many adults who care about me, but right now, I would rather have a relationship with only one adult at school and one adult at home.

People

Being Safe

Most people in the world are good people. Good people are usually kind and helpful. They are safe.

But, there are some people who are not good. There are some children and adults who might try to hurt others or make them do things that are wrong. Someone might pretend to be kind, but he or she might not really be a good person.

It can be difficult for children to know if someone is a safe person or not. It is especially hard for autistic children to know if someone is a safe person. Some children with autism try to do what someone tells them to do, even if they don't understand why. Or, they might be very fearful and think that everyone wants to hurt them, even if someone is really a good and safe person.

I will ⬭circle or highlight what is true for me. 🖉

- ▶ I think that everyone is my friend.

- ▶ I always try to do what someone tells me to do, even if I do not understand why.

- ▶ I am afraid of people I do not know.

- ▶ Even when my parent says it's OK, I am still afraid of new people.

- ▶ I wonder if _____ (name) is a safe person?

- ▶ I wonder if _____ (another name) is a safe person?

- ▶ Some children at school tell me to do certain things, and I don't know why. For example, one time someone told me to _____ _____.

More on Being Safe ...

Most students at school are nice. But there may be a few students who aren't nice. There might be a child at school or in the neighborhood who bullies other kids.

A child who bullies may tell me to do things that are wrong or bad or scary or funny. Sometimes he or she tries to scare or hurt other children. He or she might hit someone. Or, the child who bullies might laugh a lot. A child who bullies might tell me to do something that gets me in trouble. He or she may say we are friends but then do something that doesn't make sense.

If there is a child who does things that scare me, or does things that might get me in trouble, or laughs at me, or says or does things that don't make sense, I must tell an adult. I must tell my teacher or my parent or another adult what the child does.

- I can keep myself safe by telling my parent or teacher or other adult when there is something I do not understand.

- The adults will only be able to help me if I tell them what has happened. If I do not tell them, then they will not know what has happened. If they don't know, then they won't be able to help.

- It is good to tell my parent or teachers when something doesn't make sense. For example, why does _____

_____

_____ ?

My parent or teacher can make a list of some of the adults or children in my life who are safe people. These are the ones who will know what to do about bullying. Here are names of safe children and adults who can help when there is something that doesn't make sense:

1. _____

2. _____

3. _____

4. _____

5. _____

My parent and I can do these things to help me learn how to be safe:

- My parent or teacher can make me an identification card with my phone number and address to keep with me. The phone numbers of my safe people will be on the card, too.

- I can practice using different types of phones and practice calling my safe people.

- My parent can write on the back of the identification card what I need to say if I need help, so I can read the words when I practice calling for help.

- If I ever really need to call for help, I will know what to do, because I have practiced it on a regular basis.

Friends

Friends are people who are special to me, in ways that feel good. Chapter 10 is all about friends.

I will circle or highlight what is true for me. ✏

- ▶ I want to read about friends.

- ▶ I don't understand lots of things about friends.

- ▶ I used to have a friend, but he (or she) moved away.

- ▶ I used to have friends, but I don't now.

- ▶ I don't know if I have friends.

- ▶ I have a friend whom I haven't seen in a long time.

- ▶ I have lots of friends.

- ▶ I have one friend.

- ▶ I have an online friend or more than one online friend.

- ▶ I have an animal friend.

- ▶ I have more than one animal friend.

- ▶ I have at least one brother or sister who is my friend.

- ▶ I have a friend who is a cousin.

- ▶ I have a friend who is autistic.

- ▶ I don't have a friend.

- ▶ I want to have a friend who is also autistic.

- ▶ Other: _____ .

For Parents, Teachers, and Therapists

"I really enjoy spending time with another person when both people are involved in separate and independent activities; this can be ideal—a sort of solitary togetherness."

—Jade, 2012

Consider using visually structured strategies to prepare your child or student for social events and to clarify relationships with the people in her life. Although these ideas may not magically or instantly change the underlying complexities regarding people, structured strategies may help make things easier by making sense of things through predictability, familiarity, and a sense of order.

Ideas in This Chapter:

☑ Listing new people on the schedule

☑ Using a calendar

☑ Writing a schedule of events when waiting for visitors

☑ Having overnight visitors

☑ Parents going out of town

☑ Making changes to the family structure

☑ Having substitute teachers

☑ Writing Social Stories

☑ Teaching a routine for getting help in public

Listing new people on the schedule

When your child encounters someone different than the usual people she sees at home or at school, you can write it on her daily schedule. Write the new person's name alongside the appropriate entry in context, even if your child doesn't yet know whom the person is. By routinely seeing the names of new people indicated on her schedule, your child will come to handle such changes with less anxiety. Developing a routine of seeing new people listed at appropriate spots on the schedule not only clarifies the change, but this gives it added meaning. Remember that to a child who relies on routines, the routine itself is meaningful.

A short written explanation at the top of the schedule might also be reassuring. For example, a note to prepare a child for a new sitter might read:

> *Debbie is sick. She has to stay at her house on Coleman Street today. Ms Hunter will babysit starting at about 4:00. Mama will return home sometime between 7:00 and 7:30.*

Using a calendar

Give your child her own calendar. Write what will be coming up on the square for the appropriate day and point it out to her ahead of time. If possible, attach the new person's photograph to the calendar to provide more specific visual information.

Use the calendar to prepare your child for physical changes in familiar people, such as someone who gets new glasses or contact lenses, a haircut, or even a suntan from going on vacation. Mark the calendar when you or a significant person will come home with a new or changed appearance.

A few children become overly focused on an upcoming event when they see it indicated on the calendar. For some, seeing the event listed on the calendar can be anxiety provoking. Having difficulty understanding the passage of time can make this problem worse. The child may think the event is going to happen immediately. You will need to pay attention to how much preparation time works best for your child. It may be that one day's notice is better than a week's notice. As your child gains more experience with the calendar, using it may prove to be more helpful in the long run—even if it causes problems at first—as you are figuring out the amount of lead time that works best.

Do this to teach the concept of time related to a calendar: Use a large monthly calendar with squares for each day. Before going to bed, have your child draw a red X over the "finished day's square." In the morning, circle the square for "today" with a green marker. Fill the squares in with little and big significant events as you introduce what's coming up.

Writing a schedule of events when waiting for visitors

Prepare for visits by family and friends by making a checklist of the things your child may choose to do during the visit. List some solitary activities, as well as activities that include the visitor, if appropriate.

Your child will probably enjoy interacting with the visitor if the activities involve her interests and if the activities have a clear beginning and end. Examples of the types of social activities that can be structured are playing card games or lotto games, playing bingo, naming people and places in a family photo album, and being a waiter or waitress and "taking orders" from the visitors for refreshments from a list you have written on a notepad.

Having overnight visitors

For overnight visitors, mark the days on the calendar to show how long the visitor(s) will stay. Putting photos on the calendar squares may help make it clear that the visitor "will be here on these days and nights." On the calendar, write something significant that your child will do after the visit is over on that day, so she can see what will happen next.

Remember to include information about the visit on her daily schedule, as well. Next to the appropriate entries, add information that may be significant for her, such as who will sit around the table at dinnertime, who will sleep where, and which TV programs might be watched. Giving her the job of putting "name cards" at the appropriate places at the table and taping the names of the people on the guest room door will help her feel some control over the space or home during the disruption of normal daily life.

Parents going out of town

Mark the calendar to show the days when you or your spouse will be out of town. Mark when you will return. On the appropriate calendar square, write where the absent parent will be each day or

something concrete that he or she is doing: "Daddy drives to Atlanta," "Mommy's at work in the Flat Iron Building," or "Daddy visits Aunt Suzie in Charleston and Mommy comes home."

Write short letters ahead of time, to be given to your child each day you are out of town. Help her see that you haven't just disappeared, but you are somewhere, doing something, and you will return on a specific date. Date the letters as if you are writing them each day.

Remember to include significant information on her schedule, like when it is time to say goodbye and which people are going to be involved with her on which days and what they will do. Help make the changes seem more predictable. Don't make assumptions about what she knows and understands.

If you have already been using a calendar and a schedule consistently, then the whole process will be more familiar to her, and she will handle the changes more easily!

Understanding changes in the family

If there are changes or additions to the family because of separation, divorce, or remarriage, draw a diagram or a family tree (see page 143) so your child can see how she and the other people are connected. This will provide her with a sense of order about the changes. Record births and deaths of important people and pets on the calendar. Write Social Stories (see below) to provide more information about such life-changing events.

Provide ample "alone time" or "quiet time" for your child at school and at home.

Having substitute teachers

Classroom teachers may prepare students for having substitute teachers by creating a file of photographs labeled with the names of possible substitute teachers. If you are planning to be absent, attach the appropriate photo or name card of the substitute teacher to the classroom calendar or the student's individual calendar to show when the substitute is coming and whom it will be. If you don't know whom it will be, you can make a blank card on which is written "Name? _____ ," and have the substitute teacher write her name on it when she gets there. Remember to take a photo of the new substitute teacher to add to the file for future use.

Sometimes, you'll have to prepare for the teacher's absence at the last minute. Throughout the year, the teacher can have the students look through the substitute teacher photo file periodically, so they are familiar with the faces and names. Make sure to always include the blank card, as described above, so it will always be there to visually remind your student that "We may not know who the substitute teacher will be."

When the teacher is absent, first thing in the morning, have a familiar teacher, assistant, or responsible student help the autistic student locate the appropriate photo for the substitute teacher and attach it to today's calendar square. (If the student already knows this routine and can manage it independently, there may be no need for assistance.) In cases of a "new substitute" when there is no card, write his or her name on the blank card and attach it to the calendar. Before leaving at the end of the day, make sure someone takes a photo of the new substitute teacher to add to the file, for future use.

Writing Social Stories

Write a Social Story about upcoming events. It may be written about almost any life experience, concept, or skill and may applaud achievement and acknowledge success. A Social Story that is written from the perspective of the child offers accurate social information regarding what to expect, what may occur, and what may have already occurred. This provides the context for more complete understanding. Be careful, as there are widely popular misconceptions about Social Stories. They are not written to tell someone how to act or to focus on changing her behavior. The purpose of a (real) Social Story is to provide information! Most of the text in this workbook is written in the style of true Social Stories. Carol Gray, in *The New Social Story Book* (Future Horizons, 2010), states that, "… the most common misconception is that the goal of a Social Story is to change [your child's] behavior. This has never been the case. The goal of a Social Story is to share accurate information meaningfully and safely."

Try to attend a Social Story™ workshop and get information from Web sites and resources that are authorized by Carol Gray, the creator of the Social Story approach. You can also look for the trademark sign (™) on Social Story materials, which denotes that they are indeed the real thing. You will find hundreds and thousands of hits online for "social stories" that misrepresent the intent and use of the

Social Understanding approach. The author of this book, Catherine Faherty, is one of a few authorized Social Story trainers worldwide. To arrange for a workshop with Catherine Faherty in your area, visit *catherinefaherty.com*.

Here is an example of a situation and the Social Story that was written for a third-grade child who had great difficulty every time there was a substitute teacher in his class:

Because of personal health issues, Mrs Smith knew she was going to be absent many days that winter, and she worried that one of her students may have problems with the substitute teacher. After asking this student many pointed and concrete questions (by talking with him and asking him in writing), I discovered that he thought the substitute teacher was someone who just walked in off the street and started teaching the class! He did not know the reason for having this new person in the room, acting like she was a teacher. He did not understand that this different person was supposed to take his teacher's place on purpose. It is noted that the principal had intervened many times in the past and told the student that he needed to behave and listen to the substitute teacher, but the student continued to show disrespect and refused to listen or work when there was a substitute teacher. It wasn't until this student read this Social Story that it all made sense.

A Social Story: Substitute Teacher Days

My teacher is Mrs Smith. Most of the time during the school year, she is at school on Mondays, Tuesdays, Wednesdays, Thursdays, and Fridays. Sometimes, Mrs Smith has to stay at her house because she is sick or she has to go to the doctor's office. On those days, she cannot come to school.

The children in our class still need to have a teacher, even if Mrs Smith cannot come to school. On the days Mrs Smith cannot come to school, the principal assigns a different teacher to be the teacher in our class. This different teacher is called a "substitute teacher" because she is substituting for Mrs Smith. Usually, our substitute teacher is Mrs Rider, but sometimes it may be someone else.

If Mrs Smith knows ahead of time that she will have to stay home, she will tell us. Sometimes, Mrs Smith does not know when she will have to stay at home. When this happens, the other children in my class and I will find out that we are going to have a substitute teacher when we get to school in the morning.

Mrs Smith leaves directions for the substitute teacher about what to do and what to say in our class. The students in Mrs Smith's classroom try to remember that the substitute teacher is following Mrs Smith's directions on Substitute Teacher Days.

Teaching a routine for getting help in public

Have your child carry an identification card or wear an identification bracelet or necklace. One side of the card can contain the typical identification information. The other side can be a "cue card" for your child to use in an emergency. It might contain reminders, like how to use a phone or how to ask a store manager to use a phone. The written reminders would augment your actual teachings on how to make a phone call. If the necessary information cannot fit on the back of card, make a special small, folded card that can fit into a wallet, purse, or pocket.

Practice using different types of phones. Write and laminate the directions, listing the steps to follow in sequence. As your child becomes familiar with the routine, list the steps on a small card or on the back of her identification card.

Depending on your child and her ability to function independently in this kind of situation, and depending on her access to a phone, you may want to teach her to give the cue card to someone (like a store manager) for help. It may be easier for her to hand a card to a salesperson when she is feeling anxious than to try to talk. The message on the card might read, "I'm a little nervous. Can you help me call home?" Teach her a routine of going into a store, asking for the manager, and asking to use the phone (or handing over the cue card). Practice frequently—first at home, then in different public locations, like the mall. You might feel more comfortable initially by setting these situations up in a familiar store, where you are known.

Keep in mind that even though your child may be very verbal, when she's experiencing stress, she may not be able to use her verbal skills effectively. By providing her with an alternative communication system (a written cue to read or to hand to someone), she may be more able to function in an emergency.

Remember to include and list practice sessions on her schedule, from time to time. If she resists you when you try to teach her this, or if you want to get help teaching her about safety, ask another significant adult—a teacher, friend, grandparent, aunt, uncle, or older cousin—to read these suggestions and help set up a practice session. For more ideas and complete information, refer to the pages titled, "What is an emergency?", "What is a difficult situation?", and "Why should I practice the plan when an emergency is not really happening?" in my book, *Understanding Death and Illness and What They Teach about Life*. Also, make sure to read the parts of this workbook that cover "getting help" and related topics.

Chapter 6
Understanding

Workbook

Eye Contact

Eye contact means looking directly at someone's eyes. Many children listen and understand better when they look directly into the eyes of the person who is talking. Most children make eye contact when they are paying attention to someone talking to them. That is why people think that if I make eye contact, I will understand them better. When I don't make eye contact, they think I am not paying attention. This is true for many children, but it may not be true for many autistic children.

I will circle or highlight what is true for me. 🖉

▶ I can make eye contact or I can listen, but it is difficult to do both at the same time.

▶ It is difficult to understand what the person is saying when I have to look at their eyes.

▶ It is easier for me to understand what people are saying when I look somewhere else.

▶ I do not like eye contact because it is uncomfortable.

▶ Sometimes I like to make eye contact and listen at the same time.

▶ Other: _____ .

If someone says "Look at me" when they want my attention, and if I have difficulty doing it, I may say:

> **I am paying attention.
> Right now, I can listen better when I look away.**

Words: Literal Meanings and Figures of Speech

Some words and phrases have two meanings. The first meaning is literal. *Literal* is when the word means exactly what it says.

But sometimes, people use figures of speech. These phrases actually mean something different than what is literally said.

For example:

- "Hit the road" doesn't really mean to literally hit the road. When people say "hit the road," it means it is time to go somewhere else.

- "Off the wall" doesn't really mean that something is off of the wall. When people say "off the wall," it means something is unusual or odd.

- "Straighten up" doesn't really mean that someone needs to stand straight up. When people say "straighten up," it means they want you to have good behavior and follow the rules.

More Examples of Figures of Speech ...

Someone can help me list more figures of speech and what they mean.

Figure of Speech	What It Means

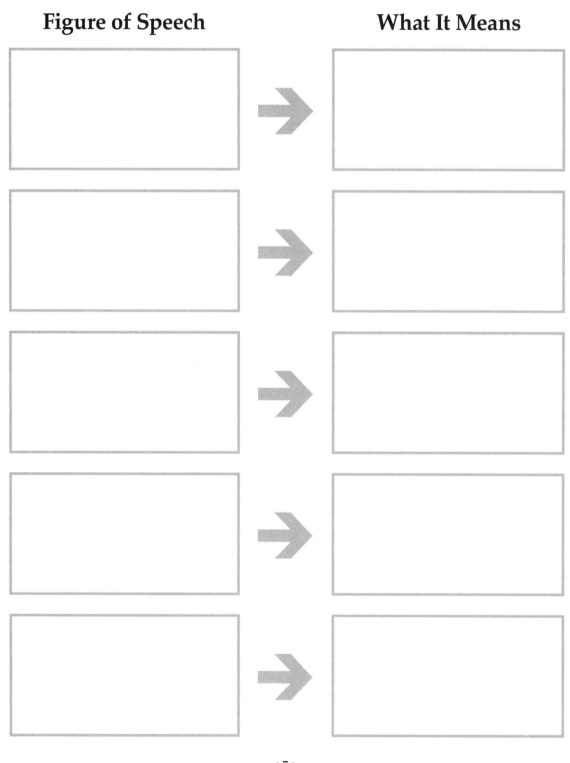

Body Language and Facial Expressions

People communicate by talking and writing. People also communicate by moving their faces and their bodies. When they communicate by moving their bodies, it is called *body language.* When they communicate by moving their faces, it is called *using facial expressions.*

- Body language means something. But, it doesn't always mean the same thing!   For example, when a person turns and puts her back to you, it might mean she doesn't want to talk anymore. Or, it might mean she has to sneeze and doesn't want to sneeze on you. Or, it can mean something else!

- Facial expressions mean something. But, they don't always mean the same thing! For example, when a person moves his eyebrows close together, making lines in the skin between his eyebrows, it might mean he is confused. Or, it might mean he is angry. Or, it might mean something else.

The meaning of body language and facial expressions is not always exact, but most non-autistic children understand them automatically. I can see that people move their bodies and faces, but I may not always know what it means. Understanding body language and facial expressions may not come naturally for children with autism.

Understanding

More on Body Language and Facial Expressions ...

When people want to communicate with me, they should communicate so I know exactly what they mean.

It is best for someone to communicate in words that are:

- Specific
- Concrete
- Literal

If I do not understand what a person is saying or writing, I may say to that person,

"Will you please be more specific?"

Examples of Typical Facial Expressions That are Happy ...

Look through magazines for pictures of people's faces with happy expressions. I will cut out four happy expressions and tape them here. ✂

Understanding

Examples of Typical Facial Expressions That are Not Happy ...

Look through magazines for pictures of people's faces with expressions that are not happy. I will cut out four unhappy expressions and tape them here. ✂

Understanding My Facial Expressions

It is true that most autistic people find it difficult to interpret and understand the body language and facial expressions of other people. But, it is also true that non-autistic people cannot always interpret and understand MY facial expressions!

For example, there may be a time when I am feeling happy or content, but my face may have a serious look, and I may not be smiling. If someone looks at my face, they may think I am angry or sad. They don't understand that I am feeling happy or content. They misinterpret my facial expression.

I will circle or highlight what is true for me. ✏

▶ What does "facial expression" mean?

▶ Sometimes people ask me, "Are you okay?" and they think I am feeling bad, when I'm not.

▶ I usually don't smile, even when I am feeling happy.

▶ I don't know what my face looks like when I am feeling content and happy.

▶ I don't know what my face looks like when I am feeling sad.

▶ Sometimes people think I am happy, when I am not happy.

▶ This page is confusing.

▶ Other: _____ .

Understanding

Difficulty Understanding People

When people talk, I hear their words. Even though I know the words, sometimes I don't understand what they are saying.

I will circle or highlight what is true for me. 🖉

▶ It is difficult for me to understand when:

▶ Others talk quickly.

▶ They use too many words.

▶ They use words I don't know.

▶ They use figures of speech.

▶ They talk when there are too many other sounds.

▶ They don't wait for me to think about what they have said.

▶ They talk with a foreign accent or a different dialect.

▶ They say "look at me" and want me to make eye contact.

▶ They talk to me when I am thinking about something else.

▶ They talk when I am worried, anxious, or overwhelmed.

▶ They don't want to type or write what they are saying.

▶ Other: _____ .

People in my life who are difficult to understand are:

1. _____   3. _____

2. _____   4. _____

Understanding People Better

Some people are easy to understand. The names of people in my life whom I understand more easily are:

1. _____ 3. _____

2. _____ 4. _____

I will circle or highlight what is true for me. 🖉

I can understand people better when they:

▶ Use fewer words.

▶ Talk at a slower speed.

▶ Pause and give me time to think.

▶ Remember that I understand words literally.

▶ Explain any figures of speech they may use.

▶ Talk to me in a quiet place.

▶ Stop to ask if I understand, before saying more.

▶ Ask me if I have any questions about what they have said.

▶ Don't insist on eye contact. It's OK if I look away.

▶ Communicate in writing—on paper.

▶ Communicate by typing.

▶ Ask me to choose: talking or typing?

▶ Other: _____

_____ .

Seeing What They Mean

Many children with autism understand people better when they can see what is being communicated. It might be easier for me to understand people when I can read what they are saying or if there are pictures.

One intelligent high school student told her teachers, "I understand when you talk, but I really understand when you write it down."

If someone wants to tell me something important, it usually helps if they write it down. A *computer conversation* is when I sit next to someone with a computer or a tablet. The other person can type, and I can read what is being said. Then it's my turn to type, or I can choose to talk.

I will mark what I like. 🖉

- ▶ I like when people just talk. I like to listen to what they are saying, even if they talk fast.

- ▶ I like when people write or type, quietly. I like to read, without having to listen. It is better for me this way.

- ▶ I like when people talk and write it down. I can understand better when I listen and read what they are saying, at the same time.

- ▶ I like when people type their words while they are talking. I can understand easily when I read and listen while we are sitting at a computer or tablet.

- ▶ I don't know how I like to have conversations.

- ▶ Mostly, I don't like conversations.

- ▶ I'd like to try some of the ideas with a tablet or computer.

- ▶ Other: _____

_____.

Tuning Out

Some children or adults might not hear or understand what someone is saying because they tune out. When they are tuned out, they miss what has been said.

I will circle or highlight what is true for me. ✎

- ▶ Sometimes I tune out.

- ▶ I never tune out.

- ▶ I do not know if I tune out or not.

Some children tune out for only a few seconds—only a very short time. Or, they might tune out for a long time. They might miss a lot of information. If I tune out, it may be because:

- ▶ I am overwhelmed by too many sights and sounds. Tuning out is taking a break from it all.

- ▶ I might be paying more attention to my own thoughts and feelings inside of me.

- ▶ I tune out when _____ .

The ideas in this book can help me with all the things I have to hear, see, feel, and understand. There is more information about understanding in the section about communication.

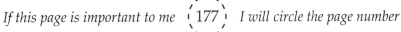

Understanding

For Parents, Teachers, and Therapists

"In general, I avoid eye contact because it adds to the amount of stuff my brain has to do. There are lovely things about this brain of mine, but it can really only do one thing at a time. So, while I can concentrate very deeply, I can't pay attention to more than one thing at once. One thing at a time, and one thing only please!"

—Jade, 2012

Ideas in This Chapter:

☑ A critical gap between talking and understanding

☑ Take a close look

☑ Eye contact

☑ Choice of words

☑ Be aware of distractions

☑ Structuring time to listen

☑ Body language

☑ Writing it down

☑ Tuning out

☑ Choice of words

☑ Pacing and Pausing

A critical gap between talking and understanding

It is now well documented that autistic children, teenagers, and adults frequently have difficulties understanding spoken language and/or processing auditory information. Typically, their auditory comprehension is weaker, compared with their overall cognitive abilities. Receptive language difficulties are often more obvious among children who are nonverbal and those who have significantly limited skills. However, making assumptions about a person's verbal skills and what she understands can complicate matters for highly verbal autistic individuals—both children and adults.

Your child can talk and read. She may be talented in one or more areas. She might perform well on some standardized tests. She may be quiet or introspective, or she may be quite articulate about certain subjects. Some children with autism are very talkative, and some are described as "little professors." It is no wonder that parents and teachers assume their autistic student understands everything that is said.

Frequently, though, there is a critical gap between expressive and receptive language skills. A complete speech and language evaluation may be indicated, with special focus on receptive language, pragmatics, and the social use of language and communication.

Take a close look

Even if your child has a large vocabulary, she might have difficulty making sense out of what she hears. So much of her understanding is related to the unique way she thinks and learns, her focus on particular subjects, how she experiences the sensory environment, how she interprets social interaction, and whether or not she is aware of the context of a situation.

Can your child digest and organize the large amount of spoken information encountered in school? How does she interpret the concepts, details, nuances, and meanings of everyday conversation?

Closely examine the manner in which you communicate. Observe your habits and notice your assumptions about communication. Most of us talk automatically, without giving thought to how well the child may be receiving the information. We need to slow down and notice how we use words, how we explain and provide information, the pace of our speech, and our assumptions about what is being communicated nonverbally. As with all the suggestions in this book, you must determine through trial and observation which of these issues matter most in helping your individual child deepen her understanding.

Eye contact

It is a commonly held belief that for the listener to understand what the speaker is saying, the listener must be looking at the speaker. Eye contact is an indication that the listener is paying attention. Logic and experience tell us that if the listener is looking elsewhere, it is proof that she is not really paying attention. So, to make sure a child is paying attention to his teacher or parent, she must first make eye contact. True?

Not always. It may be true for most typically developing children, but it is likely not true for autistic children, teens, and adults.

Autistic adults have spoken clearly about the issue of eye contact. One person explains that he can look at someone or listen to someone, but he cannot look and listen at the same time. Another autistic

person very poignantly asks, "Do you want me to look at you, or do you want me to understand what you are saying?" Yet another person said that he can make eye contact if necessary, but much of his comprehension is then "sacrificed."

"I can actually pay closer attention with my eyes closed."

—John, age 31

It appears that the issue is not only an "either/or" situation but that comprehension may actually increase for many children when they have the freedom to look in another direction while processing the spoken word. Simultaneously looking (attending to and interpreting someone's eyes and facial expression, while noticing details in the eyes and on the face), listening (processing language), reflecting on the meaning, and then noticing one's own response, is a complicated process that requires the listener to split his attention, shift his attention, and integrate these multiple perspectives.

The amount of stimulation and "social expectation" (according to one man with autism) that is present with eye contact can be experienced as overwhelming. An autistic woman has said that making eye contact is often physically painful for her.

Allow your child to follow her instinctive inclination to look away when she is listening, if that is what comes naturally to her. Acknowledge the fact that she is trying to process what you are saying as best she can. Teach your child about eye contact and how it is perceived by the mainstream, typically developing culture, but appreciate the differences. Furthermore, respect the differences, and teach other important people in your child's life to respect them, as well.

Choice of words

Remember that your child's first interpretation of a word will probably be its literal meaning. When you want something to be understood clearly, choose vocabulary that is concrete, with the intended interpretation being the literal one.

In a relaxed moment, after making sure that your child understands what you are saying, you might want to take the opportunity to teach other ways of saying the same thing. It might be fun to make a list of alternative phrases and figures of speech, paired with their literal meanings. You can introduce figures of speech, one by one, as time goes on.

Pacing and pausing

It may take your child longer than anticipated to process spoken information. Remember to pause and wait in silence before expecting a reply. Refrain from repeating yourself, unless she asks. Take a breath, be patient, and remember that your pause may seem like an eternity to you, but in reality, it isn't.

Slow down if you have a tendency to talk quickly.

Try to get into the habit of speaking in a calm, matter-of-fact tone of voice, especially when dealing with subjects or situations that may be stressful or anxiety provoking. Too much emotion in your voice may be distracting, confusing, irritating, or frightening to your child.

Try not to be too wordy. The most effective

communication from your child's point of view is concise and simple. She will be able to pay attention to what is most relevant when you limit extraneous information.

Be aware of distractions

Pay attention to the surrounding environment when communicating. If there are distractions, your child or teen may not be able to concentrate on what is being said. Wait until later when things calm down, or move to a quieter and calmer place. Say, "Let's go over here ..." or "Let's move to the other room, so we can talk and listen to each other more easily."

Try to become aware of your child's "inner environment," and notice if she is getting distracted by her own thoughts or if she is becoming anxious. If she is upset because of something that has happened, or if she is focused on a particular idea or subject, this is not the time for her to listen and take in new information.

Structuring time to listen

Use your child's daily schedule to help her manage her "inner distractions" or her need to talk about her favorite subjects. If something else needs to be done or talked about, or if she needs to let go of a particular subject right now, you can use her schedule to help clarify that it is time to move on and that she can still talk about her concern or subject later. For example:

Retrieve her schedule while she is watching, and write a new entry that shows when it will be time for her to talk about her topic. Point to her schedule as you say, "First, we are talking about [parent's subject], and then it will be time for [feeding the dog], and then it will be time for [her concern or subject]." Seeing clearly that she will get to talk or engage in "her" subject might allow her to be able to more easily shift her attention to something else.

Although this example refers to a home situation, the same strategy can be applied at school.

There may be times when you agree it is important to talk right now or deal with the subject that is of her immediate concern. Again, use the schedule to clarify what is expected. She needs to see that she cannot talk about it for the rest of the day and that there are other things to do, too. This may even come as a relief to her. Add or change the schedule accordingly. On her schedule, in the appropriate spot, you can write, "talk about _____ until _____ (time)." Then point out on the schedule what will happen next.

Body language

Except for very general poses, the interpretation of body language is nearly impossible to teach because of its transient nature and the fact that subtle changes of movement or posture can result in dramatically different meanings. Individual differences make this area all the more perplexing; identical postures or movements made by one person do not guarantee the same meaning when done by another person. Plus, the same posture looks different on a different body!

One young adult with autism went to the library in search of books that explained body language. He was able to memorize a few basics, although body language and nonverbal communication still remain a mystery to him. In the end, it may simply be enlightening for young autistic people to know that there is such a thing as body language and to realize that it can be hard to interpret. Teaching them other ways to get information may be more helpful.

On the other hand, depending on your child and his interest in exploring this complex issue, you might want to point out common gestures, expressions, postures, and stances. Label what you consider to be the most common interpretation of body language basics—especially those that occur on a regular basis with familiar people at home or in the classroom. If appropriate, have your child identify these with you or someone else during the actual act of communication, in real time. One young woman recently learned to ask important people in her life—while they are talking with her— what their body language and facial expressions mean.

If there is sufficient interest, motivation, or need, you might make a game of it, in the style of "charades." Family members or classmates can take turns modeling gestures and postures, while others have fun guessing the meaning. When typically developing people do this, they will discover just how difficult it can be to define nonverbal communication accurately.

A similar activity can be designed by using videos of dramatic programs, such as soap operas. Pause the tape at the pertinent moments to discuss the possible meaning. Rewind to more closely examine and label the various postures and gestures.

Writing it down

Visual learners respond positively and naturally to visually structured teaching styles. Although the written word is used most often among those who can read and write, pictures, icons, and photographs may enhance comprehension for some individuals. Experiment to find out.

If you want to increase your child's comprehension, write or type what you are saying as you are speaking to her. Do this especially when you want to be sure that your child understands the message.

If you must communicate with your child or student when she is anxious or upset, don't talk. Instead, write her a note. (See pages 175-176, 249, and 410)

Support communication by sitting side by side at a computer or tablet and take turns typing, with or without pairing it with speech. I started inviting my students and clients to have computer conversations like this many years ago. Happily, this strategy is becoming increasingly more accepted, even between verbal communication partners. Some children and adults can process information more easily if the verbal and the visual are not given simultaneously as you type, but rather one after the other. The sequence may be significant; for some, it may work best if the written word comes first to prepare and focus, followed by the spoken word. For others, the written word needs to follow the spoken word to confirm or enhance the meaning. For many, a silent conversation conducted by typing is exactly what is needed for authentic self-expression and mutual understanding. I usually let my communication partner on the spectrum choose how he or she would like to start off. If there is no preference, I

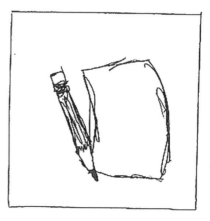

usually opt for silent communication in the beginning. There is more discussion about communicating by typing in chapter 8.

A daily schedule should be included as part of daily life. It is easier to help your child understand the big picture, including expectations at home and school, when you structure things in visually clear ways. Using a daily schedule has been introduced in detail in chapter 3 and is recommended throughout this book.

Additional visually structured teaching strategies, such as a work system, written instructions, checklists, written rules, and other visual methods to increase your child's understanding at school, will be introduced in chapter 9. Use them.

Chapter 11 deals with helping your child understand what happens when she feels upset. Visual strategies such as "Mind the gap" and "the Emotion-meter" may be helpful.

Tuning out

As introduced on page 177 of the workbook, your child's coping mechanism in an overwhelming environment may simply be to "tune out." However, most professionals recommend that children with autism undergo evaluation by a neurologist to rule out other complications. If your child or student has staring spells or repetitive eye movements, falls asleep in the middle of activities, falls asleep often, loses skills that she has previously mastered, exhibits seizure-like behaviors, has had a seizure, or seems to "tune out" several times a day, she should be referred to a neurologist.

Chapter 7
Thoughts

Workbook

What Are Thoughts?

Thoughts are what I see or hear or feel in my mind …

- When I remember something that has happened, when I see a picture in my mind.

- When I remember how something felt, when I think words quietly to myself.

Everyone has thoughts. Thoughts are words or pictures or feelings in other people's minds, too.

Here I am. I will write some thoughts I have had today, in the thinking bubble.

Who Has Thoughts?

I have thoughts. My parent has thoughts. Brothers and sisters have thoughts. Grandparents have thoughts. My teacher has thoughts. Children have thoughts. Teenagers have thoughts. Adults have thoughts.

Everyone has thoughts.

Thoughts

Hopes Are Thoughts

Hopes are thoughts about what I want to happen. It may feel good to think about my hopes. Sometimes what I hope for may happen soon, and sometimes it happens much later. Sometimes what I hope for never happens at all. Sometimes, there might be things that I can do to help make my hopes happen, someday.

I hope that _____

_____

_____

_____

_____ .

No one knows my hopes unless I tell them or show them what my hopes are. I can tell my hopes to these important people in my life:

1. _____

2. _____

3. _____

4. _____

5. _____

Fears Are Thoughts

Fears are thoughts that make me feel afraid or worried.
Everyone has fears, sometimes.

Sometimes I feel afraid when I don't know what is going
to happen. I might cry. I might yell. I might be very quiet.

When I have fears or when I am afraid, I can tell my
fears to someone who cares about me. My parent and
my teacher care about me. But they don't know my fear
unless I tell them or unless I write it down and show
them what I have written. Here are the names of some of
the important people whom I can talk to or write to when
I am afraid.

1. _____

2. _____

3. _____

4. _____

5. _____

These people will not make fun of me for being afraid.
They know that everyone feels fear sometimes. They will
listen to me. Sometimes I am afraid that _____
_____
_____ .

Imagination: A Fantasy World

Many children and adults like to think about things that they can actually see and hear and touch. Sometimes people think about things that are only in their minds—not things that they can see and hear and touch. This is called "using their imagination." It's also called "pretending."

Some people have lots of imagination.

I will circle or highlight what is true for me. 🖉

▶ I usually think about actual things that I can see and hear and touch in the real world. I do not like to pretend.

▶ I like using my imagination and being in a fantasy world.

▶ I like to pretend.

▶ Having lots of imagination means that my mind may be filled with thoughts about pretend things. Imagination may be fun. It may help me be creative and think about new ideas.

▶ Sometimes I might pretend so much that I forget I am in the real world. People may say I am in a "fantasy world." They try to remind me that the real world is my home and my school and the other places and people I can see and touch and hear.

▶ It may be fun for me to be in my fantasy world. But other people at school or at home may not understand about my fantasy world, since they cannot see it.

▶ If having too much imagination causes a problem at school or home, then my schedule can show me when it is "imagination time." I can see that sometimes it is time to think about my fantasy world, and sometimes it is time for the world of school and home.

Other People's Thoughts

Other people have pictures or words or feelings in their minds, too. They have their own thoughts. Their thoughts are silent and invisible to me. I cannot hear or see or feel other people's thoughts. Only they know their thoughts.

Other people have thoughts.

Other people's thoughts are like a box that is closed. I cannot see what is inside a closed box. I can make guesses, but I do not really know for sure what thoughts are inside other people's minds unless they tell me.

Who Knows My Thoughts?

I know my own thoughts. I can see or hear or feel my thoughts. My thoughts are in my mind.

Other people cannot see or hear or feel my thoughts.

My mind is like a box with my thoughts inside. No one knows what is inside, except me. Sometimes people can guess what I am thinking, but they don't know for sure. My parent or teacher or another person cannot know my thoughts for sure, unless I tell them.

When I tell someone my thoughts, it is like opening the box so the other person can see what is inside.

Telling someone my thoughts or writing my thoughts and giving them to my parent or teacher or friends is called *communicating*.

For Parents, Teachers, and Therapists

Assumptions

Your child may assume that you know what she has experienced at school, even though you were not there. She may assume you know what she is thinking. She may assume you are thinking the same thing she is thinking.

Matters can be complicated further; one autistic adult explained that he isn't always sure if he has simply thought something or if he has actually said it aloud. When recalling memories of his childhood, he now realizes he often assumed that he had spoken and that others had heard him, when, in reality, he had only thought the words to himself.

Comic Strip Conversations

Comic Strip Conversations can be used alongside Social Stories, as developed by Carol Gray. Comic Strip Conversations are interactive strategies to help understand the child's, teenager's, or adult's assumptions about a social situation. Comic Strip Conversations are created with stick figures, "thought bubbles," and "talking bubbles" to visually depict social interactions. With colored pens and paper, stick figures are drawn to represent the person and others involved in the interaction. Bubbles are filled in with words to demonstrate what was said and guesses at what people were thinking. Emotional content may be color coded. This strategy helps the teacher, therapist, or parent find out the child's perceptions and assumptions about what has happened. Comic Strip Conversations may be used with people of any age, not just children.

Carol Gray writes that Comic Strip Conversations "systematically identify what people say and do and emphasize what people may be thinking … each Comic Strip Conversation regards the thoughts and feelings of others as holding equal importance to spoken words and actions in an interaction." She goes on to explain that "Comic Strip Conversations often provide insights into a student's perspective of a situation and serve as an excellent prerequisite to the development of a Social Story."

Chapter 8
Communication

Workbook

Communicating by Talking Is Natural to Many People

Most people in the world automatically communicate by talking. Many people tell their thoughts and ideas to other people. They ask about other people's thoughts, and they like to listen to what other people are saying.

Communication through talking is natural and easy for many children and adults.

- This is why most children play in groups at recess. They talk and laugh and sometimes yell.

- They play games together.

- They cluster around the same tables in the classroom, talking.

- They talk a lot at lunch and want to sit next to each other whenever they can.

- Often, they work quietly by themselves only when the teacher tells them they have to.

Communication might feel different to me. Communication through talking might not always feel natural, easy, or fun to many autistic people.

Communicating May Not Always Feel Easy

Many autistic children may not automatically communicate when they are around people. They may not know what to say, or they may not have the right words. They may not know when it's their turn to talk or when to stop talking. It may be difficult to understand a group of people, when they are all talking at the same time. Some children may enjoy being alone more than being around other people. Or, they may want to talk with another person who has the same interests.

Communication

I will ⬭circle⬭ or highlight what is true for me. ✐

- ▶ I usually do not like to listen to people talking.

- ▶ I usually do not like to talk to people.

- ▶ There is nothing I want to say to most people.

- ▶ It's hard to figure out when to talk.

- ▶ I just don't seem to think of the words to say.

- ▶ Usually there are no words that match my thoughts.

- ▶ I would rather communicate with one person at a time.

- ▶ I like to talk and listen to people.

- ▶ Sometimes, talking with other children can be stressful or confusing. It is not always fun.

- ▶ Sometimes, it is fun for me to talk with others.

- ▶ Sometimes I get disappointed when I try to talk to others.

- ▶ Sometimes people don't understand me.

- ▶ I do not understand why people say _____ _____ .

- ▶ Other: _____ .

The Process of Communication

The process of communication is like a circle:

- Putting my thoughts into words

- Getting someone's attention and telling them the words

- Listening to what that person is saying back to me

- Thinking about what that person said

- Putting my next thoughts (about what the person said) into words

- Telling them the words … and continuing on …

Communication moves in a circle, around and around between people. It involves:

1. Putting my thoughts into words

2. Getting someone's attention and telling them the words

3. Listening to what that person says to me

4. Thinking about what that person said

5. And returning to the first step … making a circle …

Putting My Thoughts into Words

The most common way to communicate is by talking. I do this when I put my thoughts into words and then say the words to someone who is listening, in person or over the phone or through video chat. Another popular way to communicate is by writing or typing. After my thoughts are on paper, I can give the paper to someone or send the paper to someone in a letter. Communicating by typing may be done online through e-mail or instant messaging or in person by typing on a keyboard and sharing the tablet or computer.

I will ⬭circle or highlight what is true for me. ✎

▶ I usually like to talk to people.

▶ I usually do not like to talk to people.

▶ I like to communicate by writing. After writing, I give what I wrote to the other person.

▶ I like to communicate by typing. Then I print it and give it to the other person. Or, we can have a computer conversation.

▶ I like to communicate through e-mail.

▶ I would like to try typing or writing to communicate more.

▶ I would like to try writing a letter and mailing it to someone.

▶ There is a person with whom I'd like to communicate.

▶ The name of the person is: .

▶ I do not like to communicate, not though talking nor writing.

▶ I would rather keep my thoughts to myself.

▶ Other: _____.

▶ Other: _____.

Sentence Starters

These sentence starters might be useful to me. I can turn to this page when I want to say something but I'm not sure how to begin. My parent, teacher, or therapist can make me a copy of this page. I can use extra paper, so there will be more room to write my thoughts in words. Or, I may type on a keyboard. My parent, teacher, or therapist may write other sentence starters for me, too.

I want to _____ .

Please help me with _____ .

The teacher said that_____ .

At school, I _____ .

What does " _____ " mean?

Someone said that _____ .

I am thinking about _____ .

Is it true that _____ ?

I hope that _____ .

I am really happy that _____ .

I don't understand about _____ .

There is something I'd like to do. It is _____ .

Thank you for _____ .

Making Sure Someone Is Listening

For talking communication to happen, I must make sure that a person is ready to listen to my words. I must make sure that he or she is paying attention.

Some children think that when they talk, someone will always hear them, but that is not always true. The other person might be busy and not be listening, or thinking about something else, or talking with someone else.

When I talk, the other person might not hear what I am saying. For communication to happen, I need to make sure that the other person is ready to listen.

This is how I know if my parent or teacher or friend is paying attention and ready to listen to me:

- They are ready to listen if they have just asked me a question and they are looking at me.

- If they are standing near me and their eyes are looking toward me, they are ready to listen.

Communication

More about Making Sure Someone is Listening ...

- Sometimes my parent or teacher or friend is standing near me but might **be doing something else or listening to someone else**. Then I need to wait until he or she is ready to listen to me.

- Before I talk, I might look at the direction of the other person's eyes, to see if she is already **looking at another person who is talking**. If she is, it probably means she is busy listening to that person. She is not ready to listen to me yet. I need to wait.

- If a person is talking on the phone or holding the phone quietly next to her head without talking, it means she is having a **phone conversation**. She is not ready to listen to me yet. I need to wait.

- If I am not sure how long to wait, then I can softly tap the person's shoulder one time and say, quietly:

> **"Excuse me, I have something to tell you. Please let me know when you are ready to listen."**

- I can **wait quietly** until the person tells me he is ready to listen. If I am worried I will forget what I want to say while I am waiting, I may choose to write myself a note or draw a picture to remind me of what I want to say.

More about Making Sure Someone is Listening ...

Some autistic children, teens, and adults like to communicate by writing or typing. They might find it much easier to communicate this way.

I will circle or highlight what is true for me.

I like to communicate by:

▶ Writing with a pen or pencil on paper.

▶ Typing on a keyboard.

▶ Writing an e-mail.

▶ Having a conversation by talking.

If I want to communicate in writing, I must remember to show what I have written to the other person.

I may ...

• Hand the paper to the person

• Put it into an envelope and mail it

• Show them the computer or tablet screen

• Send the e-mail to their e-mail address

Communicate with Whom?

There may be something I want to say by talking or writing, but I may not know whom to communicate with.

These are the names of children and adults with whom I may communicate (my parent, teacher, therapist, or a trusted person can help me with this):

1. _____

2. _____

3. _____

4. _____

5. _____

6. _____

7. _____

8. _____

Listening and Responding to What the Person Says

Communication is not just talking or writing. An important part of communication is **listening** (or **reading**) and then thinking about what was said.

When listening, I try to understand what is being said. If I do not understand, I may say:

> **"I don't understand what you mean."**
> **"Please explain it again."**

For more ideas to help with understanding, see chapter 6.

After I think about what the person said, then it is my turn to talk again. **Responding** is when I say something after I consider what the person said.

When my parent, or teacher, or friend and I listen and respond to each other, we are having a **conversation**. Conversations can happen by talking or by writing.

I like to have conversations about _____
_____
_____.

For more ideas to help with understanding, see chapter 6.

Communication

Why Conversations May Be Confusing

Sometimes, conversations may be confusing.

I will circle or highlight what is true for me. 🖊

▶ Conversations might be confusing because:

▶ I may not understand what the person is saying.

▶ Trying to make eye contact while I am talking and listening is difficult.

▶ I don't know when it's my turn to speak.

▶ I would rather think about something else.

▶ People are unpredictable; I never know what they will say.

▶ I need more time to think and talk.

▶ People interrupt me before I finish what I am saying.

▶ There is too much sensory stimulation (sights, sounds, feelings, etc).

▶ I don't always agree with what is said; maybe I get angry.

▶ Someone laughs at what I say, but it's not a joke.

▶ Someone might make fun of me.

▶ I don't understand why I should talk.

▶ I don't have anything else to say.

▶ It's difficult to put my thoughts into words.

▶ The other person doesn't understand me.

▶ I am more intelligent than almost everyone else.

▶ I don't know whom to talk to, or who is talking to me.

▶ I don't know when to start or when to stop talking.

▶ I don't think I'm intelligent enough.

▶ The other person is not interested in what I am saying.

▶ The topics change too quickly.

▶ Other: _____ .

▶ Other: _____ .

Talking a Lot

Some children talk a lot. They may talk so much that no one else has a turn to talk. They may not listen to what other people say. They may not know when to stop talking.

It is difficult for most people to have a conversation with someone who talks so much. Usually, it is not fun for people to be with someone who talks so much.

If my parent or teacher says I talk too much, we can try to understand why.

I will circle or highlight what is true for me. 🖉

I might talk so much because:

▶ I don't know when I am supposed to stop talking.

▶ I like to think and talk about my special interest.

▶ I have a lot to say.

▶ I want to show others that I know a lot.

▶ I want people to like me.

▶ I am very excited or enthusiastic about something.

▶ I feel worried, upset, or anxious about something.

▶ I don't want the subject to change, so I keep talking.

▶ I want to show how intelligent I am.

▶ I don't want the other person to talk.

▶ Other: _____ .

Asking the Same Question

Sometimes people ask questions. Usually when the question is answered, they do not ask the same question many times, over and over again.

Some autistic children and adults never ask questions, but some may repeat the same question again and again. If I repeat questions, we can try to understand why.

I will circle or highlight what is true for me. ✏

I might ask the same question repeatedly because:

▶ I like to hear the answer.

▶ I want to hear if the answer stays the same.

▶ I might be worried about something.

▶ I might wonder if something is going to happen.

▶ I might wonder when something is going to happen.

▶ I want to see people's faces while they answer again.

▶ It's fun (or funny) to ask the same question again.

▶ It feels good to know what the answer is going to be.

▶ I don't remember what the answer is, so I ask again.

▶ I don't understand the answer, so I ask again.

▶ I want to ask something else, but I can't find the words.

▶ Other: _____ .

Not Talking

Some children do not talk very much. They may be quiet most of the time. They may be quiet at school, or with certain people, or about certain subjects. Teachers and parents may say that they are "quiet children."

Parents and teachers sometimes worry about quiet children. They want to know what the children are thinking and feeling. They want the children to communicate more.

If my parent or teacher says I don't talk enough, or if I don't communicate at all, we can try to understand why.

I will circle or highlight what is true for me. 🖉

I am quiet because:

▶ There is too much happening at the same time.

▶ I may be feeling upset, worried, anxious, or angry.

▶ I may feel something, but I can't describe it now.

▶ It may not be the right room or the right place to talk.

▶ I may not be with the right person to talk to.

▶ I don't know when to talk.

▶ There is no reason for me to talk.

▶ I would rather communicate by typing on a keyboard.

▶ I would rather communicate in writing.

▶ Other: _____ .

Communication

I will circle or write the ways I'd like to communicate:

By talking	By keyboard	By writing with a pen or pencil

I will fill in the blanks if I know what is true for me. ✏

Through art, by doing: _____ (See chapter 4.)

I do not like to talk to (name) _____ .

I like to talk to (name) _____ .

I want to talk to (name) _____ .

I'd like to communicate by typing or writing with these people: _____ .

Other: _____ .

I want to talk about (what topic) _____ .

I do not want to talk about (what topic) _____ .

Other: _____ .

Communication

Styles of Speaking

People have different styles of speaking.

People who grow up in different geographic areas might speak with an accent or in a dialect. Accents or dialects make words and sentences sound different than what I am used to hearing. There are different styles of speaking, even for people who live close to each other. Everyone has his or her own voice.

I may ask someone to help me mark what is true for me. 🖉

My style of speaking is:

▶ Formal, serious

▶ Soft, quiet

▶ Loud

▶ Precise, meticulous

▶ High-pitched

▶ Low-pitched

▶ Monotone

▶ Fast

▶ Slow, with frequent pauses

▶ In a different accent than my family

▶ The same as other members of my family

▶ Other: _____ .

▶ I am the only one who talks like me!

▶ I have my own voice!

Ending a Conversation

Some conversations between people are brief; they may last less than a minute. Some conversations are long; long conversations may last for many hours. It may be difficult for some people, especially some autistic people, to know when a conversation should end.

I may like to talk about something so much that I keep talking and talking. I may not notice if the other person has stopped listening or wants to do something else.

Sometimes, the other person talks too much and doesn't know I am finished listening. I don't know how to end the conversation.

Every conversation is different, and every person is different. The same person might sometimes need a short conversation and other times need a long conversation.

- My teacher or my parent or someone else can help me practice ending a conversation.

- If I talk a lot, I may learn to ask, ***"Is it time to end this conversation?"***

- If I don't want to listen or talk at all, I can politely say ***"I am sorry, but I can't listen or talk right now."***

(For more information on conversations, see the workbook section of this chapter for older children, teens, and adults.)

Talking to Myself

Most of the time people talk when they want to communicate with someone. Most people do not talk aloud to themselves. My parent will tell me if people often hear me talking to myself.

I will circle or highlight what is true for me. ✏

If I talk to myself, it might be because:

▶ I am repeating something I have heard.

▶ I am saying words or sounds that are pleasing to me.

▶ I am saying what I am thinking about.

▶ I don't realize I am saying my thoughts aloud.

▶ I am getting ready to talk to someone—I'm practicing.

If others hear me talk to myself a lot, they might laugh. That does not mean it is bad or wrong. They laugh because most people don't talk to themselves. It is different from what they expect.

If I want to change this, I can try to:

• Whisper very quietly.

• Think the words in my mind, not aloud.

• Write my thoughts on paper, a tablet, or a computer.

• Talk to myself when I am alone.

Asking for Help

It is natural for most children to ask for help. One of the first things babies learn is that when they cry, someone will come to help them. Soon, they learn to ask for help by pointing, and eventually they ask for help by talking. Asking for help comes naturally for most children.

It is usually different for autistic children. Some may not like to ask for help. Some do not know how or when to ask for help. Many autistic children don't realize that they can get help or that someone is there to help them. Sometimes older children might need help but don't want to ask because they think it means they are not intelligent. Sometimes a child will get into the habit of asking for help all the time, even when it's not needed.

Asking for help does not mean I am not intelligent. In fact, it is intelligent to ask for help when:

- I don't understand what someone is saying.

- I don't understand what I am supposed to do.

- I know what I am supposed to do, but I can't do it.

- I have tried my best to do something without help, but it just does not work out.

The words to say are, **"Can you help me, please?"**

I may cut this out on the lines and tape it to my desk to remind me what to say. ✂

Being Honest and Polite

Being honest means saying what is true. It is good to tell the truth. When my parent or teacher asks me a question, it is important to answer with the truth.

Sometimes, though, I might say something that is true, but it hurts a person's feelings. Being polite means not saying things that will hurt someone's feelings.

To be polite, these are examples of what NOT to say:

- That a person is fat, skinny, ugly, or ignorant.

- That a person has a hairstyle that looks funny.

- If I don't like something else about the person's appearance.

- Other: _____ .

- Other: _____ .

Saying these things may hurt a person's feelings. We may make a list on the next page of other things that I should probably not say aloud about a person, even if they are true.

It is good to be honest and to tell the truth, but I should try not to hurt someone's feelings. This is being polite.

Communication

More on Being Honest and Polite ...

It is difficult to know which words will hurt someone's feelings. If I need to say something, but I am not sure if it is polite, I may start by saying:

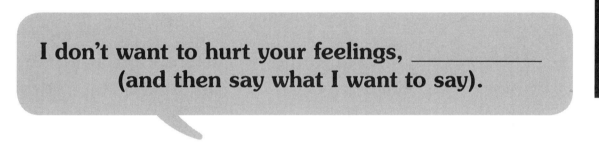

I don't want to hurt your feelings, _____
(and then say what I want to say).

If I often say things that aren't polite, my parent or teacher or friends may help me make a list of things I can try to avoid saying. I will try not to say:

1. _____

2. _____

3. _____

Instead, here are statements I may say that are polite and honest.

1. _____

2. _____

3. _____

Communication

Humor

When people have a sense of humor, it means they say and enjoy funny things. People with a good sense of humor can also laugh about themselves. There are different types of humor. I may ask my parent or teacher to help me fill in the lines below.

- *Slapstick* is the kind of humor in cartoons and in some movies. The "Three Stooges" are famous for slapstick. Other slapstick we have seen is: _____

    _____ .

- *Dry humor* is when people seem serious but they are really saying something funny. If I know someone who uses dry humor, his or her name is:

    _____ .

- *Puns* are jokes that use words that sound the same but mean different things. Examples of a pun are:

    _____ and

    _____ .

- *Exaggeration* is when things are described differently on purpose to make them sound funnier. An example of this was when:

    _____

    _____ .

- *Sarcasm* is when you say the opposite of what you really mean. It can hurt people's feelings.

More on Humor ...

Jokes and riddles are memorized statements or questions and answers that may be funny. If I have a favorite joke or riddle, it is:

_____

_____

_____

_____ .

Everyone might not laugh at my jokes. Everyone doesn't have the same sense of humor.

I will circle or highlight what is true for me.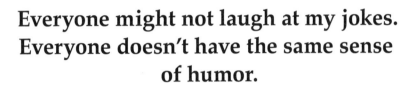

▶ Sometimes I try to say funny things or tell jokes, but people don't laugh.

▶ Sometimes I think of something funny, but I don't say it aloud.

▶ Sometimes I make people laugh without even trying. I didn't tell a joke. I don't know why they laughed.

▶ Sometimes I laugh when I hear or say particular sounds, words, phrases, and questions.

For example, something that makes me laugh is:

_____

_____ .

Why People Laugh When I'm Not Making a Joke

There are times when children or adults say something that isn't a joke, but other people laugh.

I will circle or highlight what is true for me. 🖉

▶ Sometimes people laugh when I say something, but I am not making a joke or trying to be funny.

▶ I do not like it when people laugh when it's not a joke. They seem to be laughing at me.

▶ Sometimes I get confused when people laugh.

▶ I like when people laugh, even if I do not understand why. It makes me laugh too.

People may laugh when they hear something that they do not expect; because they are surprised, they laugh. The surprised feeling makes them laugh. Many autistic children understand things literally. Some literal things are funny, like puns.

If people laugh, it doesn't mean there is something wrong with me. It might mean that people enjoy being with me. If I want to know more about this, I may try to find out why they laughed. I may say to a trusted person

> **"Please explain why people laughed when I said**
> _____ .

Communicating with Art

Some people like to express themselves creatively. They like to communicate with art. There are many examples in chapter 4 of this book.

I will mark what is true for me. 🖉

▶ I like to be creative. I like to _____ .

▶ I try to communicate with my art. I want other people to understand what I am saying with my art.

▶ My art is not for communication. I am not trying to express my ideas to anyone. I just like doing it.

▶ I am not interested in making art.

> **If I try to communicate my ideas and thoughts with art, I have to remember that people who see or hear my art will think their own thoughts. When they hear or read or see my art, their ideas might be different from what I want to communicate. They might not understand exactly what I am trying to express.**

If I want my parent, teacher, or friends to know something important, I can do it through art, but then I also need to do one of these things:

1. Put it into words and tell the person.
2. Write it down in words and give it to the person.
3. Type it and show it to the person.
4. Send the words by mail or e-mail it to the person.

I can still enjoy doing my art, but I should also try to communicate in one of those four ways.

Especially for Older Readers

The previous topics in this chapter are relevant when individually selected for older children, teenagers, and—in some cases—adults. Relevant supplementary information that is specifically for older readers can be found on the following pages.

This section provides information on and opportunities for self-awareness as related to the act of communication. It covers the reasons for communication, why it is valued, how to know when to communicate, miscommunication, the importance of honesty and kindness, asking for help, and self-advocacy. It encourages the reader to embrace autism-friendly ways to communicate, as an alternative to "talking in the moment" if and when desired … and to reassure the reader (and educate his or her typically developing communication partners) that it is perfectly okay to do so!

Parents, teachers, and therapists can simplify these topics to use with younger children, where indicated.

 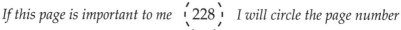

What's the Big Deal about Communication?

It is commonly agreed that communication is important, but why is it so important?

Communication is often the first step in understanding one another. It is a way for people to connect with each other. In fact, it is considered to be one of the most important activities in which a person can participate, because it is a way to build connections with others and be a part of a community. No one really knows what thoughts are in someone else's mind or what feelings are in someone's heart, unless the thoughts, ideas, or feelings are communicated.

Communication can help us understand one another. It is one of the factors that may contribute to a more peaceful life.

I will circle or highlight the ways in which I like to communicate: ✎

- ▶ Talking face to face with another person

- ▶ Talking by phone

- ▶ Writing and sending e-mails

- ▶ Writing and mailing letters by post

- ▶ Typing with someone on a tablet or computer

- ▶ Using manual sign language

- ▶ Drawing or painting

- ▶ Creating comics for people to read

- ▶ Making computer graphics

- ▶ Playing a musical instrument

- ▶ Writing song lyrics

- ▶ Doing dance or creative movement

- ▶ Writing stories or essays

- ▶ Writing a blog

- ▶ Other methods of expression: _____

- ▶ Other: _____

Communication

Miscommunication

To communicate effectively, I must talk to another person at a time when the other person is able to pay attention and listen carefully. Or, I may write what I want to say and make sure the person receives the message. But sometimes, it doesn't work perfectly. There may be a miscommunication.

What is a miscommunication?

When one person tries to communicate, but the other person is confused about what was said (or written), it is called a *miscommunication*.

How do I know if there is a miscommunication?

Here are some clues to detect if a miscommunication has happened:

If I said (or wrote) something, but the person's response is unexpected or doesn't make sense to me, there may be a miscommunication.

If the person gets angry or upset or expresses another emotion that is unexpected or doesn't make sense to me, there may be a miscommunication.

Generally, if something doesn't make sense during or after a conversation or if there is an unexpected response to what I have said (or written), it may mean there has been a miscommunication.

If someone says (or writes) to me that what I have communicated doesn't make sense, it means there is a miscommunication.

What Should I Do If There Is a Miscommunication?

After detecting there may be a miscommunication, a person may politely say (or write), "I think there may be a miscommunication."

The next step could be one or both of these:

I can politely request that the speaker explain what he or she said. I may say, "Please explain that again." This is an intelligent response to use when something doesn't make sense.

I can politely request of the speaker, "Please write it down, so I can read what you are saying." This is also an intelligent response to use when something doesn't make sense.

Asking for more information in writing is an intelligent and responsible thing to do.

Sometimes, other people may say they don't understand what I am saying or what I mean. This is also an example of miscommunication. If someone asks me to explain it again, it means the listener needs more information to better understand what I mean.

It is intelligent and responsible to try to ask for—and give—more information by talking or through writing.

How Do I Know If I Have Something to Communicate?

The reasons to communicate are divided into three general categories:

> 1. One category consists of communication that expresses the need for a change to make things better.
>
> 2. The second category consists of communication that expresses pleasure and gratitude about how things are.
>
> 3. The third category consists of communication that shares information about ideas, thoughts, or feelings.

I will circle or highlight what is true for me. 🖊

▶ There are times when I wish certain things would change for the better.

▶ There are times when I like to share information about some of my ideas.

▶ There are times when I like to share information about some of my thoughts.

▶ There are times when I like to share information about some of my feelings.

▶ There are times when I am glad that some things are the way they are.

▶ Other: _____ .

The First Category: Expressing the Need for a Change (for the better)

A person may notice inner feelings of discomfort or emotions, such as impatience, frustration, anger, sadness, fear, confusion, or another uncomfortable feeling.

Other physical sensations are sometimes clues about emotions that signal the need for communication to make things better. Examples of physical sensations are feeling a fluttery or heavy feeling in the stomach, having a stomachache or heaviness in the area of the heart, the heart beating rapidly or hard, feeling tightness in the throat, or having itching skin or blushing or another physical sensation. Each individual has his or her own physical reactions to discomfort, confusion, and emotions.

When a person notices physical reactions in the body, it is a good time to ask oneself, *"Is something bothering me?"* or *"What is bothering me?"* Another important question to ask oneself is, *"What do I wish was different about this situation?"* Asking these questions—and answering them honestly—is a way to decide whether to communicate and what specifically may need to be communicated. It may mean it's time to ask for help about something.

I will (circle) or highlight what is true for me. 🖉

▶ Something is bothering me. It is: _____
_____ .

▶ I wish something would be different. It is: _____
_____ .

▶ I have something to communicate. It is: _____
_____ .

▶ I don't know if something is bothering me.

▶ Sometimes I experience one of those physical sensations when I am in these locations or situations: _____
_____ .

▶ Sometimes I experience one of those physical sensations when I am near the following person or people: _____
_____ .

▶ Other: _____ .

▶ Other: _____ .

▶ Other: _____ .

When Asking for Help, What May Happen?

Help means assistance doing or understanding something. (See pages 221 and 232-233)

Asking for help is one important part of communicating. When receiving help, the "help" may happen in one of these six ways:

1. *The helper does it all.* The person asking for help watches or listens, while the helper does it all.

2. *The helper tells the person who asked for help what to do (or gives written instructions).* Then the person follows the directions and does it.

3. *The helper does some of it, but not all of it.* This may happen in like this:

    - The helper starts … and the person asking for help finishes.
    - The helper waits for the person to start … and then the helper finishes.
    - The helper and the person needing help work together.

4. *The helper may make suggestions about what to do.* The person who needs help can choose what to do from the suggestions.

5. *The helper may ask questions that allow the person to think about it in different ways.* Then the person figures out what to do and does it by him- or herself.

6. The person you ask may not know how to help, may not want to help, or can't help. In this case, the person asking for help may say, *"Thank you. Do you know who might be able to help me with this?"*

The Second Category: Positive Experiences and Expressing Gratitude

Positive experiences are usually things that result in feelings that are pleasurable. A positive experience may give a feeling of relief, satisfaction, comfort, contentment, peace of mind, relaxation, or another good feeling. Some people may feel joy, happiness, or a sense of well-being.

Positive feelings usually happen automatically when something is going well in a person's life. Or, a person may choose to experience life with a peaceful or positive feeling, even when there are things that he or she doesn't like.

When a person learns to experience life with a feeling of gratitude and acceptance, positive feelings may be felt, even when things don't go the way you want. (More information about this can be found in chapter 12.)

Another reason to communicate is to express good feelings, or gratitude, for things that feel good.

I will circle or highlight what is true for me. ✏

▶ Sometimes I feel positive feelings. I will underline the words above that describe the positive feelings that I have felt.

▶ The situations or places where I have felt these positive feelings are:

_____ .

▶ Here are the names of people in my life whom I'd like to tell when I am feeling these positive feelings: _____

_____ .

▶ I don't remember feeling pleasure or any of those positive feelings.

▶ Other: _____ .

The Third Category: Sharing Ideas, Thoughts, and Feelings

Communication is a good way to make connections with other people. Sharing ideas, thoughts, and feelings with one another is a good way to build social connections. People do this by talking and writing, listening and reading, and thinking about and responding to other people's ideas and thoughts.

When family members, friends, teachers, therapists, and other important people ask questions about my thoughts, ideas, and feelings, it may be time to communicate by trying to answer the questions. If it is difficult to answer at that moment, it's okay to say, *"I'll try to answer those questions, but not right now. Let's find another time—or another way—to talk about these things."* Then a time can be written into the day's schedule or on the weekly calendar.

Remember, there are other good methods of communication besides talking. Try having a computer conversation by sitting side by side at a keyboard or tablet and taking turns typing. Sending e-mails is another good option.

I will circle or highlight what is true for me. ✏

▶ Sometimes I like to talk about my thoughts and ideas.

▶ Sometimes I like to write or type about my thoughts and ideas.

▶ I usually do not like to talk or type about my thoughts and ideas.

▶ Sometimes I like to talk about my feelings.

▶ Sometimes I like to write or type about my feelings.

▶ I usually do not like to talk or type about my feelings.

▶ I'd like to talk about thoughts, ideas, or feelings, but the words just don't come.

▶ I'd like to try writing or typing about my ideas, thoughts, or feelings.

▶ Other: _____ .

▶ Other: _____ .

▶ Other: _____ .

Communication: There Are Options!

Typically, most people expect to communicate with each other by talking, in the moment. However, there are other methods of communication that may allow communicators to express themselves with greater clarity. For many people, especially autistic people, using one or more of the suggested alternative methods opens the door to lucid self-expression and true authenticity that would not otherwise have been accessible, had the person been restricted to talking in person, in the moment.

I invite all communicators, especially those on the spectrum, and their willing communication partners to experiment and choose what is best for them personally.

When there is a desire or need for communication, review the suggestions described on the following page. Experiment. Have fun. Find the ones that allow the most fluidity of thought and ease of expression. **Use the methods that help you communicate what is true for you.**

Communication

I will circle **or** highlight **what is true for me.** 🖉

▶ Usually people expect me to talk to them, in person, in the moment.

▶ Sometimes talking in the moment is okay for me.

▶ Sometimes I am blank, and I don't know what to say.

▶ Sometimes I just say a rote phrase I have memorized.

▶ I usually need more time to think about what I want to say.

▶ Sometimes I feel pressured to respond in a conversation, so I just say something—anything—but I don't even know if it is really true for me.

▶ I wish I could express myself clearly and authentically.

▶ I like being in a conversation by speaking.

▶ I like being in a conversation by writing e-mail.

▶ I have tried typing instead of talking with a person.

▶ I'd like to try to type more.

▶ I wish the other person would say, "Do you want to type instead of talking? We have plenty of time, we don't have to rush …"

▶ I am not interested in trying other methods. Talking is my favorite way of communicating.

▶ Other: _____ .

▶ Other: _____ .

Find Your Favorite Way to Have a Conversation

Read about these eight options. Experiment with them.

1. *Take time to think, and respond in a few minutes.* Say, "I want to respond, but I need a few more minutes to think quietly about this topic. Please wait while I think about it."

2. *Think about the topic and respond later.* Say, "I want to continue this discussion, but I need more time to think. I'll think about this and respond later." Agree on the time when the discussion will be continued. If it will be later today, write it on the day's schedule or write a reminder note. If it will be on another day, agree on the day and time and write it on the calendar.

3. *Use e-mail.* Say, "I'd like to continue this discussion, but I'd rather think and type my thoughts when I have more time to think. Let's continue this conversation by e-mail."

4. *Use instant messaging (IM).* Say, "I'd like to continue this discussion, but I'd rather type. Let's continue this conversation by IM."

5. *Have a conversation by typing (a "computer conversation").* Say, "Let's continue this conversation on my tablet or computer. We can take turns typing."

6. *Ask for a Communication Form. (This option is meant for communication partners who are familiar with creating Communication Forms or for those who want to learn to use them.)* Say, "Could you please give me a communication form about this topic?"

7. *Suggest looking through this list together.* Say, "Let's look at this list to choose a way we'd both like to try."

8. *Other.* You may have another idea. Say, "I'd like to suggest another way we can communicate. Let's try _____."

Communication

Communicate with Honesty and Kindness

Sometimes a person who tries to be honest all the time may unintentionally hurt other people's feelings. Statements made about other people's appearance and other types of personal comments may be unintentionally hurtful to other people.

At these times, other people may say that their "feelings are hurt" or that what was said was "rude." They may think that the honest person is trying to be cruel or critical. They may feel the hurt so much that they misunderstand what is really being communicated by the honest person.

It is possible to be an honest person without hurting someone's feelings or being rude. The way to do this is to say what is true, while speaking respectfully and kindly. In some situations, learning not to say certain things out loud is regarded as respectful and kind.

It is possible to learn how to be honest—and be respectful and kind at the same time. It is a communication skill. Honesty that is tempered with kindness and respect is an honorable trait. It is worth learning. More information about honesty and kindness is provided in chapter 12.

I will (circle) or highlight what is true for me. 🖉

▶ I am usually honest.

▶ I think I unintentionally hurt someone's feelings in the past.

▶ I don't know if I have hurt someone's feelings by being honest.

▶ Sometimes people have told me I have hurt their feelings.

▶ Sometimes people have told me I am rude.

▶ I really don't want to be rude or hurt someone else's feelings.

▶ I am not sure how to be honest and kind at the same time.

▶ I need more specific information about this.

▶ I'd like to talk with _____ (name) about this topic.

▶ Other: _____ .

Self-Advocacy

Self-advocacy is communicating what is true for me. Self-advocacy emphasizes communicating for myself, and, while doing so, I may include educating others about autism. This may mean requesting assistance, support, and/or understanding from others related to particular situations or general conditions.

Depending on a person's interests, skills, and desires, it may also include political activism related to significant issues for the welfare of the autistic community at large.

The author of this book has identified three significant elements underlying the ability to self-advocate. They are:

- Self-knowledge

- Specific communication skills (initiating asking for help)

- Identifying a receptive audience and/or educating an uneducated audience about autism

I will circle or highlight what is true for me. 🖊

▶ I understand what is meant by self-advocacy.

▶ I want to learn more about self-advocacy.

▶ I am not sure what self-advocacy is.

▶ I have self-advocated about: _____ .

▶ I am would like to self-advocate about: _____ .

▶ I am interested in activism related to the autistic community.

▶ How do I find out about activism and advocacy for the autistic community?

▶ Other: _____ .

▶ Other: _____ .

Communication

For Parents, Teachers, and Therapists

When discussing an incident at work that resulted from a lack of communication with a coworker, an autistic man said that the coworker was …

"… just some guy making noise. That's what people do. I don't really see why I was supposed to respond, or how I was supposed to respond. What was I supposed to say? I guess I don't go by the same rule book as most people."

Ideas in This Chapter:

☑ Language and communication are two different things

☑ Being verbal does not necessarily mean a child is communicative

☑ Significant differences occur from an early age

☑ Get a speech and language evaluation

☑ Use this book

☑ Experiment with writing or typing

☑ Provide written cues

☑ Check these out!

☑ Make conversation easier

☑ Experiment with other methods

☑ Make new agreements about communication

☑ Use Communication Forms

☑ The pages "especially for older readers"

Communication

Language and communication are two different things

Communication is more than the development of verbal skills. In fact, communication and talking are often two distinctly different things, as will be discussed below. Many, if not most, children on the autism spectrum develop verbal language skills separately from learning to communicate. From the very beginning, learning to say words is not automatically linked with communication. An often-cited example is the child who repeats commercials or recites the complete dialogue from animated videos but rarely uses these highly developed verbal skills for communicative intent in daily life.

In young typically developing children, the acquisition of language and communication is one and the same. For most of them, words automatically and powerfully function as tools for communication, from the very beginning.

Being verbal does not necessarily mean a child is communicative

Most children on the autism spectrum, even those with highly developed verbal skills, have significant natural differences in their awareness and understanding about essential aspects of communication and conversation. Pragmatics—the social use of language—usually lag behind other areas of language development, even in very verbal children. Social communicative functions, such as the ability to get someone's attention; initiating communication; using conversational skills, such as responding and building on what is being said; and having the ability to sustain a reciprocal interaction are surprisingly not what parents or teachers expect from a child whose cognitive development is at, around, or above the average range.

Significant differences occur from an early age

Discrete skills and behaviors that form the backbone of communication generally emerge between infancy and the toddler years for most typically developing children. It is said that an infant's eyes first focus at the distance of approximately 10 inches—the distance from his eyes to his mother's eyes when cradled in her arms. This illustrates the early bonding that connects one to another. During the first 2 years of life, most children become proficient at following another's line of gaze and using eye contact and gestures to meet their needs and to develop communication and social interaction.

These powerful communicative behaviors happen easily and naturally. They do not have to be intentionally taught to most babies. Whatever it is in the brain that ignites awareness of being connected to others, perceives multiple perspectives, and drives social communicative skills is already present in typically developing infants at birth. Communication skills  are the culmination of an elaborate cluster of versatile behaviors and perceptions that merge to create meaningful engagement. The ease with which this takes place is a result of the way the typically developing—non-autistic—brain functions.

The distinct communicative styles found in autistic children also result from the way the brain functions from infancy. Autism results in particular patterns of thinking, attention, and learning styles. Maybe these babies' perceptions are flooded with sensory experiences that are so entertaining, distracting, overwhelming, or even disturbing that these experiences take precedence over the

need to communicate. Maybe these children are paying attention to isolated and unconnected details and do not see the relationships between them. Maybe they become so engrossed in one thing that they don't notice other factors in the environment. Most toddlers with autism demonstrate that they don't fully understand that there is a powerful connection between their needs and purposeful spontaneous action that results in desired changes. Simple accomplishments, like getting someone's attention and directing their attention to something–even the simple act of initiating communication—seem to be foreign concepts, like part of a different language or culture.

According to parents' reports, we learn that some babies who received a diagnosis of autism later in life were extremely passive as infants. Others were very demanding and cried but could not be comforted. Their mothers' attempts to ease their cries didn't seem to soothe them. Who can begin to imagine what this baby experiences as he tries to make sense of the big sensory world around him? Autistic adults often point out that the world runs on rules that weren't made for them—and they are right!

Get a speech and language evaluation

A speech and language therapist should look carefully at your child's pragmatic use of language and his everyday functional and social communication skills. Which specific areas need focused teaching and practice? *On the other hand, which areas necessitate more education and understanding on the part of his typically developing communication partners?*

Use this book

Reread the appropriate pages in this chapter with your child when he encounters awkward or troubling experiences due to communication difficulties. You might add a time on his

schedule for rereading particular pages. With the book open, identify and review the basic elements of communication and conversation, while relating them to the real issue that has occurred.

Experiment with writing or typing

Have a keyboard or pen and paper available for frequent use. During relaxed times, free time, or recreational time, experiment by communicating in writing. Do it for fun, not just for "problems." Do it frequently enough that it becomes familiar. Help your child

become used to writing or typing in a variety of situations, for a variety of reasons. By being proactive and practicing on a regular basis, you will lay the groundwork for the most effective use of written communication for those difficult moments when there is a desperate need for communication. When your child resists or is unable to communicate verbally during times of stress, or if his attempts at communicating are ineffective, the tools of written communication will already be familiar to him and to you—his partner in communication. (*You* need to become familiar with this and practice too!)

There are times that your child needs to (or is expected to) communicate, but he is unable to do so. Instead of demanding speech, offer him the now familiar keyboard or pen and paper. Free from the complexities of face-to-face talking, he may discover this to be a clearer route to communication. You might write sentence starters for him, as demonstrated earlier in this chapter. Allow his attention to be on the written or typed word and not on you. Eye contact is irrelevant while using this strategy ... unless it happens naturally.

Provide visual cues

In situations when your child isn't spontaneously communicating or when he doesn't get someone's attention or won't ask for help for something he needs or wants, you can provide visual cues to make it easier. For example, let's say your child doesn't ask for help when he needs it. He might sit passively and not do anything at all. He might get stuck in one activity because he can't move ahead. He might become very frustrated, anxious, or upset. The following ideas are examples of written cues that can help him initiate communication. Notice how the level of structure and specificity are slightly different in each of the four ideas. Your child might need more or less structure, depending on the situation and how he feels on a particular day. You can try one or more of the following as models:

1. *Write a rule.* Be concise, specific, and concrete. Post it where it can be seen.

> **"When I don't understand what to do, I may raise my hand and ask for help."**

2. *Write a list of phrases to fit the situation.* Have him review it frequently, especially prior to entering the situation. If necessary, post it in the situation where it is needed.

> **"I can ask my teacher for help when I need it. I can say, 'Can you help me please?' or 'Please help me,' or 'I don't understand what to do now.'"**

3. *Write a "cue card" with the exact wording for a specific situation.* Place this written cue in an appropriate location. When you notice your child needs help, draw his attention to the cue card so he will read it. Have the appropriate person respond to his request. For example, a card with this wording could be posted in the inside of his locker. Keep it in his locker as a cue that he can refer to it, by himself, in the future.

> **"Will you please help me with the zipper on my coat?"**

4. *Provide a card with a question or statement for him to hand to you.* In this example, the card is posted in the locker with Velcro, within sight and within reach. This strategy is intended for a child who is too anxious or otherwise isn't able to always rely on his verbal skills to ask for help. In this case, he may take the card and give it to the teacher. By doing this, he is practicing "initiation" without the added demand of having to use verbal language—doing it in a way that is easier if and when he is overwhelmed. Keep the card accessible in his locker to remind him that he can get help in this manner. If you use this strategy, make sure the teacher responds to him positively and accepts this method as 100% valid. In other words, the teacher shouldn't respond by saying, "Use your words" or "I want to hear you ask," or other similar prompts to get him to talk. There will be time for that later. For now, accept, respect, and reinforce this powerful (and often difficult) act of initiation.

> **"Will you please help me with the zipper on my coat?"**

5. *Supplement with a Social Story to clarify the situation.* Describe the situation in a straightforward manner, from the perspective of the child. Give relevant information, including the perspective of others, if important, as demonstrated in this

example. The Social Story may give the child a way to more accurately interpret what is happening, help make sense of it all, and, in this case, offer a suggested course of action … with background understanding. Have him read the story ahead of time and keep it available for rereading prior to recess.

Asking for Help with My Puffy Blue Jacket

Our class goes outside for recess almost every day. On days when it is very cold, I wear my puffy blue jacket. I try to zip it up, and sometimes I can do it myself. But other times, the zipper gets stuck.

While the kids are getting ready for recess, they usually say, "Hurry up." They tell me to hurry up because they are happy it is recess time. They cannot go outside until everyone, including me, is standing in line.

Having a stuck zipper is a perfect time to ask for help. I can try to remember to walk over to Ms Bea and say, "The zipper is stuck. Will you please help me?"

After asking for help, my puffy blue jacket will get zipped up, and then I may stand in line. When everyone is ready, the whole class, including me, will be able to go outside for recess.

Check this out!

Typically, you would make visual cues to fit specific purposes. I've always made them by hand or with the help of my computer. There are books and tons of resources online where you can find icons, symbols, and other graphics to borrow, copy, or purchase to help you make visual cues.

For fun, I'd like to draw your attention to another resource. One autistic blogger-artist and very creative person is also an alternative communicator. Her name is Annabelle (*anabellelistic.com*), and she makes and sells buttons with graphics, words, and phrases to help other alternative and nonverbal communicators. These buttons are attractive visual cues that are used for communication, support, and humor. I recommend visiting the online store at *etsy.com* to look at these options for visual cues that may fit a purpose in your family or classroom. Her online shop can be found at *etsy.com/shop/unspokenvisuals*.

Make conversation easier

Explore ways that a conversation can be depicted visually, so your child can see the reciprocity, the "back-and-forth essence" of the interaction, and the connection and the relationships between the statements, in a concrete way. Try strategies that add structure and order to the potentially confusing, distracting, or annoying qualities of conversation:

Use a computer or tablet.
Have a conversation at a keyboard, sitting side by side. Take turns typing and talking simultaneously. Watch the dialogue appear on the screen as it is spoken. Or, have a silent conversation in this manner. This takes more time than talking—enjoy getting used to a slower pace of communicating.

Write e-mails.

Much like colleagues in the same office who keep up a dialogue via e-mail, your child might build and sustain communication with you or his friends more readily in this manner.

Use a topic hat.

Make a game of staying on a topic. Take turns drawing from a "topic hat." Topics that are personal favorites can be placed into the hat, along with a variety of other subjects. Make up rules that would be most appropriate on the basis of your child's unique needs. One of the rules might be to stay on each topic for a certain amount of time. A variation of this rule might be for each person to make a certain number of statements and/or ask questions about the topic before the next one is chosen.

Create Comic Strip Conversations.

As introduced on pages 197-198, this strategy combines a visual representation of conversation, along with the speaker's unspoken thoughts. Variations of this strategy can be tried to meet an individual's needs. Carol Gray has described Comic Strip Conversations as "the art of conversation."

Experiment with other methods.

As suggested several times in this book, try to experiment with methods that have been found to be helpful—and a relief—for many children and adults on the spectrum. If your child is sensitive to being "different," you can turn it into a game. Choose your timing wisely; for example, make sure you try having a computer conversation at a stress-free time and NOT during a crisis. Go to the keyboard frequently, so when you really need communication, you will both be well versed. Even if your child is younger, you can supplement the basic workbook pages with the previous pages that are especially for older readers: "Communication: There Are Options!" and "Find Your Favorite Way to Have a Conversation."

Make new agreements about communication.
Treatment options and teaching strategies in the field of autism abound, and most, if not all, dictate that autistic individuals must ultimately change something about themselves: how they act, how they respond to others, the way they think, what they think, and how they interact and communicate. Most typically developing people may not be aware of nor acknowledge the courage it takes for children and adults on the spectrum to respond to a teacher's or parent's unquestioned expectations that they change something about themselves as basic as their natural way of interacting and communicating. On top of that, our students, more often than not, experience our teaching objectives and "their" educational goals as nonsensical demands.

We must recognize that the autism spectrum denotes a different style of communication—different from the widespread, mainstream style of communication that most (non-autistic) teachers, therapists, and family members are familiar with and therefore automatically and unconsciously expect. Many of these unconscious expectations are based on assumptions about communication—assumptions that emerge from a non-autistic point of view.

In my workshops, consultations, and books, I propose a broad, truly inclusive, and arguably more courageous approach. As its foundation, I ask communication partners who are not on the spectrum—a family member or friend, teacher, or therapist—to examine their automatic assumptions about interaction and communication and then be willing to make changes in their natural and instinctive way of interacting and communicating, just as they expect their student or child on the spectrum to change.

Consider the notion that miscommunication and misunderstanding can result from a mismatched style of communicating—and, finally, that all of us are responsible when desiring improved communication, interaction, and a positive educational environment for those on the spectrum whom we live with, work with, and play with. This is true whether it involves being in a relationship with a family member or friend or in the classroom with teachers and peers or in consultation with a therapist. To reach through these differences and meet the other person in a place of clarity, ease, and understanding, each communication partner must adapt or modify at least some parts of his or her automatic way of communicating.

In its broadest sense, teaching style is informed by how we communicate, interact, and provide instruction, as well as how we understand and interpret our student's behavior. I propose to teachers, therapists, friends, and family members who desire to better understand and relate to their communication partner on the spectrum that they adopt a specific set of "new agreements" for communicating. These new agreements are guidelines that consist of modifications in communication, interaction, and therefore teaching style. The beauty of the guidelines I propose is that all of them can be described as win-win, whether they are suggested for the autistic student or the non-autistic teacher, therapist, or family member. All communication partners benefit from every guideline. In my book, *Communication: What Does It Mean to Me?* (Future Horizons, 2010), I have distilled simple guidelines and made new agreements, written in the form of a contract for communication to improve mutual communication. For more information, you can either read the book or, for a summary, visit my Web site, *catherinefaherty.com*, and look for the article titled, "Making New Agreements."

Use Communication Forms

I came up with and have been experimenting with and using what I eventually titled "Communication Forms" in the early 1990s. These are typically multiple-choice and/or fill-in-the-blank lists intended to engage the communicator and support self-knowledge by inviting the user to discover, identify, and indicate what is personally true. You have already seen many versions of Communication Forms in this workbook! The title includes the word "communication," designed as a reminder for the user to share the information with someone—to communicate. These forms help the communicator on the spectrum connect with others by making it easier to initiate and share his or her personal thoughts, ideas, and questions in an accessible, structured manner. The use of Communication Forms usually sets the stage for further interaction on a particular topic. The hundreds of Communication Forms in my book, *Understanding Death and Illness and What They Teach about Life*, facilitate communication about common and intimate topics that present challenges for everyone, sometime in their life. Helpful hints about creating your own Communication Forms, along with yet more examples, are found in my book, *Communication: What Does It Mean to Me?*.

Parents and teachers may automatically notice clues as to how our children are feeling, based on our unconscious, intuitive interpretations of facial expressions and body language (from the unwritten typical development rule book!). For this reason, most teachers often unknowingly make false assumptions about the emotional status of their autistic students. I strongly recommend that parents and teachers design a generic, daily Communication Form to be used at school—one that fits the abilities and level of understanding of the individual child—and, while you are at it, make one for home, too! An example of a "generic" daily Communication

Form for school can be found in the workbook section of chapter 12. *The best Communication Forms are ones that you design to fit the individual and the situation.*

The pages "especially for older readers"

Even if your child is too young to benefit from the information on the workbook pages written especially for older readers, parents, teachers, and therapists may find them useful. Notice the style in which the information is presented—a nonjudgmental and calm approach; the clear, concrete, and specific choice of words; and, of course, the Communication Forms on most of the pages to help the reader reflect, discover, identify, and express what is personally true. In this chapter, I chose to expand on specific aspects of communication from the point of view of the older child or teenager. I attempt to explain the importance of communication and miscommunication, knowing when to communicate, honesty and kindness, alternative methods of communication to facilitate authenticity, and the concept of self-advocacy.

Chapter 9
School

Workbook

School

Different Kinds of Schools

Most big towns and cities have many different schools. Preschools are for very young children. Children in kindergarten or first grade begin elementary school. Middle school usually begins in the sixth grade. Sometimes there are junior high schools instead of middle schools. Students begin high school in the ninth or tenth grade.

People who attend school are usually called "students."

There are public schools and private schools. There are charter schools and parochial schools. Some children do not go to a school at all. They are homeschooled. There are combinations of home schooling and attending school.

I will circle or highlight what is true for me. 🖉

▶ I go to a public school. I am in the _____ grade.

▶ I go to a charter school. I am in the _____ grade.

▶ I go to a private school. I am in the _____ grade.

▶ I go to a parochial school. I am in the _____ grade.

▶ I am homeschooled. _____ (name) is my teacher.

▶ Other: _____ .

The ideas in this chapter may help me learn and feel good about learning, no matter what kind of school I attend.

Knowing What Will Happen Today

Most students like to know what is going to happen in school. After I get used to a new teacher, I usually remember what will happen in that class. But, things can *change*.

I will (circle) or highlight what is true for me. ✏️

▶ Often, teachers announce what is going to happen, but I don't always understand exactly what they mean.

▶ Sometimes I think something is going to happen, but it doesn't.

▶ Sometimes things change, and I don't understand why.

▶ The children and the teachers all seem to know what is going to happen, but sometimes I get confused.

▶ I wonder when it will be time for my favorite things.

▶ I usually ask my teacher when things are going to happen. For example, I wonder when _____ will happen?

▶ I often tell the teacher when something is supposed to happen. I get worried or angry if it doesn't happen on time.

▶ I like to be able to know when things will happen.

If I have a schedule, I can see *what* is going to happen and *when* it is going to happen. I can use it every day.

Detailed information about using a schedule for parents, teachers, and therapists can be found on pages 96-114.

A Place to Work

Everyone has a place to work.

Some teachers let students choose where they want to sit. Sometimes students sit anywhere they want to, around a large table, with other students. Sometimes they sit at different places every day.

In some classrooms, students have their own desks. The desks might be touching other desks, in groups or pods.

In other classrooms, the desks are lined up in rows, and they are not touching each other.

Sometimes students are always supposed to work at their own desks. Sometimes students are supposed to go to different desks or tables to work.

Some children might go to a special place to work. It might be a flat desk, or it might be a desk with walls or a study carrel. Sometimes a desk is called an "office."

The teacher decides how the desks will be arranged in the room. Sometimes the teacher might move the desks.

In the classroom, I work at _____ .

At home, I do my work at _____ .

My Own Office

An office is a special place for working. The school principal works in an office. Many adults work in offices. Maybe my parent works in an office. Offices are just for working. Offices help people stay focused on their work.

I may have a special type of office at school. For instance, my office can be made by putting up three short walls on my desk. The office walls help me pay attention to my work instead of other things in the room.

This is what my office might look like.

More on My Own Office ...

My teacher may help me find the best place for my office. I might try working in different places until we find the best office place. My office might be:

- *At my desk.* I put the office walls up when I work, and I take them down when I am finished.

- *At a different desk in the classroom*—a desk used just for my office.

- *At a desk outside of my classroom*, where it is quiet.

- *At a desk in a different classroom.*

Other students might use offices, too. Offices help people focus on their work.

In my class, my office is located here: _____
_____ .

My schedule shows me when it is time to work in my office. I might work in my office many times every day.

Why It Might Be Hard to Work Independently

To work independently means that students work by themselves, without someone sitting next to them to keep them working. In school, students have to remember which assignment to do, when to start, how to do it, where it goes when it's finished, and what to do next. It might be difficult for students to start working and then remember everything they have to do.

I will circle or highlight what is true for me. 🖊

It might be hard to work by myself because:

▶ There are too many things to remember.

▶ I don't know how to get started.

▶ I don't know what to do first.

▶ I don't understand the directions.

▶ There might be too much noise in the room or out in the hall.

▶ I may get distracted by other children in the room.

▶ I don't know when the work will be done.

▶ It's better to wait until someone comes to help me.

▶ There is too much work to do.

▶ I may be thinking about something else.

▶ I wonder what is going to happen later on.

▶ I would rather do something else.

▶ Other: _____ .

School

Being Independent and Organized with a Work System

When I do my work, I may follow a **work system**. The work system is a list of things to do. I don't need my teacher or assistant to *tell* me what to do, because the work system *shows* me what to do.

The work system shows me:

1. **How many assignments I am supposed to do.**

2. **What exactly the assignments are.**

3. **When they're finished.**

4. **What I am supposed to do next, after I am finished.**

My teacher or assistant will teach me how to follow the work system.

The work system helps me be more **organized**. I follow the work system by crossing out or checking off each assignment, **one at a time**. I can see exactly **how many assignments** I have left to do, the progress I am making, and what will happen **next**, after I am **finished**.

☑ I don't need my teacher or assistant to help me all the time. My work system helps me work by myself.

Written Directions

Sometimes my teacher says I must do an assignment or a job by myself. I try to remember what to do, but sometimes I wait for someone else to tell me what to do.

Sometimes when I am supposed to be working, I might:

▸ Forget the directions.

▸ Get mixed up.

▸ Start thinking about something else.

▸ Have trouble staying focused.

There is a way for me to learn to do my assignments and jobs by myself. My teacher or assistant can teach me how to follow **written directions**.

They can keep the written directions with each assignment or with the materials for each activity or job. The directions will be written clearly and literally, in the right order. I'll read the first line, mark it, and then do it.

After doing the first thing, I'll read the next one on the list, mark it, and do what it says. *I'll follow each step until I am finished.* Then, the job or assignment is finished!

School

Knowing What Is Most Important

Students are supposed to read or listen to a story and figure out what is important in the story.

My teacher or parent might tell me that I need to find what is most important in a story, or they might tell me to pay attention to something important in the directions.

- Most autistic children and adults are very good at focusing on details, especially the details that are very interesting to them.

- Many of the details I pay attention to may not be considered important to my teacher or my parent. They want the students to find the information that relates to the "most important" things or "the main idea." Main ideas are usually considered most important.

- It helps if someone can show me which information is most important. The teacher or assistant can:

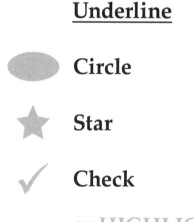

<u>Underline</u>

Circle

Star

Check

or HIGHLIGHT

the most important details in an assignment, on a story, on my schedule, and on my written directions.

Handwriting

Some children and adults like to print or write. They like the way it looks and feels, and their handwriting is easy for other people to read.

But there are many children and adults who find it very difficult to write. They might know what they want to write, but when they try to use a pencil or a pen, it just doesn't look right.

When that happens a lot, students may not want to do their school assignments or their homework. It might be too difficult or frustrating.

It is good for young children to practice writing or printing. Therapists can give teachers and parents ideas that can help. *But children should also be able to do their work and put their ideas on paper, without always getting frustrated!*

If writing frustrates me, I may be able to learn to do my work by typing on a tablet or computer. **I will mark what is true for me.** 🖉

▶ I like my work to look good.

▶ I would like to learn to use a keyboard with a computer or tablet for my classroom assignments and homework.

▶ I do not want to do my assignments on a tablet or computer. I want to write my work with a pen or pencil.

▶ I'd like to do some work by writing and some with a keyboard.

▶ Other: _____.

School

Using My Focused Interests

There are a lot of things to learn about in school. But sometimes, a lesson just doesn't make sense. I may not be able to concentrate on it.

But, my focused interests mean a lot to me. I may more easily understand and remember when I read about my focused interests.

I may be able to learn new things easily if my teacher remembers to involve my focused interests!

The classes that sometimes don't make sense to me are:

1. _____

2. _____

3. _____

My focused interests are:

1. _____

2. _____

3. _____

There is more about my focused interests on page 68.

Technology

Most children like to use tablets and computers. Many children with autism are very skilled with technology, like tablets and computers.

I like technology. (Circle one:)

YES   NO   I DON'T KNOW

Sometimes, it is easier to learn something new with a tablet or computer than to learn it from a person.

Computers and tablets can be used for many things: school assignments, homework, free time, communication, entertaining myself, or playing with someone else.

I may be very good with a tablet or computer. I may want to use it all the time. My schedule will show me when it is time for technology and when it is time to do other things.

- Sometimes my schedule will allow free time with the tablet or computer. Then I can make a choice of what I want to do with it.

- Sometimes my schedule will allow work time on the tablet or computer. This means I have a particular assignment to do. At work time, it is not my choice. It is the teacher's choice.

School

School Jobs

The principal has a job. The cafeteria workers have jobs. The custodians have jobs. The teachers have jobs. Students have the job of doing their work and learning.

Some students might have other jobs, too. Other school jobs for students may be:

- Sorting mail in the office
- Delivering messages
- Taking reports to the office
- Collecting attendance sheets
- Shelving or straightening library books
- Dusting shelves
- Taking lunchroom chairs down or putting them up
- Watering plants
- Cleaning mirrors
- Sorting and recycling
- Other: _____
- A job that sounds interesting to me is

_____ .

Maybe I will have a job in school. First, someone can teach me how to do the job. Then, I can work independently by following the written directions.

Free Time

Sometimes, the teacher says it is free time. Free time is usually different with every teacher. Free time can be confusing!

Some teachers say that students must be quiet. Other teachers say that students can talk with each other. Some teachers say that students must stay at their desks. Other teachers say that students can walk around the room. Some teachers say that students can walk or sit only in certain areas of the room. Other teachers might say that free time starts at a different time for each student, after their work is finished. Another teacher might say it is free time for everyone at the same time, or only at the end of the day.

Free time usually means that children can make choices. But even though it is called "free," certain things are not allowed. Teachers have their own rules for free time.

Free time may be especially confusing for autistic children.

I will circle or highlight what is true for me. ✏

- ▶ I am not sure what I am supposed to do at free time.
- ▶ Sometimes it is confusing or too noisy.
- ▶ Sometimes I get in trouble during free time.
- ▶ If I see the choices, I can pick what I want to do.
- ▶ I would like to do something involving my focused interest.
- ▶ Sometimes, I'd like to play with someone during free time.
- ▶ Sometimes, I'd like to play alone during free time.
- ▶ Other: _____ .

Knowing More about Free Time

▶ I would like more information about free time.

▶ There is free time in my classroom, in the after-school program, in Boy Scouts or Girl Scouts, in clubs, at other places, or at _____.

I may make a copy of the previous page and this page. I'll take it to my teachers or my activity leaders and ask them to please write down important, specific information about their free time.

Specific Rules and Choices for Free Time at _____

1. _____

2. _____

3. _____

4. _____

5. _____

6. _____

School

Rules

Rules are everywhere. There are rules in stores and in restaurants, on streets, in the neighborhood, at home, and at school. There are rules about what to say, how and when to talk, how to behave, what to do, when to do it, and so on.

Sometimes rules are written on signs, like traffic signs or in stores, but many important rules are not written down. These are called *unwritten rules*. Most people learn the *unwritten rules* just by watching and listening to others. Most children and adults learn and follow *unwritten rules* without even thinking about it.

- Many people with autism have difficulty figuring out the *unwritten rules*.

- Rules are most helpful when they are written in a literal, concrete, and specific manner.

- It is fair and safe for me—and for everyone—if the rules that others know automatically (the *unwritten rules*) are written on a sign or piece of paper so I can read them.

School

More on Rules ...

Most students follow the rules because the rules make sense to them. When people understand the reasons for the rules, they can follow them more easily.

I may know a rule, but I may forget to follow *it because it may not make sense to me.*

I may need **more information** about some rules. Rules at school or at home that *do not make sense to me* are:

1. _____

2. _____

3. _____

4. _____

5. _____

6. _____

If there are more, I can write them on a separate piece of paper.

Social Stories are one way to get more information about the situation surrounding a particular rule that doesn't make sense to me. **If I have more information I can read, then that rule may make more sense!**

Homework

Students have four different types of work. The first two types of work happen when *I am in school*.

1. **Independent work in school**—This is work I do at my desk or in my office at school. This is when I work by myself, using a work system or written directions.

2. **Work in school with another person**—This is work I do in school with a teacher, assistant, tutor, or another student.

The other two types of work are done *at home*. This is why it is called "homework." There are two kinds of homework:

3. **Independent homework**—This is the work I do by myself at home. I may use a work system and written directions at home so I can work by myself.

4. **Homework with another person**—This is the work I do with someone's help, at home.

When I get home from school, I may check my after-school schedule. I can see when it is time to do homework and when it is time for free time and other events or responsibilities.

Good Grades

Students earn grades for their work. Some grades are letters, and some grades are numbers. Everyone likes to get good grades. The highest grades are usually an A+ or 100, but there are other good grades, too.

For example, depending on the student, good grades may be C, C+, B-, B, B+, A-, A, and A+.

I will circle or highlight what is true for me. ✏

- ▶ I like to get good grades.

- ▶ Getting good grades makes me feel happy and proud.

- ▶ I feel like I have to get the highest grade possible.

- ▶ I do not like to make mistakes.

- ▶ I get angry or upset if I do not get the highest grade.

- ▶ It is OK if I make some mistakes.

- ▶ My parents want me to get good grades.

- ▶ I get in trouble if I don't get good grades.

- ▶ I want to know which grades are good grades for me.

- ▶ If I get good grades, then I earn rewards.

- ▶ I do not care about grades.

- ▶ Other: _____.

If I am concerned about getting good grades, I should get more information about this. My teachers can write down the numbers or letters or symbols that are considered good grades for me in their classes.

More on Good Grades ...

Different teachers use different grading systems. Grades can be letters, numbers, checks, or other symbols. I am concerned about getting good grades.

(My parent or teacher and I can make a copy of the previous page and this page. I will show them to my teachers and ask them to fill the pages in.)

Teacher's name:

Good grades for me in this class are considered to be:

Teacher's name:

Good grades for me in this class are considered to be:

Teacher's name:

Good grades for me in this class are considered to be:

Teacher's name:

Good grades for me in this class are considered to be:

The Quiet Area

There are a lot of sounds and people. There are a lot of things to remember and things to do. School takes a huge amount of concentration and energy for autistic students.

Sometimes I feel overwhelmed. *Overwhelmed* means there is too much going on at the same time. When I am overwhelmed, I may get very confused. I may not know what to do.

I will circle or highlight what is true for me. 🖉

Sometimes in school:
▶ I feel worried or anxious, angry or sad.
▶ I may not do my work.
▶ I may cry or yell.
▶ I may get very quiet and want to disappear.
▶ I feel overwhelmed.
▶ I wish I could be by myself, where it is quiet.

A quiet area is a good place. It is not a punishment. It is perfect for taking a break. I may practice going to the quiet area to help me stay calm during the school day. After taking a break in the quiet area, I simply go back to work or to the classroom activity that is going on.

My schedule shows me when it is time to practice going to the quiet area for a break. Eventually, I will learn how to know when I need to go to the quiet area, before getting overwhelmed.

Teaching Other Children about Me

This book is helping me learn about me, and autism.

Other students and teachers need to learn, too.

When children and teachers know about autism, they might understand me better. They will learn that I am perfectly OK just the way I am … just like they are OK the way they are. They will learn that there are different ways of being in the world. They will learn that autism is one of the ways of being. (See page 12.)

I will circle or highlight what is true for me. 🖉

▶ I want my classmates to understand about autism.

▶ I want a particular student, _____ (name), to know about autism.

▶ I would like to show this book to _____ (name).

▶ I want classmates to see this book.

▶ I want a teacher to see this book: (name) _____ .

▶ I don't want most students to see this book, except maybe one person in particular: (name) _____ .

▶ I want a friend to see certain pages of this book. I will show my parent which pages are important to show.

▶ I want someone else (name) _____ to see this book.

▶ Other: _____ .

My Thoughts about School

1. My favorite thing about school is _____ .

2. In school, I also like _____ .

3. In school, I do not like _____ .

4. _____ is the hardest thing for me at school.

5. _____ is the easiest thing for me at school.

6. The things that help me the most at school are

   _____ .

7. It bothers me when _____ .

8. I wish that _____ .

9. I would like to learn more about _____ .

10. I do not understand about _____ .

11. I would like to be friends with (name, if known)

    _____ .

12. Other: _____ .

Especially for Older Readers

Many of the previous topics in this chapter for children are relevant when individually selected for older children, teenagers, and—in some cases—adults. Relevant supplementary information specifically for older readers is provided on the following pages to support their understanding, development of self-advocacy, and authentic participation in the Individualized Educational Program (IEP) or transition-planning process.

Because of the wide range of students and their needs, the examples of Communication Forms contained in this section are offered to IEP and transition team members as examples. Please keep in mind that written information and Communication Forms must be individualized to fit the learning style, issues, needs, and strengths of each student.

My book, *Communication: What Does It Mean to Me?* (Future Horizons, 2010), is recommended to support authentic communication between autistic and non-autistic communication partners. The use of Communication Forms and other ideas are included.

IEPs

Most students who have a diagnosis of autism may receive support at school through the Exceptional Student Services in their school system. The type of support they are supposed to receive is described in a document called an IEP. The next few pages will provide more information to students about the IEP process.

I will circle or highlight what is true for me. 🖉

▶ I have heard my parent talking about the IEP.

▶ I have an IEP.

▶ I don't know if I have an IEP.

▶ I don't know what an IEP is.

▶ I have attended an IEP meeting with my parent and teachers.

▶ I have never attended an IEP meeting.

▶ I need more information about IEPs.

▶ Why do I have an IEP?

▶ What is written on my IEP?

▶ I have other questions or concerns about IEPs.

▶ Other: _____ .

▶ Other: _____ .

IEPs: What and Who?

What is an IEP?

IEP is the abbreviation for Individualized Education Program. The purpose of the IEP is to help the student in school. The IEP is a legal document that lists the student's strengths, skills that the student needs to learn, and type of support and accommodations a student will receive to help the learning happen.

Student's Name: _____

IEP Meeting Date: _____

Who writes the IEP?

The IEP is written by the IEP team. The IEP team includes the student, teachers, other school staff, therapists, and family members. It can also include other people the student and parents invite.

The people on my IEP team are: _____

_____.

When is the IEP meeting?

IEP meetings happen one or more times, each school year. They usually happen at the beginning or end of the school year. Sometimes they happen in the middle of the school year. My parent and teachers will let me know when my IEP meetings are to be scheduled. I may ask them to write it on the calendar.

School

My IEP Meeting Checklist

This blank checklist should be given to my teacher before the IEP meeting. It will show me what will be discussed at my IEP meeting, in the order it will be discussed. This is recommended so I know what to expect at my IEP meeting.

The schedule for my IEP meeting is as follows:

☐ _____

☐ _____

☐ _____

☐ _____

☐ _____

☐ _____

☐ _____

☐ _____

☐ _____

☐ _____

The IEP Team Needs Information

To write an IEP, the IEP team needs information about the student. They get information from teachers, parents, grades, and test scores. They also need information from the student. This is important!

The other members of the IEP team cannot really know a student's thoughts, feelings, or ideas about school unless the student communicates with them. The members of the IEP team will want to ask the student questions and hear what the student has to say. The IEP team members should use methods of communication that most easily allow the student to communicate this important information. The teachers and parents should not only talk, but they should try using written communication via pen and paper and/or keyboards.

Communication can occur through *talking* in person and *writing* with a pen or pencil or on a *tablet or computer keyboard*. Some students may also want to *draw pictures or comics*; it may be a helpful way to communicate their ideas and thoughts. Filling out a *Communication Form* can be an easy way to begin communication about the student's ideas about school.

The IEP Communication Form on the following page is an example of how members of the IEP team may learn about the student's opinions, desires, and needs. By using a Communication Form, students will be able to give "input" into the decision-making about their school life. On the IEP Communication Form, the student may circle or highlight the statements or questions that are personally true, as on other pages in this book. Afterward, the IEP team may want to get more information by talking or writing. Reading and listening to what a student has to say is an important way for others to truly understand the student.

School

IEP Communication Form

(Example)

My Name: _____

IEP Meeting Date: _____

I am an important member of the IEP team. I have information about me and my school that the IEP team needs to know. The people on my IEP team do not automatically know my thoughts about school unless I communicate with them. (They might guess, but their guesses might not be accurate, unless I give them honest information.) This IEP Communication Form will help my IEP team know my opinions, worries, successes, and desires about my school life. Because of what I may say or write, some things at school may be adjusted or adapted in ways I would like or in ways to help me be successful, feel better, and learn more. Using this form honestly will provide accurate ideas about me and my school. What I mark and write may help others understand my point of view about school. This is a first step in making things better.

I will circle , highlight, or fill in the blanks what is true for me. 🖉

▶ This semester I have _____ (how many) classes.

▶ There are classes I usually like. They are: _____
_____ .

▶ There are classes I usually don't like. They are:_____
_____ .

▶ I have a favorite class. It is:_____ .

▶ Some teachers are easy to understand. Their names are:

_____ .

▶ Some teachers are difficult to understand. Their names are:

_____ .

▶ I want to learn more about certain subjects or ideas. They are:

_____ .

▶ I usually have homework most days after school.

▶ I almost ALWAYS have homework every day after school.

▶ Homework is easy most of the time. I usually do it without problems.

▶ I usually like homework from this/these classes: _____

_____ .

▶ I usually don't like homework from (class name): _____ .

▶ Homework gets finished quickly, in 1 hour or less.

▶ Homework gets finished, but it takes longer than an hour. It often takes _____ (how many) hours.

▶ I am not sure how long homework takes. I will ask my mom or dad or another person who may know. The answer is:_____(how many) hours.

▶ Sometimes my homework does not get finished.

▶ Usually my homework does not get finished.

▶ I usually don't do homework.

▶ I usually remember homework assignments, and I bring the books home to use.

▶ Sometimes I don't remember the assignments, and/or I forget to bring the books home. This happens: (circle)

A LOT   SOMETIMES   NEVER

▶ There is a student who is friendly to me. This student is in one or more of my classes. This student is in my _____ _____ class(es).

▶ I know the name of that student who is friendly.

▶ I don't remember the name of that student who is friendly.

▶ There is something I want to announce or ask about school, teachers, classes, other students, homework, or something else:

_____ .

School

Giving More Information to the IEP Team

After my IEP team reads the Communication Form, they may want more information from me about a specific class, subject, teacher, or student, my homework, or another aspect of school life. We can communicate by talking or through other methods of communication. Communication is how I may help other people understand me better.

If more information is needed, please consider using a method that is best for me now.

I'll (circle) or highlight or the ways I'd like to communicate: 🖉

▶ I'd like to talk to one person on the IEP team. (Who?_____)

▶ I'd like to talk to the whole group (the IEP team).

▶ I'd like to write with a pen or pencil.

▶ I'd like to use a computer keyboard or tablet.

▶ Please ask me questions by typing in silence.

▶ I will answer the questions by typing.

▶ I may want to talk, after typing for a while … but I am not sure.

▶ I'd like to fill out another Communication Form about the specific information that is needed.

▶ Other: _____ .

Chapter 9

For Parents, Teachers, and Therapists

"My pace is not school's pace."

—Maria White at age 16

Ideas in This Chapter:

☑ The educational environment

☑ Remember the schedule!

☑ Problems when teaching independent work skills

☑ The one-on-one assistant

☑ Making an office

☑ How can I use a work system to teach my child to work independently?

☑ Providing written directions

☑ Written directions can be used at home, too

☑ Organizing the workspace, supplies, and materials

☑ Modifying worksheets

☑ Folder tasks

☑ Student satisfaction and motivation

☑ Incorporating special interests

☑ Outlines, diagrams, models, notes, and mapping

☑ Nine types of lesson adaptations

☑ Group instruction

☑ The computer: a cautionary measure

☑ Homework

☑ What are the most important skills I should teach?

☑ The quiet area

☑ Why is he like that?

☑ Programs to teach peers about differences

☑ Talking about autism and your child

☑ Authentic IEP participation

The educational environment

Which classroom is best for my child? Where will he learn best? Where will he be the happiest? Calmest? Most motivated? Most challenged? Successful? Independent? Accepted? Should the school system hire a special assistant for him? Should he be homeschooled? Should he go to a private school? What about full inclusion? What about a special-education class? What is the best educational environment for children on the spectrum?

Parents and teachers often agonize over these questions, and rightly so. Your child may not fit perfectly in any of the options available in your community. There is no single right answer for all students. Both informal and formal assessment is necessary. Take a close look at your child's skills, strengths, interests, needs, and learning style. What level of structure is optimal for him to function in school successfully, independently, interdependently, and happily? What qualities in the environment allow him to thrive? What has worked in the past? What hasn't worked? Do any ideas in this book help? According to the TEACCH program,*

> The basic aims of structured teaching remain relevant when teaching children with high-functioning autism and Asperger syndrome. First, structured teaching seeks to make the world, in this case, the classroom environment, as meaningful as possible. When the child genuinely understands what is happening and what is expected, learning is enhanced, and behavior problems decrease. Second, teaching children with autism involves a two-prong approach that focuses on helping the child develop skills and competencies while also recognizing the need for environmental modifications to maximize student strengths and minimize student deficits.

* Kunce L, Mesibov GB. *Educational Approaches to High-Functioning Autism and Asperger Syndrome.* New York, NY: Plenum Press; 1998: 230.

These organizing principles underlie the primary strategies for structuring the classroom environment for students with high-functioning autism and Asperger syndrome. The strategies include: *(1)* understanding autism, *(2)* understanding the unique child through both formal and informal assessment, *(3)* making events consistent and predictable, *(4)* clarifying instructions and expectations, *(5)* structuring tasks and assignments to promote success, and *(6)* cultivating and fully utilizing students' compelling interests.

While determining the best educational program for your child, review the previous workbook pages in this chapter and make a list of the strategies to try. Some of these strategies are discussed in greater detail here.

Remember the schedule!

The schedule has been introduced and recommended again and again in subsequent chapters. It is no coincidence that it is at the top of the list of strategies to use with your child. The schedule, usually in the form of a checklist with icons, pictures, and/or the written word, serves as a premier organizing strategy.

Your child's schedule should be designed in a way that makes sense to him. Period. You might have to try different adaptations until you see what is most effective. Examples of several different types of schedules, as well as tips for using a schedule, can be found on pages 77, 96, and 266.

Your child's ability to use the schedule independently will have far-reaching results, especially after graduation! In North Carolina, we have found that the adults who use a schedule and follow a work system independently have greater success at keeping a job. (See pages 109-114.)

Problems when teaching independent work skills

It is not unusual for families to sit hour upon hour every night, fighting a never-ending battle to keep up with class assignments. You may find yourself constantly prompting, encouraging, directing, bribing, pampering, bargaining, or actually doing the homework.

Most autistic students have difficulty with one or more features of independent work.

For some children, the idea of doing work for school at home (called *homework*) is so absurd that they flatly refuse to do it. One high-school student completed every assignment but didn't understand it was important to return them to the teacher. It was only at the end of the semester, after he had failed the class, that the school counselor discovered all the assignments stacked neatly in his locker.

It is an obvious but often-overlooked fact that to develop independent work skills, the child must already know how to complete the work in question. In some classrooms, it is not unusual to find that the assignments require skills that the child has not yet mastered. If this is the case, you cannot expect the child to practice working independently, if he cannot do the assignments by himself to begin with. The level or amount of work might be inappropriate on the basis of your child's abilities. In some cases, the assignments will need to be modified. Ways to organize, clarify, and modify assignments will be suggested later in this chapter. In other cases, the student's educational program may need to be reevaluated on the basis of an updated and accurate assessment of his skills and abilities.

More than likely, your child has developed the habit of waiting for someone to help, even if he knows what to do. The routine varies from child to child. He may need a prompt to begin, constant prompts to continue, someone sitting next to him, or someone telling him when he is done and what to do next. This can become a firm, well-established routine. No amount of explaining why he must work on his own seems to make a difference. Waiting him out only seems to delay and lengthen the inevitable. It appears that he simply can't or won't work independently.

If this is true for your child, then learning to work independently should be a primary educational focus and take top priority in his yearly educational goals. From TEACCH's long-range perspective of supporting children with autism as they grow into adults who are entering the job market, the ability to work independently is even more crucial than acquiring specific academic skills.

The one-on-one assistant

One solution that school systems may frequently use is to provide a personal assistant or a "one-on-one" assistant. This well-meaning assistant does what is necessary to get your child to pay attention, participate in the classroom, and complete his work. And although the goal is to reduce this level of personal support over time, independence may be elusive.

Whether your child has a personal assistant or requires a great deal of attention from the teacher or prodding from other students, it is recommended that his helpers be clear on what the goal is and how to reach it. They must understand that the goal is to teach him to use the structure that will allow him, in turn, to practice and develop independent work skills. Your child must learn how to make sense of his environment and how to organize his behavior without an outside voice or presence prompting him. He must know how to find the most relevant information in the situation and use this information to function independently. This is one of the foremost reasons for providing additional "structure."

On the previous workbook pages, you and your child have been introduced to the office (page 263), the schedule (page 261), the work system (page 265-266), and written directions (page 267). These basic and essential tools are the keys to achieving and sustaining independent work skills during the school years—and beyond.

Making an office

Making an office provides the physical structure to help your child focus on the work in front of him. When the office is set up, or when your child sits at a special desk designated as his office, he is reminded that it is "independent work time."

An office should be portable, yet sturdy. A good, inexpensive office can be made easily from a science fair display board, which you can find at office supply stores. Cut the folding board in half, horizontally, creating two tri-folding cardboard screens. (Each display board makes two offices.) This inexpensive, sturdy office is preferable, in most cases, to buying expensive new furniture or study carrels. It is portable, allowing for individualized use, and can be folded and stored when not needed.

I recommend that you keep a large stack of "offices" in your classroom for other students to pick up and use when they need to concentrate, too. This will help eliminate any possible stigma that the office may imply about this student and others who may need to use it. You may find that many students enjoy setting up an office on their desks.

The work system has been taped to the inside wall of the "office."

How can I use a work system to teach my child to work independently?

The work system is a logical way to organize a series of assignments. For children who have good reading abilities, the work system is usually provided in the form of a written checklist. It provides four important pieces of information:

1. **What work am I supposed to do?**

2. **How much work is there to do?**

3. **How do I stay on track and know when I am finished?**

4. **What will happen after all my work is finished?**

A work system is used when your child must complete a series of assignments or tasks.

> **11:00 Independent Work in Office**
>
> ☑ 1. Reading - "Recipe Questions"
> ☐ 2. Geography - "Bordering States"
> ☐ 3. Spelling - Chap 16 words (5 times)
> ☐ 4. Fold Up office + Choose activity
>   in _Activity Center_

After checking his schedule and seeing that it is time for independent work, your child goes to his designated office or sets up the cardboard "office" on his desk. He locates the work system, which has been written on a piece of paper, a clipboard, or a notepad. It may have been placed in or on his desk, or perhaps it is taped to the inside of his office (see the diagram on page 298). The work system will show him what he is to accomplish during this period of time.

It is important to note that the work system differs from what we typically think of as an "assignment list," in that it always contains the four essential pieces of information listed above. The tasks or assignments are listed in sequence. Your child checks them off or crosses them out as they are completed. The last entry on the list shows what to do next, after completing all the assignments. This final piece of information, "What will happen after all my work is finished," is an integral part of the work system that is not normally found on assignment lists. By doing this, you have reinforced the concept of "finished," and you have structured the next transition. This provides your child with a sense of order and clarity about what will happen next.

Providing written directions

Written directions show each step needed to complete a single task or assignment. Each task is broken down into smaller steps, based on your child's organizational needs and how much detail he requires. The steps are listed in sequence, and your child is taught to check off or cross out each step as he proceeds. On the basis of his responses, you might need to highlight certain words or pieces of information.

Below are two sets of directions for completing the same assignment, but they are written for two different children. Both students require a high level of structure to work independently. Both sets of directions provide a clear sequence to follow; however, the directions are different—they have been individualized for each student. The difference is that the directions on the right are even more specific and concrete and provide more details than the directions on the left.

DIRECTIONS FOR
"Recipe Questions"

___1. Get "Recipe Questions" sheet for garlic bread.

___2. Get cookbook.

___3. Answer circled questions on sheet.

___4. Return cookbook to shelf.

___5. Put sheet in "finished work."

___6. Check work system.

Follow Directions for
"Recipe Questions"

☐ 1. Get what is needed:
   ☐ cookbook
   ☐ pen
   ☐ "Garlic Bread" sheet

☐ 2. Write name on sheet.

☐ 3. Open book – page 56

☐ 4. Read question #1

☐ 5. Write answer on sheet.

☐ 6. Read question #4

☐ 7. Write answer on sheet.

☐ 8. Read question #5

☐ 9. Write answer on sheet.

☐ 10. Fold sheet + put in book.

☐ 11. Put book in "finished" tray.

☐ 12. Check to see what to do next (on work system).

School

Written directions can be used at home, too

Visual strategies can be used at home. Schedules, work systems, and written directions in the form of checklists can be a valuable aid in teaching independent self-care skills and household responsibilities. A short list for packing swim gear was written into Adam's schedule on page 112. A checklist to use at bath time was referred to in Catie's schedule on page 111. Catie's bath time checklist might look like this:

☐ **Tell Mom, *"Mom, I'm ready for the bathwater, please."***

☐ **Undress and put clothes in hamper.**

☐ **Choose four bathtub toys.**

☐ **Get clean washcloth.**

☐ **Set the timer for 15 minutes.**

☐ **Get in bathtub.**

☐ **When timer rings, playtime is over—put toys in the bucket.**

☐ **Wash—Mom will help. (On June 1, Catie washes by herself.)**

☐ **Dry body and hang towel on rod.**

☐ **Put pajamas on.**

☐ **Tell Mom, *"It's time to check the calendar."***

Several strategies have been built into the checklist to help Catie become more independent. The first and last directions prompt her to communicate. Rather than just having a passive role, she is learning to take the initiative to organize her evening routine. The checklist prompts her to tell Mom it is time for the bathwater. Notice the specificity in the direction about getting the bathtub toys. It is clear that she cannot dump her entire collection of bath toys into the bathtub tonight. Within the structure, she takes an active role (by setting the timer) and can see exactly what the expectations are (when to put toys away).

Notice the entry about washing. Mom has decided that when summer vacation begins, she wants Catie to begin to wash herself independently. She knows it might take a long time, and there will be small steps to take along the way. She also knows that Catie is used to Mom washing her, so she might resist or refuse to change the old routine. So, Mom is preparing Catie by showing her when the new routine for washing will begin. Mom writes it on a calendar, too. (See page 155 about using a calendar.) When June 1 arrives, Catie will expect a change in the routine, and, hopefully, she'll experience it with minimal resistance.

Before June 1 arrives, Catie's mother will write a list, probably with a sequence of pictures to help Catie learn the steps of washing by herself. They will use it together, so Catie can practice referring to the pictures that show the steps of washing herself.

Organizing the workspace, supplies, and materials

The location of your student's desk may significantly affect his behavior while working. Try placing his desk to the side of the room, away from the door. Some children do better at the front of the room so as not be distracted or annoyed by classroom movement. Others feel more comfortable in the back. You may need to try a few different locations until you determine the best place. Carefully observe your student when deciding where he can most easily learn to work independently. Provide a Communication Form with options for desk locations.

It may be that your student will use only one desk. He will set up and take down the cardboard office when needed or as indicated on his schedule. However, children work better when there is a different, permanent location reserved just for independent work. The office can be set up permanently at a second desk, typically in a quieter location with fewer distractions. The schedule will indicate when it is time to sit at the office.

There are children who work best when the office is located outside of the classroom, either in the hall, in an extra room, or perhaps in a smaller, quieter classroom. It is not unusual for some special-education teachers to renovate an unused, outdated time-out room, completely changing its purpose. Now it is a distraction-free, well-defined space in which a student can practice independent work. It becomes a "real" office!

Many students with autism have difficulty keeping their school supplies organized. Designate a nearby shelf, table, or counter for the necessary materials, supplies, and books. Label shelves, cupboards, containers, plastic baskets, or trays with what is to be stored inside. Identify and label where completed work is to be placed. Color-code folders by subject. Keep pencils in the folders with the work. Label the place where the "office" is to be kept when not in use. Provide and label a spot where the schedule is to be kept, if your student does not carry it with him.

Modifying worksheets

Assignments come in many forms, depending on the grade level, the skills to be practiced, and teacher preference. Worksheets and related written formats are widely used. For some children with organizational difficulties and problems distinguishing relevant information from details, even the most basic worksheets can be baffling.

Worksheets, workbook pages, and other assignments can be modified in ways that help students become more organized in their approach to working.

Clarify what is important, while minimizing extraneous details. Rearrange the visual format of worksheets by using colored markers, scissors, tape, and even the copy machine. Through careful observation of your student, you will learn which types of modifications are most supportive. One of the teacher assistant's jobs can be to make the necessary worksheet modifications for the week. Below, you can see a "before and after" example of the same worksheet that has been modified to meet the needs of a particular student.

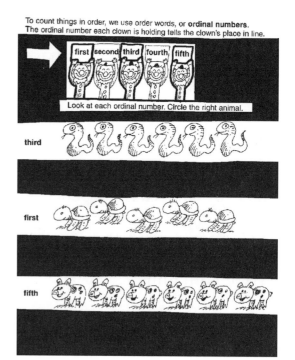

Try these methods when modifying worksheets and other written assignments:

- **Color code**
- **Label**
- **Highlight**
- **Limit extra information**
- **Outline**
- **Frame**

- **Underline**
- **Offer partially filled-in answers**
- **Use contrast**
- **Cut things out**
- **Enlarge**
- **Circle**

Folder tasks

More structure might be needed for students with significant organizational difficulties and/or students who cannot complete assignments independently because of handwriting difficulties. Actually manipulating and arranging materials in a concrete manner, rather than only writing the correct answer with pen and paper, may elicit greater motivation and cooperation from your student. Folder tasks can easily be used for supplementary skill practice.

Folder tasks are created out of manila folders, like those used for filing. Materials such as laminated pictures from magazines, books, workbooks, or textbooks, and flat objects such as plastic counters, puzzle pieces, and cards make up the raw materials for folder tasks. Instead of accomplishing the task by writing the answers, the student manipulates the pieces by sorting, matching, or otherwise arranging them to complete the work. The finished work is kept in place by slipping the pieces behind paperclips, placing them in pockets, or fastening them in place with Velcro.

Each folder task is self-contained; all the materials required to complete the task are stored in the folder itself. Folder tasks are an excellent

School

alternative to pencil-and-paper assignments, especially for students with significant organizational and/or handwriting difficulties. Folder tasks are also an excellent alternative to letting your student become too dependent on someone else's assistance to complete his work. Folder tasks can be a valuable aid in helping students work independently. Here is one example of a folder task created to practice reading comprehension and social studies facts. New sentences and new pictures can be added and rearranged to create additional tasks.

Sentences are tucked into the pocket on the left. Student matches the sentences to pictures on the right, by attaching them to the Velcro pieces.

Student satisfaction and motivation

Once structured teaching strategies have become routine, you may find, delightfully, that your child's level of motivation increases along with his independence skills. For many children on the autism spectrum, the acts of following the list, checking things off as they are accomplished, and "finishing" become motivating and fundamentally satisfying in and of themselves. The systems are predictable and clear. Your child knows what to expect and what will happen

when he is finished. It becomes intrinsically motivating to the student to follow the schedule, the work system, and written directions.

Usually, when these visually structured teaching strategies are individualized properly and used consistently as a dynamic, flexible, and active part of the school day, systematic reliance on traditional behavioral management techniques decrease. Parents and teachers frequently find that they no longer experience the urgent need to use eternal motivators or "reinforcers" to get the child to work.

Incorporating special interests

A student's satisfaction and motivation increase dramatically when teachers and parents consider his interests. Fascination and devotion to a special interest can open many doors for the student of the creative teacher who is willing to cultivate what moves him.

Incorporate your child's special interests to capture his attention, introduce new skills, illustrate difficult concepts, motivate and stimulate, increase positive social experiences, and add overall pleasure and satisfaction to learning. Review the following examples:

> *1. Allow him to use his special interest when working on an "unrelated" project.*

Student's interest:	Buildings
Art project:	Design a Christmas card
Try:	Allow the student to include his interest in the Christmas card design. For instance, Doug loved drawing buildings. (See the drawing for a Christmas card, above, by Doug Buckner. Notice the hint of a Christmas tree at the bottom of the drawing.)

2. *Introduce a new topic in a way that relates to his special interest.*

Student's interest:	Weather
New social studies topic:	Cities, suburbs, and towns in your state
Try:	Record temperatures for designated cities

3. *Teach a new or difficult skill by relating it to his special interest.*

Student's interest:	Electrical poles and wires
Skill:	Multiplication
Try:	If there were four lines attached to the top of an electrical pole, and there were three rows of these lines going down the pole, then how many … ?

4. *Teach abstract concepts by relating them to his special interest.*

Student's interest:	Star Trek
Concept:	Empathy and taking another person's perspective
Try:	Picard changes form and becomes a foreign entity (taking another person's perspective). He now understands what they feel and think (empathy).

5. *Motivate by allowing the time to partake in special interests when finished working.*

Student's interest:	Washing machines

Try:	When work is completed, the student gets to look through Laundromat specialty catalogs.

6. *Increase social contact through his special interest.*

Student's interest:	Years and makes of automobiles

Social skill goal:	Initiate social contact

Try:	Poll classmates, one at a time, as to the types of cars their parents have. Make a chart and share the results with classmates. Then poll classmates as to the type of car they "want." Make another chart to share the results.

Outlines, diagrams, models, notes, and mapping

When information must be presented verbally or through lectures, it will help if you augment the lecture with visual aids. Whenever possible, demonstrate concepts with models, charts, photographs, and pictures.

☑ **Minimize visual distractions.**

When writing information on the whiteboard, wipe it clean of extraneous information that distracts from what is relevant.

☑ **Use the overhead projector or Smart Board and highlight items.**

School

Display an outline of your presentation and lists of relevant points. Highlight key words with colored markers as you talk. "Mind map" (see below) to show connections as you talk.

☑ **Provide written notes.**

Give your student a copy of the lecture notes or an outline of the information you are presenting. Or, arrange with another classmate to duplicate a copy of his or her notes to share.

☑ **Try "mind mapping."**

Show how the information fits together, concretely and visually. "Mind mapping" visually depicts the relationships and connections between pieces of information. This is also known as "graphic organizing." See below.

About mind mapping

Mind mapping is a technique used for planning, organizing, and seeing the connections between concepts or ideas. Variations of mind mapping are also known as clustering, webbing, bubbling, and mapping. They are sometimes referred to as "semantic organizers" or "graphic organizers." Mind mapping can be used for taking notes, reviewing and remembering information, problem solving, making plans, and presenting information.

Teachers may provide visual input during verbal presentations and lectures through mind mapping. The mind map highlights and emphasizes the flow of information and shows how the separate pieces are connected. For group instruction, use an overhead projector or Smart Board. For individual instruction, use a blank piece of paper and pens, while sitting with the student.

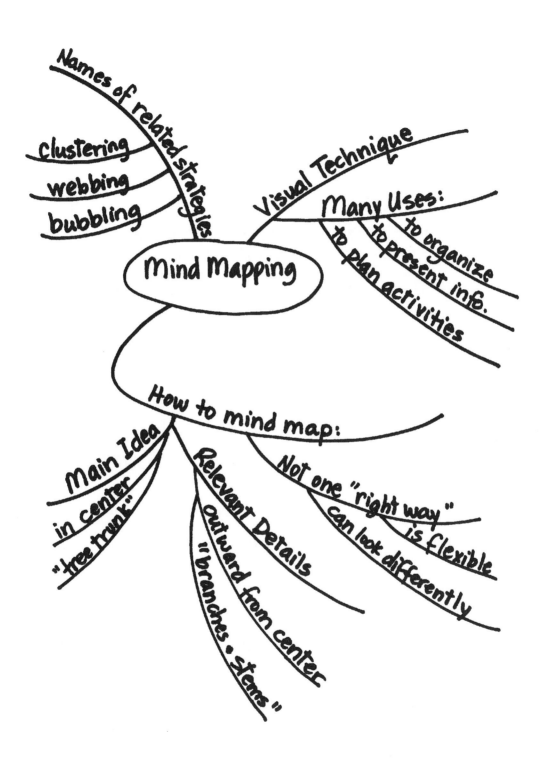

Mind Mapping

Names of related strategies
- clustering
- webbing
- bubbling

Visual Technique

Many Uses:
- to organize
- to present info.
- to plan activities

How to mind map:

Main Idea
in center
"tree trunk"

Relevant Details
outward from center
"branches • stems"

Not one "right way"
is flexible
can look differently

I have often used mapping with teenagers and adults in coaching sessions to help them identify, review, and organize their thoughts; make plans; and help them look at the connections between their ideas, behavior, and desired outcomes. The therapist creates the mind map as the student talks and responds to questions. The mind map serves as the visual focal point during the discussion.

How to mind map

A mind map is created by starting with a main idea or topic that is written in the center of the page with a circle drawn around it. Ideas relating to the main idea are written on lines that are drawn outward from the center. Think of the center of the mind map (the main idea) as the trunk of a tree. You are actually adding "branches and stems" (relevant details) that are growing out from the trunk. Each new group of "branches and stems" coming out from the middle should be drawn in the same color. Use a new color for additional ideas that are related to the main theme by creating new branch and stem systems. Mind maps can look many different ways. Here is my mind map about mind mapping.

Nine types of lesson adaptations

Cathy Pratt, director of the Indiana Resource Center for Autism at the Institute on Disability and Community, located at Indiana University, promotes the use of educational strategies to support special learners within the general-education setting. She identified the following nine ways to adapt and individualize lessons. They are included here with permission.

Teachers should review these ideas when they create an individualized program to accommodate their student's learning style, skill level, and interests. Consider the following, if and when appropriate for your student:

1. *Size*

    Adapt the number of items that a learner is expected to learn or complete. For example, reduce the number of social studies terms a learner must learn at any one time. Or, in cases where a student has highly developed skills, such as spelling, increase the number of spelling words he is assigned.

2. *Time*

    Adapt the minutes, hours, or days you allow for task completion or testing. For example, increase or decrease the amount of time allotted for an assignment according to your student's pace. For a student who is working at a slower pace, consider giving him a head start, so his work will be due at the same time as the other students' work.

    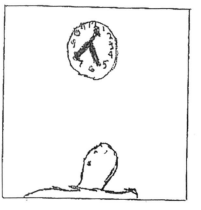

3. *Input*

    Adapt the way information is delivered to the student. For example, use visual structure, plan more concrete examples, and provide hands-on activities.

4. *Output*

    Adapt the way the student can respond to instruction. For example, instead of answering questions in writing, allow a verbal response (or vice versa) or allow students to show what they have learned by completing folder tasks and using other hands-on materials.

5. *Difficulty*

Adapt the skill level to the student's needs. For example, allow the use of a calculator, simplify directions, break down the steps with written directions, or change the rules to accommodate the student's unique learning style.

6. *Participation*

Adapt the extent to which the student is actively involved in the task. In geography, have a student hold the globe, while others point out locations. Allow a student to work with a partner, instead of working alone. Or, in the case of a student who finds group work confusing  or unbearable, allow him to work with one person or alone, instead of assigning him to a group of three or more. For group work, provide written information that describes the specific role of each group member, including his role.

7. *Level and type of support*

Increase or decrease the amount of interaction and provide other types of support, such as visually structured strategies. For example, assign peer buddies, teacher assistants, and peer tutors and provide small-group instruction. Teaching him to use a work system, instead of relying on a helper or assistant to keep him on task, is another way to individualize the type of support.

8. *Alternate goals*

Adapt the expectations while using the same materials. For example, in social studies, expect one student to locate just the states, while others learn to locate the state capitals, as well. Or, expect one student to learn more information about a particular subject, especially if it relates to his area of special interest. If it doesn't relate, show him a possible connection to his special interest.

9. *Substitute or parallel curriculum*
    Provide different instruction and materials to meet a student's individual goals. For example, while most of the students are taking a test, one student is practicing computer skills in the computer lab. Or, during a German language lesson, the student is engaged in an independent work session at his "office."

Group instruction

Expecting a student with autism to participate in and benefit from group instruction can be frustrating to both teachers and students. Group instruction can be confusing, bewildering, confusing, or even upsetting to some children. This can be due to having difficulty in knowing where to focus; having problems shifting attention; dealing with simultaneous sounds, words, sights, motion, touch, and other sensory stimulation; and having challenging auditory processing skills. In addition, group work involves spontaneous interaction, on-the-spot interpretation of what is being communicated, and the pressure to respond quickly. Many children cope by "tuning out."

Careful observation is necessary to determine if and how the student can benefit from large-group instruction. Try the suggestions that have already been mentioned, concerning ways to enhance verbal instruction (pages 309-312). Typically, working in a small group is better than working in a large group. Give the student a written list or a work system (pages 266 and 300) to prepare him for what is going to happen. This, of course, becomes more complicated during active group discussions or when the teacher's spontaneity leads to last-minute changes in the plan.

In some cases, teachers are often surprised when the student responds to questions with answers that show he had been paying attention (even though it looked like he wasn't). Remember what we know about eye contact and autism (pages 166 and 180-181). It may be easier for your student to pay attention to what is being said when he isn't looking at the speaker. He may also need more time to process—to attend, understand, and prepare to respond to what is being asked. If this is the case with your student, you can try the following:

- **Keep a stack of blank index cards and a pen with you.**
  As you ask a question, write it on the card. Place it in front of the student and do not repeat the question once you have already asked. He will probably immediately look at what is written (it's visual!). Then, wait for his answer. Depending on your student, you might just have to jot down a few key words.

- **You can use the index cards with the entire group, at random.**
  The children will see that some of your questions are only spoken, and some of them are paired with a written note. Most of the children will think this is fun; wondering if and when they will get a card might also increase their attention level on the topic.

The computer: a cautionary measure

A computer, tablet, or other type of technology can be a useful tool for students with autism. It can teach and reinforce cognitive skills, be used as an alternative to handwritten assignments, encourage and support communication and social interaction, serve as a leisure activity or a vehicle for creativity, and be an excellent prevocational skill. However, when using the computer with your child, do not overlook one important caution:

Your child must learn that there are two kinds of activities with the computer. One is doing what pleases him (*computer free time*). The other is following directions to complete a prescribed task or assignment (*computer work time*).

Future vocations in technology may be a real possibility for some children. However, there are many talented autistic adults with computer expertise who are unable to come close to getting a job that allows them to use this talent. Why?

It may be that over the years, the computer was primarily used as a free-time or leisure activity. It had become a routine so ingrained that a person is virtually unable to do what someone else wants him to do on the computer. The combination of the computer being a compelling special interest and the long-established routine of doing what he wants makes for an extremely inflexible and difficult habit to break when there are specific job requirements in the office or workplace. From his point of view, it just might not make sense.

Especially if your child is highly skilled with technology, it is imperative for him to learn from the very beginning that there is computer work time and computer free time, and he should engage in both (page 271). This should be clearly indicated on his daily schedule. As he matures, give him a variety of jobs and assignments to do and lots of different directions to follow, so he must sometimes do things not of his own choosing. This will help expand the ways he is able to use his talent and help him become more flexible when using technology. By doing so, you are keeping the door open for a possible future vocation. It may be too late if you wait until he is older and has already established rigid habits that are difficult to stop.

In the situation of an adolescent who is skilled on the computer but cannot stand to do what someone else wants him to do, realize that he has a wonderful leisure skill but acknowledge the fact that he first needs to master the prevocational skill of following someone else's instructions, even if he is very talented. **The most fruitful vocational training for individuals with autism begins in childhood and continues through the school years.**

Homework

As was clarified in the workbook on page 277, there must be a clear distinction made between work that is meant to be completed independently and work that requires help. *With this in mind, teachers need to hear from parents about what happens at home. Teachers and parents should work as a team to ensure that homework is a positive learning experience.* Try the following suggestions:

- Allow your child to **take a break** immediately after arriving home from school. Refrain from immediately asking questions about the day and making demands. Give him quiet time to recover from the day.

- Provide an **after-school schedule**. The activities should be appropriate for your child's age, interests, and needs. Include ample quiet time, time for being alone, and times for having a snack and doing favorite activities. Schedule chores and homework. Alternate unappealing activities with favorite ones. (See page 111.)

- Before leaving school, your child should get the homework assignment list from the teacher. **Do not insist that the *child* write this list himself, unless he can do it independently and easily.** For many, the act of copying down the assignments from the board is too difficult, overwhelming, and frustrating. In addition, it usually takes place when everyone in the classroom is rushing to prepare to go home. This may not be a current priority.

- At home, you can modify the assignment list to create **a work system for homework**. Remember to include what he will do after finishing at the end of the list. (Review pages 265-266.)

- If not included already, **add written directions** for specific assignments (page 267).

- Keep a record of how long it takes your child to complete his homework. Communicate with his teacher and compare it with the standard amount of time that his classmates typically spend on homework. If there is a significant difference, assignments should be modified appropriately. **Consider further timing modifications to meet your individual child's needs for more or less homework.**

- Keep **a duplicate set of textbooks** at home if other organizational methods (checklists, routines, backpack) don't help him remember his books on a consistent basis.

What are the most important skills I should teach?

There are many different subject areas, curriculum guides, courses of study, and educational philosophies. Schools have their own guidelines, while individual teachers and parents have their own biases and opinions. Each student comes with particular strengths, interests, and needs. There is limited time in the school day, and there is a lot to do.

The TEACCH program works with children, adolescents, and adults who have been educated in very different settings—from home schools, private schools, self-contained special-education classrooms, and resource programs to full-time general-education settings. We see the kinds of skills these adolescents and adults have by the time they leave school and enter the job market. With this long-range view, we are constantly able to evaluate educational programs based on how they realistically affect the lives of adults with autism.

No matter how skilled and talented your child may be or how much knowledge he possesses, sooner or later, he will fail to keep a job if he is inflexible and cannot handle change, if he is disorganized and requires constant prompts, if he obsesses on certain topics and cannot switch his attention, if he cannot follow directions or becomes resistant or angry when he is told what to do, and if he cannot communicate when he needs help.

Simply stated, by the time a child reaches adulthood, it is critical that he has learned to be organized, to function (work and play) independently, to use his strengths and skills in a positive and/or productive manner, to communicate effectively, and to have a method to help him understand times when he encounters confusing information.

☑ **The schedule and other structured strategies play a crucial role for most working adolescents and adults with autism when it comes to living an adult life and functioning on the job.**

Review the introductory information about the schedule (pages 96-114). When used dynamically and consistently, the schedule can help your child become more flexible, stay organized and involved, monitor obsessions or time focused on special interests, handle leisure time, follow directions and work independently, soften resistance to authority, and get along with others more easily. These are the life skills and vocational behaviors he must have in the workplace!

If a child, even one with a high level of intelligence, has been educated without becoming proficient in using a schedule or other types of structured strategies and without understanding about how and when to communicate the need for help, he will often find that he lacks the tools to help him function successfully and independently when dealing with the daily—and overwhelmingly complicated—demands of work and home life, no matter how smart or talented he is.

A job provides more than a paycheck. The workplace is an important source of daily social contact. Many of us actually spend more time with our coworkers than with our families and friends. And, sometimes, coworkers become friends. The constancy a job provides often fulfills many social needs.

☑ **The most effective vocational and life-skills training begins when an autistic child is young.**

Incorporate the schedule and other structured teaching strategies daily. Use them in creative and flexible ways, in a multitude of settings, at home and at school. Teach your child that checklists are meaningful tools by using them often. Even though it sounds simplistic, your child's ability to use checklists independently can have long-lasting, significant, and overall positive effects on his adult life—more than most other skills he might learn in school. When planning his educational program, make sure that you:

- Review the results of formal and informal assessment.

- Consider his innate style of learning.

- Capitalize on his natural gifts and strengths.

- Pay attention to his greatest needs.

- Determine educational goals based on these factors.

- Teach your child to independently use and follow a schedule, work system, and written directions. (See pages 96, 261, 266-267.)

- Assess his ability to function interdependently—specifically, the ability to know when, where, how, and whom to ask for help. (See pages 221, 233-235.) Besides mastering the art and science of using visual organizational strategies, as discussed previously, it is imperative that your child or student is educated about the concept of "help" and all the skills that surround it. This will lay the foundation for future self-advocacy (page 244).

The quiet area

As mentioned in chapter 9, the quiet area may provide a welcome respite from the demands, frustrations, and overwhelm that accompany daily life for many children with autism. Identify a place for the quiet area that will work for the teacher, the student, and the rest of the class. It may be a corner in the classroom or a designated place in the hall or in another room. One adult said it would have made a big difference for him in school …

"... if I could have been allowed to go somewhere where it was quiet, when it got to be too much, so I could have gotten calmed down. That would have helped."

A concern of some teachers is how to justify this special area for one student and not for others. Ordinarily, all it takes is a matter-of-fact statement: "John needs to take a quiet break once in a while to enable him to stay focused and calm." Children will accept an explanation that is simple, clear, and honest. You may even consider making the quiet area available for other students, as well—those who may benefit from having a preventative break in a quiet area. Two positive results of the quiet area may be the following:

1. *Prevention*

    By including time for the quiet area on your child's schedule throughout the day, you'll help prevent overwhelm, which can otherwise snowball into distress and anxiety. The distribution of quiet area times on the schedule should be determined through careful observation and informal assessment. Some children might only need one visit to the quiet area all day. Others might need frequent periods of respite—as many as four to six short visits throughout the day. You may discover that your student benefits from a routine visit to the quiet area before or after a particular activity. An individual child's needs will undoubtedly fluctuate, depending on the levels of calmness and anxiety and the day's circumstances.

2. *Self-awareness*

    Through consistency and familiarity with the quiet area, as well as the child's growing awareness about the purpose of the quiet area, he may learn more about himself. A goal is that over time, he will learn how to take care of himself, before a meltdown occurs. Your student may learn to gauge his need for respite and know what to do about it. He may learn to estimate, at the beginning of the day, how frequently or when he might need to visit the quiet area. In this case, happily be willing to adapt his schedule accordingly. This is an incredibly valuable life skill for your student to develop! Other strategies to help relieve and prevent anxiety are discussed in chapters 2, 11, and 12.

Why is he like that?

Some parents are hesitant to talk directly with other students and significant people at school about the fact that their child is on the autism spectrum. Most parents do not want the child to be thought of as different. They hope that maybe if the differences are not mentioned, then the child will be "just like every other child." Or, perhaps by not mentioning the differences, they will be minimized.

Of course our ultimate goal is for every individual to be respected and appreciated, with all of our personal quirks and uniqueness. This is what diversity is all about. The challenge is, though, how do we make this happen? How do we create an environment of mutual respect, where every child's humanity is embraced and celebrated? How do we create an environment where "difference makes no difference anymore," as stated so eloquently in the opening quote of this book?

The truth is this: Even if you or your child's teacher does not educate your child's classmates about autism or how he is different in certain ways, they already know it. But, they don't know why. As a result, you run the risk that his classmates will fill in the missing pieces

with wrong information. "He must be crazy or stupid or weird …"
Consequently, behaviors ranging from ignoring, whispering, and
name-calling to other overtly rude or hurtful actions may typically
result. The classmates' responses largely depend on the particular
combination of the general classroom climate and your child's
unique traits.

There is an alternative. It is education.

Programs to teach peers about differences

Uncensored questions and honest answers can lay the groundwork for
understanding, empathy, and acceptance. Since 1985, I have spoken
with thousands of students from kindergarten through high school
about their autistic peers. In almost every instance, an immediate
positive change in attitude was observed after the presentations.
Among a few students, a long-term interest in and understanding
of the child with autism began to sprout. I created the program
"Understanding Friends" for the purpose of educating peers about the
differing abilities that are found in every person. It is a simple program
that can be adapted to fit all grade levels and individualized to explain
autism as it relates to a particular classmate. The children learn that
even though all people are different in a multitude of ways, we are all

the same in one major way: Each of us deserves to be understood and accepted for who we are.

"Understanding Friends" begins with an introduction in which the class explores how everyone is unique. Then the children rotate between experiential centers that are set up to simulate "different abilities," including fine-motor, visual, sensory, perceptual, and auditory processing differences. Afterward, the term *autism* is introduced, and questions and answers follow. Depending on the grade level, the program concludes by reading a related children's book. Questions are encouraged, and the mystery about the "different" peer may shift to a new understanding. Depending on the ability and interest level of the student with autism, getting him involved in this program is an option to explore with him and his parents. To download a free lesson plan for presenting "Understanding Friends," including ideas on how to involve the student, go to *catherinefaherty.com*. Look under "Publications" and then "Articles."

"The Sixth Sense" was developed by Carol Gray to explain why some people have a different experience with social understanding. It is a short presentation that begins with a discussion about the five senses and introduces the concept of the "social sense" as the sixth sense. The ability to take another person's perspective is defined as this social sense. This program is meant to be used with children in the third grade and older and is an effective way to explain autism to groups of adults, as well. The lesson plan for presenting "The Sixth Sense" can be found in the booklet, "The Sixth

Sense II," by Carol Gray.

Susan Moreno, in her booklet, "High-Functioning Individuals with Autism: Advice and Information for Parents and Others Who Care," published by MAAP (More Able Autistic People), describes a way to simulate sensory processing problems, which are common to many individuals with autism. By using a strobe light, a radio, gloves with different textures, and verbal directions, typical students experience what it might feel like to receive confusing or distorted sensory information.

CoulterVideo.com, a family business focused on making videos related to the autism spectrum, has produced short videos in which autistic children and teens are interviewed. These are titled "Intricate Minds" and "Intricate Minds II." They are useful to share with classrooms to educate, raise awareness, and stimulate thoughtful discussion among students.

There are many new children's books written to educate and nurture understanding about one's family members and classmates on the autism spectrum. I invite you to explore the Future Horizons online bookstore for ones that fit your child's grade level, age, and needs.

Invite children, teens, or adults on the spectrum who want to educate others, speak to the class, and answer questions. Depending on the presenters, it is most supportive to structure the discussion with previously determined questions that are written down in sequence.

Talking about autism and your child

A formal program is not necessary to talk with your child's peers about his autism. Your willingness to invite open discussion and to answer questions is the key. Keep your explanations simple, open, direct, matter-of-fact, and reassuring. Information from the pages of this workbook can help you plan your talk. Most children want to understand, and, when they do, the transformative power of education is realized.

Depending on the age and maturity levels of your child and his classmates at large, it may be better to arrange for your child to be out of the classroom during these presentations or discussions. Classmates are more apt to ask the questions that are really on their minds if their peer with autism is not in the room. In most cases, depending on your child, he should be told there is going to be a presentation about autism (or differences, or whatever term you use). Usually, the child himself prefers not to be present, although he might want to hear "what happened" when it is all over.

In cases where the child chooses to be present for the discussion, it is imperative that he knows ahead of time what is going to happen and what is going to be said. If your child is going to be present, he should already have an understanding about autism. This program should not be his first introduction to autism. If he is to be present, he should already feel secure about himself as an autistic individual. In this case, he may want to answer some of his classmates' questions himself. (Refer to the lesson plan for "Understanding Friends" at *catherinefaherty.com*.)

If you are a teacher who wants to educate your students about autism and how it relates to their classmate, it goes without saying that it must be done with the full permission of the child's parents. Depending on the child's age and level of understanding, it is important to get his permission, as well. However, there may be individual situations where it may not feel right yet for a particular family or child. Even beyond the ethics of confidentiality, which obviously apply here, it is imperative that the desires of those parents and children who are hesitant to share such personal information with others must be fully respected.

Authentic IEP participation

Look carefully at the last six workbook pages I have included in this chapter, called "Especially for Older Readers." You will find that the information is not only for the student, but will support the rest of the IEP team as they encourage the student's participation as a full member of his team. If it's structured in a way that is easy for him to understand, he may play a vital role in advocating for himself by assessing his program and determining his goals. Provide visually clear structure, as shown in the examples, to help him self-advocate. Provide information in autism-friendly ways through Social Stories (about IEPs, etc), and elicit information through Communication Forms and other preferred methods of self-expression. Please do more than invite him to sit in on the meeting and ask him if he has anything to say or ask about the discussion going on around him.

Chapter 10
Friends

Workbook

Friends

What Is a Friend?

A friend is a person who is not in my family but who is important to me, in a good way.

A friend is important because both of us like each other. Friends like to spend time together sometimes. We like to do many of the same things.

I will (circle) or highlight what is true for me. ✎

▶ I do not have friends.

▶ I wish I had a friend.

▶ I do not want a friend.

▶ I have one friend. My friend's name is .

▶ I have many friends. Their names are:

_____

_____ .

▶ Other: _____ .

These are the things I'd like to do with a friend:

1. _____

2. _____

3. _____

4. _____

Playing

Some children like to spend a lot of time with other children, playing and talking. Some children like to play by themselves.

I will mark what is true for me. 🖉

1. I like to:

   ▶ Play with one child at a time.

   ▶ Play with a group of children at the same time.

   ▶ Play by myself.

   ▶ Sometimes play with others, and sometimes by myself.

2. I like to:

   ▶ Play with boys.

   ▶ Play with girls.

   ▶ Play with children who are younger than me.

   ▶ Play with children who are older than me.

   ▶ Play with those who are the same age as me.

   ▶ Play with adults.

   ▶ Play with (name) _____ .

3. When I am with others, I like to:

   ▶ Play by myself, in the same room as other children.

   ▶ Watch them play, but not join in.

   ▶ At first watch them play, and then join in later on.

   ▶ Most of the time, play together with them.

   ▶ Not be with them at all; I would rather play by myself.

Pretend Play

Most children like to pretend. *Pretending* is when children make up things that aren't really here, but they act like it is real. They might talk in a different voice or say they are someone else. They might pretend they see something. They know it is not real. For some children, pretending is fun.

Many children with autism don't like to pretend.

I will circle or highlight what is true for me. 🖉

▶ I don't like to pretend.

▶ I don't know how to pretend.

▶ I think pretending is silly or useless.

▶ I wish I could pretend.

▶ Pretending is not fun for me. I like to play in other ways. The ways I like to play are: _____

_____ .

Some autistic children do like to pretend. They might imagine a fantasy world and pretend they are in it.

If I like to pretend, I will mark what is true for me about pretending. (If I do not like to pretend, I do not have to read more on this page.) 🖉

▶ I like to pretend.

▶ I usually like to pretend, when I'm playing by myself.

▶ I usually like to pretend with other children.

▶ I want other children to imagine my fantasy world.

▶ I like to get new pretend ideas from other children.

▶ Other: _____ .

Playing Outside

Most children like to play outside. There are many things to do outside.

I will circle or highlight what I like to do. ✎

I like being active, like:

▶ Playing on playground equipment—swings, slides, climbing bars, or _____ .

▶ Throwing and catching balls

▶ Shooting baskets

▶ Riding a bike

▶ Jumping rope

▶ Playing hopscotch

▶ Rollerskating or rollerblading

▶ Doing cartwheels or somersaults

▶ Running or jogging

▶ Digging holes in the ground

▶ Other: _____ .

I like being outside, being quiet and not too active, like:

▶ Sitting still

▶ Lying down

▶ Watching the clouds in the sky

▶ Listening to birds and other sounds

▶ Looking at small things like grass or insects

▶ Playing in a sandbox

▶ Other: _____ .

Running and Other Motor Skills

Running is a big part of many games. Running is called a *motor skill*. The word "motor" refers to movement.

Some children have the kind of motor skills that let them do some or all of these things easily, quickly, and smoothly: run, jump, climb, hop, and play catch. They may have good balance and coordination. It is said that they have "good motor skills."

For other children, running, jumping, throwing, and catching may be difficult. They may not be able to move quickly or smoothly. Some children with autism have very good motor skills, and others have more difficulty with motor skills.

I will circle or highlight what is true for me. ✏

- ▶ I can run and jump easily.

- ▶ It is easy for me to throw and catch balls.

- ▶ I like doing these things … running, jumping, etc.

- ▶ It is hard to throw and catch balls.

- ▶ I don't like to run.

- ▶ I often bump into things.

- ▶ It's easy for me to bump, trip, or fall.

- ▶ I like to run fast.

- ▶ Doing these things (using my motor skills) is fun for me.

- ▶ I don't care much for these things (using motor skills).

- ▶ Other: _____ .

Winning and Losing

Most games end with winning or losing. Usually, only one player or one team can win a game each time it is played. It is said that the other players have lost that particular game.

Most people enjoy winning. Sometimes, people might get angry or sad when they are losing. When children or adults play a game and get very, very, angry, they are being "bad sports." Being a "bad sport" is when a player yells, says bad words, throws a piece of equipment, tries to hit someone, or does something else that is not polite or is hurtful. Being a bad sport ruins the fun of playing a game. No one likes to play with a bad sport.

Some children think they should win all the time. They think that winning is right. They think that losing is wrong. That's why they get upset if they do not win.

But, winning and losing are not the same as right or wrong, or good or bad. It is impossible for someone to win all the time. A famous saying is, "I win some, and I lose some!" Winning sometimes and losing sometimes is part of being human.

**Children and adults can lose a game and still be a good player. This is called *being a good sport*. I can learn to be a good sport when I win and when I lose.
Being a good sport is the best way to play.**

Being a Good Sport

Good sports are children and adults who try their best to play the game, no matter if they win or lose. A good sport remembers: "I win some, and I lose some!"

How to Be a Good Sport:

When the game is finished, try to shake hands with everyone in the game, the players who won and the players who lost, and say, "Good game!"

People like to play with good sports. We may practice being a good sport by saying "Good Game!" at home with my family while I shake their hands. Then we say what wise people say:

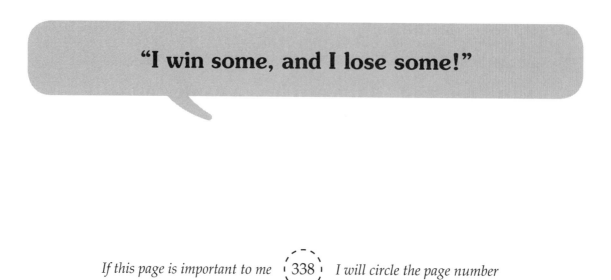

"I win some, and I lose some!"

Teams

Some games are played with teams. Teams are groups of players who play together, against another team. Some teams have only a few players. Some teams have many players.

Games and sports that require the team members playing all together might be difficult for children with autism.

I will mark what is true for me. 🖉

Playing on teams may be confusing to me because:

▶ I don't remember who is on my team.

▶ I really don't understand what to do.

▶ There is too much going on at the same time.

▶ I have difficulty throwing, catching, or running.

▶ It doesn't make sense.

▶ Other: _____ .

Some children have more fun if they participate in individual sports. They might be on a team, but the team members do not all have to play together at the same time. Examples of individual sports are:

- Swimming
- Cross country or track
- Skating
- Bicycling
- Chess
- Other: _____

A Friend Coming to My House

Playing with friends can be fun for many children.

Some autistic children want to have friends, but they don't know how to make friends. Or, they may try playing with someone, but it's not very fun.

I will circle or highlight what is true for me. 🖉

▶ I want to go to a friend's house.

▶ I would rather play by myself at home.

▶ I want to have a friend come to my house. I can get ready by following this checklist:

☐ Invite a friend to my house for an hour or two.

☐ Before my friend comes, my parent and I can make a list of the things we may do. (Including having a snack!)

☐ Some of the things on the list will be my special interests, and some of the things can be my friend's special interests.

☐ My friend and I will take turns choosing from the list what we will do. We can spend 5-10 minutes on each choice. (Or a different amount of minutes: _____.)

☐ Or, ahead of time, my parent can make a schedule for my friend and I to follow.

☐ The last thing we do will be my friend's choice, because he or she is a guest at my house. This is a friendly way to end the visit.

Getting Along with a Friend

A friend usually does not make fun of me. A true friend is nice to me. I try to be nice to my friend, too.

I like my friend, but sometimes we might not agree on what to do. We might want to do different things.

There is something to do so we both have fun and get along with each other. We may follow this "Get Along" checklist:

☐ If we argued, both say "I apologize" or "I'm sorry."

☐ Then we say, "Let's play together now."

☐ We'll write a list of the things I like to do.

☐ We'll write a list of the things my friend likes to do.

☐ We will circle the things on the lists that match; these are the things we both like to do.

☐ We'll write a new list: "The Things We Want to Do Together."

If there are things that I want to do, but my friend does not want to do, that is OK. I can do those things later by myself or with someone else. Good friends learn to get along.

Being Friendly

There are many children in my classroom and in my school. There may be many children in my neighborhood and other places. I may know other children, but it doesn't mean we are automatically friends. Some children may not be my friends.

However, even if someone isn't a friend, it is okay to be friendly.

Being friendly means being kind and pleasant. When children are friendly, they may greet each other, talk with each other, work together, eat lunch at the same table, or:

_____ .

Sometimes children who are friendly to one another for a long time may eventually become good friends. Or, they may simply continue to just see each other sometimes at school, in the neighborhood, or other places. This is okay, too.

Teachers usually try to teach their students to be friendly to each other.

I will circle or highlight what is true for me. ✏

▶ I am friendly to some other children.

▶ Some other children are friendly to me.

▶ I am not sure if others are friendly to me.

▶ I am not sure how to be friendly.

▶ Other: _____ .

I Wonder Why ...

There are some things I don't understand about other children. I wonder why they do some of the things they do. Here is a list of the things that are puzzling to me. Why do kids do these things?

(I do not have to fill in all the lines. I only should fill in questions I have about other children.)

1. Why does _____?

2. Why does _____?

3. Why does _____?

4. Why does _____?

5. Why does _____?

6. Why does _____?

7. Why does _____?

8. Why does _____?

Should Friends Know about Autism?

Other children might not understand some of the things I do or some of the things I say.

One part of being a friend is trying to understand each other.

A friend might understand me better if he or she knows I am autistic. I can help her or him understand me.

My parent can help me figure out whom we want to talk to about me and about autism. We are thinking about these children:

_____

_____

_____

_____

See chapter 9 for information about teaching other children about autism.

Finding Autistic Friends

Friends are a part of life for many children, teens, and adults. Some people have a lot of friends. Some people have one friend. Some people have no friends. Some people might have tried to make friends, but it doesn't work out. Sometimes a friend has to move away. Some people decide they don't want friends. Sometimes when a person is alone, it feels good. Other times when a person is alone, it does not feel good. He or she may feel lonely or sad.

Sometimes another thing happens for children, teens, and autistic adults.

They may meet other children, teens, or adults with autism … and discover that they have similar ideas and feelings. They may find out that they feel the same about being with other people and making friends. They may feel the same about sounds, sights, touch, odors, stimming, and more. Then, they may not worry so much about making social mistakes or stimming when they are with other autistic children or adults. They may not feel alone anymore! (See chapter 12, page 435.)

I will circle or highlight what is true for me. 🖉

▶ I know other kids or adults on the autism spectrum.

▶ I want to meet others on the spectrum, in person.

▶ I want to meet others on the spectrum, online.

▶ I have one or more autistic friends.

▶ My best friend is autistic, too.

▶ I don't know if I want to meet other autistic people.

▶ I want to meet other autistic kids (or teens or adults).

▶ I have something to say or ask about this:_____

_____ .

Animal Friends

Some children, teens, and adults have animal friends, such as a dog, cat, or other pet. Some people don't have an animal friend, but they would like to have one. For people who like dogs or cats, an animal can be a wonderful friend and companion. Some dogs and cats are specially trained to be companions and service animals for autistic people.

(If I am allergic to animals, or if I am afraid of animals or just do not like being around animals, or if animals are not allowed at home, then I do not have to read any more on this page.)

I will circle or highlight what is true for me. ✏

▶ My family has a pet or more than one pet.

▶ My group home has a pet or more than one pet.

▶ Circle which we have:

   dog   cat   bird   other animal: _____

▶ The name(s) of our pets is: _____ .

▶ Our pet is my animal friend.

▶ Our pet is not my animal friend.

▶ I wish I had an animal friend.

▶ My favorite kind of animal friend would be: (circle)

   dog   cat   other animal: _____

▶ There is something I'd like to say or ask: _____

_____ .

Having a Mentor

A mentor is a special kind of friend. A mentor is an adult who likes me and likes the same things I like. Spending time with a mentor may be fun. A mentor can be a good friend, especially as a child grows into an adult.

- A mentor can help me learn more about myself and help me learn more about the world.

- A mentor can try to answer questions and help me find the answers.

- A mentor can encourage me with my hopes and dreams and can help me find good ways to use my talents, skills, and special interests.

- A mentor may also be autistic, or maybe not.

I might have a mentor someday. A mentor is usually not my parent, but my parent can help me find a mentor. A mentor might be a teacher, a friend of my parent, an aunt, an uncle, or someone else.

I will mark what is true for me. 🖉

▶ I would like to have a mentor.

▶ I have a mentor whose name is _____ .

▶ Other: _____ .

Friends

Friends and the Internet

Important information is contained in the next section of this chapter, which is especially for older readers. In the next section, we will discuss the similarities and the differences between friends I meet in person at school or elsewhere, and another category of friends called **Internet acquaintances**.

> The first category of friends can be referred to as *in-person* friends. The new category of friends is **Internet acquaintances**.
>
> The word *acquaintance* generally refers to someone who is similar to a friend, although not as close as a friend. Meeting someone online, on the Internet, is in this category.

If I chat with other kids, teens, or adults online, or if I want to make friends online, then it is important for me and my parent, teacher, or therapist to read the following pages.

Especially for Older Readers

Many of the previous topics in this chapter for children
are relevant when individually selected for older children,
teenagers, and—in some cases—adults. Relevant supplementary
information *specifically* for older readers is provided on the
following pages.

This section provides information and opportunities for self-
awareness and subsequent communication about aspects of
Internet use and safety. Here, the subtle differences between
friends and acquaintances will be introduced, as well as
the complex issue of meeting and chatting online. This
information is meant to be a starting place, to be continued in an
individualized manner for each person.

In-Person Friends

In-person friends are what people usually think of when they talk about friends. I might have an in-person friend at school, at church, or in other places. An in-person friend might come to my house, or I might go to his or her house. The author of this book named this type of friend an "in-person" friend because when we spend time together, our bodies are in the same place—*in person.*

Usually, my parents know my in-person friend and meet the parents of my in-person friend. This is how my parents and I know if my in-person friends are safe, good friends. We know who they are, where they live, how old they are, and information about their family. In-person friends may even be members of my own family, like cousins and other family members.

I will ⬭circle⬭ or highlight what is true for me. 🖉

▶ I do not have an in-person friend.

▶ I wish I had an in-person friend.

▶ I want an in-person friend at school or in another place. (Where:

_____)

▶ I do have an in-person friend. His or her name is:

_____ .

▶ I do have more in-person friends. Their names are:

_____ .

▶ Sometimes, we make jokes and laugh about things.

▶ Sometimes, we like to talk about certain subjects.

▶ Sometimes, we may argue about certain subjects.

▶ I see my in-person friend at school.

▶ I see my in-person friend another place: _____ .

▶ I have been to my in-person friend's house.

▶ An in-person friend has been to my house.

▶ My parent knows my in-person friend, whose name is

_____ .

▶ My parent knows the parent of my in-person friend.
(Name: _____)

▶ I have something else to say or to ask about in-person friends:

_____

_____

_____ .

Friends

Acquaintances

An **acquaintance** is in the general category of a friend. The dictionary defines **acquaintance** as, "a person one knows, but not as a close friend." An **acquaintance** can be described as someone whom a person knows slightly. If someone is an acquaintance, I do not know a very much about them. I may know a few things—like their name and maybe a few other things about them. However, acquaintances are not close friends.

Often, a person may have several acquaintances. Acquaintances may be other students in school. Often, acquaintances are friendly to each other. If my locker is next to another student, we might be friendly to each other when we are at our lockers at the same time. We might say "hi." We might know each other's names. Sometimes, we might take a few minutes to chat. If that's the only time we see each other, we would be considered acquaintances.

Acquaintances may be other people I see repeatedly in certain places, whom I chat with when I see them. Another example of an acquaintance may be cashier at a store where I go regularly. If I see the same cashier often, we might begin to recognize each other, and, if it is not busy, we might sometimes take a few minutes to smile and talk with each other. We may know each other's names. We could be considered acquaintances.

Acquaintances are other people I may see often, regularly, or in certain places, like the library, the YMCA, the store, a coffee shop, a class, church, temple, or another place in my life. If we eventually learn each other's names, and take some time to chat, we could be considered acquaintances.

Once in a while, acquaintances may evolve into being in-person friends, if we both want to spend more time with each other. However, most of the time, acquaintances simply remain acquaintances. This is natural and okay.

I will circle or highlight what is true for me. 🖉

▶ I have one or more acquaintances in my life. These are places where I see my acquaintance(s): _____

_____ .

▶ We sometimes chat about: _____

_____ .

▶ I have something else to say or to ask about acquaintances:

_____

_____

_____ .

Friends

What Is an Internet Acquaintance?

Sometimes when a child, teenager, or adult is on an Internet Web site, he or she may chat online with someone else who is on the same Web site. If I do this, the people I chat with are in the category of Internet acquaintances.

Internet acquaintances are people whom I have met on the Internet, but not in person. We might "virtually" be on the same sites online, but our bodies aren't in the same place. We might play games. We might make jokes. Sometimes we even might tell each other our ideas, thoughts, or feelings. Communicating on the Internet is called *chatting*, *Instant Messaging (IM)*, or *voice chatting*. Chatting is a popular activity among Internet acquaintances. Sending e-mail is also another way of communicating with Internet acquaintances.

These "friends" are really in the category of **acquaintances** because, even though I feel like I know them, there are many things about them that I don't know OR that I can't be sure of. More information about Internet acquaintances can be found on the following pages.

I will (circle) or highlight what is true for me. 🖉

▶ I have an Internet acquaintance, whose name and age is:

_____ .

▶ I have more than one Internet acquaintance. They have told me their names and ages are:

_____

_____ .

▶ I met my Internet acquaintance(s) on these sites:

_____

_____ .

▶ We make jokes and/or have fun.

▶ Sometimes, we chat about these topics or ideas:_____

_____

▶ Sometimes, I think about wanting to meet my Internet acquaintance in person.

▶ An Internet acquaintance has told me that he or she wants to meet me in person.

Safety with Internet Acquaintances

While I am chatting with Internet acquaintances, our bodies are in different locations, different cities, or different countries. It can be fun and interesting to have Internet acquaintances. Some Internet acquaintances are honest and good people. They may eventually (someday) become good friends.

But, some Internet acquaintances may be dishonest. They might not tell the truth. It is difficult to know some things for sure about an Internet acquaintance, because I cannot see him or her in person, and my parents cannot see or meet him or her. For example, an Internet acquaintance might say he is 13 years old, but he might really be 50 years old. Because he isn't here in person, I cannot know for sure if an Internet acquaintance is telling the truth. It might sound true, but not really be true. There are some teens and adults who go to sites to find children and other teenagers for bad and unsafe reasons. This is called "taking advantage" of the child or teenager, or even other adults who don't know about Internet safety. These dishonest Internet acquaintances sound like they are good friends, but in reality, they may be unsafe and criminal.

When chatting on the Internet, no one knows for sure if Internet acquaintances are honest, truthful, or safe. Intelligent Internet users learn to stay safe with Internet acquaintances.

I will (circle) or highlight what is true for me. 🖉

▶ My Internet acquaintance named _____
   has asked questions about me.

▶ I will underline the type of information that my Internet
   acquaintance has asked me: my last name, my age, where I live, my
   e-mail address, my street address, my city, where I go to school,
   other: _____ , _____, _____ .

▶ My Internet acquaintance named _____ wants
   to meet me in person.

▶ I want to meet my Internet acquaintance named _____
    in person.

▶ I don't want to meet my Internet acquaintance named _____
   _____ in person.

▶ I have already told my parent about my Internet acquaintance(s).

▶ I don't want to tell my parent about my Internet acquaintance(s).

▶ I have already met my Internet acquaintance named _____
   _____in person.

▶ I have something else to say or to ask about Internet acquaintances:

   _____

   _____ .

Responsibility while Chatting

When chatting online, sometimes people say things that are unkind, mean, inappropriate, or gross. They think it is okay because they are on the Internet, and Internet acquaintances cannot see them.

I have a responsibility when writing with Internet acquaintances, just like with in-person friends, about the way I communicate. It is not okay to be unkind and mean. It is not okay to bully or say things that will hurt someone's feelings. It is not okay to say gross or inappropriate things, or talk about private body parts, or do sex talk, or send photographs in those categories. In fact, these things are not okay to do … in person or on the Internet.

It is important to communicate responsibly. If the conversation becomes unkind or mean, or if bullying is happening to me or to others, or if it becomes gross or inappropriate, or if it involves sex, then I do not have to continue with the chat. My responsibility is to say I don't want to chat like that. If the chat continues to be unkind, mean, bullying, sex talk, or otherwise inappropriate, my responsibility is to log out immediately.

I will (circle) or highlight what is true for me. 🖊

This has happened on a site that I have been on: (**Underline** which **things have happened.**)

▶ Unkind talk or mean talk

▶ Bullying (targeted at me)

▶ Bullying (targeted at someone else)

▶ Gross talk or other inappropriate talk

▶ Talking about parts of bodies or sexual things

▶ Showing photographs about any of those things, sexual or otherwise

▶ Other: _____

▶ The name of the site was: _____ .

▶ I stayed online but stopped chatting.

▶ I stayed online and continued chatting.

▶ I want more information about this topic.

▶ Other: _____ .

Friends

6 RULES ABOUT INTERNET ACQUAINTANCES

1 DO NOT give out personal information on the Internet. Personal information is defined as my name, my age, what I look like, my e-mail address, my home address, my school, my city, or the personal information of other people. If an Internet acquaintance asks me for information about myself or my life, I should first check with my parent* or guardian* to make sure it is not also in the category of personal information before I answer. If it is in the category of personal information, then I won't answer.

2 If an Internet acquaintance wants to meet me in person, I should tell my parent* or guardian.*

3 In some cases, my parent or guardian might want to meet my Internet acquaintance and his or her parent with me. If my parent or guardian agrees that we can meet each other, my parent or guardian will make the arrangements for us to meet and go with me to the meeting.

4 If my parent or guardian says I cannot meet an Internet acquaintance, then I must not meet him or her.

* If I am quiet or shy, or if I am worried, or if it is too embarrassing to tell any of this to my parent, guardian, or therapist, then I should hand this book to them, open it to this page, and point to the rule that applies. If I am not sure which rule applies, then I should point to this sentence."

5 If my Internet acquaintance tells me to do something private or embarrassing, or sends me sexual photos, or starts chatting about his or her body, or asks me questions about my body, or asks me about private information (like sex or other personal topics), or invites me to meet him or her without my parents, or makes fun of me if I don't do any of these things, I should stop chatting immediately and tell my parent* or guardian* about this.

6 I have responsibility to chat in an appropriate manner. It is not okay to write things that are mean or gross or to bully someone else. It is not okay to talk about my own private body or to ask someone about their own body. It is not okay to do sex talk on the Internet. It is not okay to share sexual photos or talk about illegal things. If I notice any of these things, I should log out immediately. If this happens two times or more, then it is time to tell my parent, guardian, or therapist. I need to get help stopping it, so it doesn't turn into a habit that will get me in serious trouble. Other people who have done these things online have gotten arrested, gone to court, and gone to prison.

Why It May Be Easier to Interact Online

Sometimes, in-person friendships can be easy and fun. Sometimes, in-person friendships can be difficult. Some children and teenagers, including children and teens with autism, may find it difficult to make and keep in-person friends. They may not know what to say or when to talk. Sometimes, children and teenagers can feel "out of place" or "left out" around other children and teenagers. They might feel lonely and wish they could have more friends. This is a common experience for many children, teens, and adults on the autism spectrum.

Sometimes, it is easier to interact online. When chatting with Internet acquaintances, a person can stay at home where it is quiet and not have to go anywhere. A person can start chatting and stop chatting whenever he or she wants to, taking time to think of what to say and how to respond. He or she doesn't have to worry about what he or she looks like or what to say. He or she can communicate by typing on the keyboard, which might be easier. Many pressures of interacting are easier when communicating on the Internet. These are some of the reasons it feels easier to interact online with Internet acquaintances.

However, for the reasons that have already been written about Internet acquaintances, every child, teenager, and adult must be EXTRA CAREFUL when chatting and playing with Internet friends. (See the Six Rules about Internet Acquaintances on pages 360-361.)

In some cases, an Internet acquaintance can eventually become a good friend. But always, the Six Rules about Internet Acquaintances must be followed.

For Parents, Teachers, and Therapists

"If the point of social interaction is to have it be a positive experience, to feel better as a result of it—not worse— then finding what works for me and doing that tends to do the trick."

—Dave Spicer, on social situations

Ideas in This Chapter:

☑ Start with respect

☑ Assessment

☑ Identify what is fun from your child's perspective

☑ Assess social comfort level

☑ Provide the necessary structure

☑ The equation for a successful social experience

☑ Peer helpers and other partnerships

☑ Individualizing the social event: A big party is not always big fun!

☑ Social Stories

☑ We are all in this together

☑ True friends

☑ Social groups

☑ A final word on social development

☑ Animal friends

☑ Internet safety: a plea

Chapter 10

Start with respect

The subject of friends is often a sensitive issue for parents of children with autism. It may be painful to watch other children in the neighborhood playing and building friendships with ease and spontaneity. It is so effortless, compared with your child's hesitation, awkwardness, resistance, or downright failures. Difficulties in the area of socialization (especially in social gatherings filled with typically developing children and adults) are primary for children and adults with autism. And, while many individuals with autism struggle with this issue, it is important to remember what one young woman with autism told me to pass on to the participants of an upcoming teacher training:

"Tell them not to judge the degree of my happiness by what makes them happy. Tell them that I like to be alone."

First and foremost, we need to respect the child's current and natural desires. A situation that may be upsetting to you about your child's social life may not matter one bit to him.

At the same time, respect also includes helping our children make sense out of the complex social arena by adding structure to shared activities that could possibly develop into a fun social experience. By doing this, we are giving them the freedom to enjoy social activities that would otherwise be unpredictable, stressful, and obviously not fun.

Now that's something to contemplate—Structure that fits the individual's unique level of social comfort, at a given point in time, allows greater freedom!

Assessment

Just as in other areas of your child's development, successful acquisition of social skills must start with a realistic and objective assessment. Consider the following three key principles that are introduced in TEACCH trainings when talking about social

development: Identify what is fun for your child, assess his current level of social comfort, and provide the structure needed for him to have fun. These three assessment areas are presented below. (Upcoming TEACCH training programs are posted on *teacch.com*.)

Identify what is fun from your child's perspective

Being together with other children is fun for most typically developing children. Social contact can immediately transform a boring day into a fun time. It is probably different for your child. When teachers and parents want to increase successful social opportunities for their child or students with autism, they must first recognize what is truly fun from the individual child's point of view. What does he consider enjoyable? What captures his attention? What sustains his attention? What does he do for fun?

Remember, just because an activity is considered fun for most children in the mainstream culture does not necessarily mean it will automatically be fun for all children. When you consider truly inclusive environments, you must keep this in mind.

Assessment #1: What is fun?

Make a list of what your child enjoys. Don't stop at the obvious (computer, drawing, etc) ones—also notice the little things. What gets his attention while looking out the car window? What pictures does he stop at when leafing through magazines? What was he doing or looking at when you heard him laugh? What does he like to look at? What textures or actions feel good to him? What responses does he give on a Communication Form you design as an interest survey? When you notice something that captures his attention, even for a moment, remember what it was and record it here:

_____

_____

_____

_____

_____

Assess social comfort level

Just as teaching new cognitive skills starts with an accurate assessment of mastered and emerging skills, the teaching of skills in the area of social development must start the same way. At what level is your child most comfortable? What levels of social interaction has he mastered?

While most children typically master each of the following steps before entering kindergarten, it is not uncommon for individuals with autism to be most comfortable at one of the more basic levels, even into adulthood. Read the following list and note which are most natural, spontaneous, enjoyable, and relaxing to your child. What does he do, with whom, without your prodding? What are his current levels of spontaneous social interaction?

I have labeled these levels "social comfort" rather than "social interaction" to reflect more closely what you will be observing. They are independent of the age of the person and his or her level of cognitive development, functioning level, or any other quality, skill, or developmental level.

1. Proximity

Is your child able to tolerate the presence of others close to him while he is playing? A young child who is emerging into or has mastered this level is one who will tolerate or enjoy being near others while he plays. No interaction is necessary, but he can play in proximity to others. If he consistently moves away when others come near, he may be indicating that he has not yet achieved comfort at this level. An adult with autism once remarked that:

"I might be awkward in the company of people … but I enjoy proximity, even if I'm not interacting. I like being near others."

2. Looking

Does your child notice others and what they are doing? Does he look or glance at others while they are playing? Is he interested in watching what others are doing?

3. Parallel Play

Does your child play alongside others who are engaged in their own, but similar, activity? An autistic adult pointed out that this is the level at which he is consistently most comfortable. Taking a silent walk with someone or jogging alongside another person are the social activities he finds easiest and most enjoyable.

4. Sharing

Is your child comfortable sharing materials or toys while he is playing? Is he willing to let others play with "his" toys?

5. Cooperation

Is your child able to play together with another child or a group of children, with the same materials or toys, at the same time? Examples of cooperative play are completing a floor puzzle with someone else, pulling clay to build something from a common lump of clay, building a large structure with other children in the block center, or making cookies by sharing cookie cutters and using the same dough.

6. Taking Turns

Does your child understand taking turns? Is he able to follow the sequence and anticipate when it is his turn and when it is someone else's turn? Does he take turns willingly? Does it make sense to him? Does he tell others when it is their turn?

7. Rules

Traditional table games, as well as physical games played in the gym or outside, are organized by rules. Does your child understand and follow the rules in relationship to other players? How about unwritten rules of playing on the playground or in the neighborhood? One man remarked that, as a child, "Everyone seemed to know what to do, and I did not."

I strongly recommend that you watch a 4-minute video clip of John explaining his experience of the game of "tag," which can be found at *vimeo.com/45213497*. It is excerpted by permission from the documentary by Adam Larsen, "Neurotypical," which has been featured on the U.S. Public Broadcasting Service (PBS) program series "POV."

Assessment #2: Level of social comfort

Try to be an objective observer of your child. Look over the seven levels again, and answer these questions about him at this current time:

What level(s) are most difficult?

_____

What level(s) does he enjoy the most … without problems?

_____

At what level(s) is he most comfortable?

_____

Circle your answers to the last two questions above.

After you have assessed *(1)* what is fun for your child and *(2)* your child's current level (or levels) of social interaction, then you are ready to determine *(3)* the structure your child needs for the particular social activity.

Provide the necessary structure

Look carefully at the specific social situation through the eyes of your child. Does he know what to do, where to stand, when it starts, how long it will last, when it is done, what to expect from the other person, and so on? Be aware of the type and degree of sensory stimulation in the environment. Try to imagine how your child might experience the circumstances through his eyes, mind, and particular sensory responses.

Add structure wherever necessary for your child. You might consider setting up an activity in a quiet room, away from extraneous, loud, or distracting activities. Use his schedule so he will be able to anticipate

when the activity will begin and what will occur when it is over. Written directions help organize the activity by breaking down the steps and showing the sequence. Visual structure, such as labeling, color coding, use of a turn-taking card, and visual markers, will clarify other assumptions: where to stand, whose turn it is, where to put objects, and what happens where. Communication cue cards may take the stress out of knowing what to say at significant intervals during the game or interaction.

Take the guesswork out of the situation for him, as much as possible. Do what is necessary by adding structure to create a successful experience, so it will be fun … and he may just want to do it again! Isn't that the goal?

Assessment #3: Structure

Imagine yourself being from another culture or another planet. What kinds of questions would you have about the social situation? Notice your assumptions about what "everyone knows," observe your child, and try to imagine it from his perspective. Ask yourself these types of questions:

- Where am I supposed to stand/sit/move?
- Is it my turn?
- What do I do next?
- How long will this last? When is it done?
- What happens when it's done?
- Why is it so loud/hot/cold/itchy/busy/distracting here?
- Where can I go to get away from the noise/discomfort?
- What's the purpose, or goal, of this activity?
- Who are the other people, and what are their names?
- Is it okay to have questions? How can I ask?
- How and when can I share something I like to do?

Add structure to clarify, simplify, and make easier. Write Social Stories to facilitate understanding about details and about the big picture— the purpose. What is the goal of the activity? And, what are the underlying assumptions, so the goal makes sense? (Please remember to watch the video clip about "tag" as recommended on page 369.)

Now you are ready to put all the assessment information together.

The equation for a successful social experience

Keep the three key principles in mind and refer to this equation to guide you in planning social activities for your child.

What is fun for your child

His social comfort level

+ Structure

_____

Social Success

Your plan:

At home, consider these ideas when planning your child's next birthday party or family gathering. At school, remember these principles when writing "social goals." Set up the social situation by using information you noted in the three assessments:

1. Something that is fun for your child is: _____

_____ .

2. Currently, his most comfortable and enjoyable social level is:

_____ .

3. Specific structure that helps is: _____ .

How will you set up the particular social situation you have in mind by using the equation to create a successful social experience?

_____

_____ .

For a discussion on the importance of success, refer to page 92.

Peer helpers and other partnerships

In the early days at the TEACCH Center in Chapel Hill, North Carolina, some of the therapists identified common roles played by typical friends at school. By examining these roles, we can get ideas of ways to help identify partners for children with autism to fulfill some of the roles of friends and to facilitate the development of friendships. According to your child's needs and the school environment, consider identifying a peer or a group of peers to fulfill one or more of these roles.

1. Tutor (according to subject)

2. Lunch partner

3. Companion for art and music classes

4. Partner during free time

5. Extracurricular buddy (school clubs, etc)

6. Homework partner

7. Project partner

8. Travel companion (to/from the bus, walking home)

9. Neighborhood playmate

The success of these relationships usually depends on both children having interests and experiences in common, as well as the peer's willingness to understand and empathize with your child and your child's authentic desire for companionship. Teach the typically developing peer how to use the specific structured strategies that are helpful for the autistic peer. Help your child's peer understand the unique qualities, challenges, interests, and skills of your autistic child. Keep in mind that for most children and adults on the spectrum, it is easier and more fun to interact with one person at a time!

Individualizing the social event: A big party is not always big fun!

The widely accepted practice of providing a child with plenty of social opportunities by including him in a large group of peers may actually result in further isolation. Close observation of your child before, during, and after spending time in a large group may reveal that inclusion in the large group may not be very fun from his point of view. If this is true, being in large groups of children for extended periods of time could possibly hinder your child's social development, rather than support it.

When most people find themselves invited to a social event that might be awkward or aversive, the natural inclination is to avoid attending the event, or, at the least, plan to go home early! Why would it be any different for a child with autism, who struggles with the social aspects of life all the time? Since social relatedness is said to be a core area of difficulty, it is imperative that the methods used to help the acquisition of social skills are structured and thoughtful. It must be more than simply making sure your child is physically "part of the group."

You might discover that a regularly scheduled, structured activity with one peer will offer your child the most enjoyment, confidence, and desire for future social interaction. In contrast to struggling or withdrawing in a large group of children, he may actually relax and begin to have fun when he is in a simpler, more structured situation. Try both and then ask him which he prefers.

A next step could be to merge the structured one-on-one activity with the larger group. This would only take place after success and mastery are accomplished first in the quieter, smaller, or more structured environment.

By acknowledging and respecting a child's sensory, cognitive, motor, communicative, and social uniqueness, we often find that small steps, built on the principles of fun, comfort, predictability, order, familiarity, and individual preference, nourish true social enjoyment.

Getting to know and developing friendships with other autistic children can be a deeply life-changing experience that is discussed later in this chapter.

Social Stories

In *The New Social Story Book* (Future Horizons, 2010), Carol Gray writes:

> The most common misconception is that the goal of a Social Story is to change [your child's] behavior. This has never been the case. The goal of a Social Story is to share accurate information meaningfully and safely. Admittedly, it is often a behavior that draws attention to a specific concept, skill, or situation. However, if our goal were simply to change behavior, we would likely focus on "telling the child what to do." The chances are that the audience [your child] has already been told what to do, perhaps many times. Instead, the focus is on the underlying causes of frustration or misinformation. Authors of Social Stories work to identify and share information that supports more effective responses. The theory is that the improvement in behavior that is frequently credited to a Social Story is the result of improved understanding of events and expectations.

For further understanding and support in writing Social Stories, read *The New Social Story Book*, an in-depth resource that includes guidelines, instructional support, and many examples of Social Stories. Attend a Social Stories™ workshop that is taught by an authorized trainer. For more information, go to *thegraycenter.org* or *catherinefaherty.com*.

We are all in this together

Besides promoting social success by considering what is fun, assessing your child's level of social comfort, adding visual structure, encouraging buddies, nurturing friendships with other autistic children, and writing Social Stories, there is another essential component in promoting successful social functioning.

Help the other important adults and children in your child's life rethink their assumptions and automatic interpretations of your child's behavior.

Commonly held judgments, like "He must not like me because he is not looking at me," or "He is not having fun because he is by himself," may not be true.

Help the key people in your child's life understand that the behavior they observe in your child can't always be interpreted accurately through a lens of typical social rules and assumptions. Show them this book and let them see what your child has marked on its pages.

Help children identify what they do that may be confusing to their peer with autism. It is not only the job of the child with autism to change and learn new things! Friendship, by definition, is a mutual and reciprocal relationship; therefore, the changing, learning, and understanding must be mutual. We are all in this together!

True friends

There are probably people in your child's life who find him to be a wonderful and fascinating individual, just the way he is. There will probably be others who will feel the same way in the future. As he grows, help him appreciate, enjoy, and care about these people. In the coming years, find a mentor—someone in addition

to you or your spouse—who will be there for him as he grows into adulthood. Meaningful reciprocity between your child and others will develop its own form that may look different from the outside but will be sincere and true in its own way.

In addition, explore and support opportunities for him to get to know autistic peers, and nurture the sense of having an autistic community!

Social groups

Since the 1980s, TEACCH therapists and directors across the state of North Carolina have organized social groups for children, teenagers, and adults with autism. In many regions of our state, chapters of the Autism Society of North Carolina organize social groups for their children. All over the country, grassroots social groups are

emerging. The groups vary in makeup and purpose, depending on the range of abilities, needs, desires, and interests of their members. An increasing number of social groups are run by and for autistic adults. In the early years, many professionals and parents who facilitated social groups concentrated on the teaching and development of social skills as a primary focus of these groups, with the secondary (but still important) purpose of having fun. Over the years, as familiarity has grown and relationships have emerged among group members, priorities have shifted. Fellowship and fun have taken the lead. The main goal of the first social group for older teens and adults that I started in 1991 was to create a regularly scheduled safe place and time for people with a new diagnosis to meet and get to know each other. This group, with many of the original members, is still going strong at the time of this writing!

Depending on the group and the area, the makeup of the groups is sometimes balanced between autistic and typically developing peers, or, in the case of adults, participation with volunteers from local colleges and the community at large. In most situations, though, these regular events have evolved into social gatherings made up almost exclusively of people with autism. According to many members of long-running social groups, they have stated that they feel more relaxed within  this group than they are "outside" the group. Some group members talk about the comfort, reassurance, and self-validity that they feel while together. Perhaps as a consequence, increased social spontaneity emerges in delightful ways. Humor and self-expression abound.

In more recent years, as autistic self-advocates have taken a leading role and created autistic communities, meet-up groups and regularly scheduled local gatherings of autistic adults are emerging and flourishing in many cities and towns across the country. Some are local chapters of national groups, and others are homegrown, like the group Autistic Adults United in Asheville, North Carolina.

As your child matures, consider starting a social group with autistic peers. It could be founded on common interests, like one social group for teenagers in Asheville, North Carolina. The members, along with TEACCH therapists and adult autistic volunteers, met to explore computers, computer games, the Internet, creating Web pages, and other related high-interest activities. As group members got to know one another, the activities broadened and expanded into non–computer-related activities, as well.

Another early variation of a social group was one I organized to bring together teenagers with new diagnoses, along with their adult counterparts. This group's focus was twofold: to discuss issues encountered by the teenagers and to provide a social gathering. What made this group unique was that as the TEACCH therapist, I facilitated the discussion in partnership with the adults with autism, whose distinctive perspective of having "been there and survived it" was reassuring and enlightening to the younger members.

Social groups for younger children consist of activities appropriate for the age level, interests, and desires of the members. Members of social groups for older children, teenagers, and adults have sometimes enjoyed the following types of activities. Remember to develop visual structure on an individual basis to ensure understanding and enjoyment. Add to the list by including the group members' focused interests.

★ Bingo (a big hit with fans of letters and numbers!)

★ Pictionary (second to Bingo in popularity)

★ Games such as checkers, Uno, Othello, Jenga, and other board games

★ Spectator sports, such as baseball and basketball (usually adult outings)

★ Birthday parties—planning, shopping, and setting up

★ Doing crafts and making things

★ Making and sending cards to one another or someone else

★ Doing seasonal crafts, such as making ornaments at holiday time

★ Roasting marshmallows (at a campfire or in a fireplace!)

★ Group singing (display the words on posters or a video screen)

★ Making a video of the group and then watching it

★ Playing miniature golf

★ Bowling

★ Rollerskating

★ Swinging in a park

★ Having dances, with a DJ

★ Flying kites

★ Having costume parties

★ Cooking and baking

★ Interviewing each other

★ Having tell-a-joke time

★ Staging talent shows (remember to videotape!)

Whatever the focus and makeup of the group, consider the following to accommodate the need for familiarity and allow for greater relaxation and fun. Follow these general guidelines and choose what's most supportive for your particular group members:

1. Meet on a consistent basis throughout the year.

2. Keep the group small or divide a larger group into smaller units.

3. Begin the group meetings with a familiar routine.

4. Display the schedule for the group meeting and provide individual schedules when needed.

5. Provide structure and visual cues.*

6. Write Social Stories to clarify problematic situations and to acknowledge good times, enjoyable events, and positive behaviors.

7. Have a snack or a meal.

8. Discuss and/or vote on what the group will do next time.

9. Conclude with a familiar, routine activity.

10. Make reminder phone calls and send reminder e-mail messages prior to the next group meeting.

---

* Respect individual choices of how each member chooses to participate. Be sure that each person is familiar with or is able to find out what the range of options is for participation. Don't assume that a group member will automatically know how to participate in the game or discussion. Visual cues and written information are beneficial and are always appreciated by members. For an example of how information about sharing in an adult group was made clear, read my article, "Ways to Share in This Group," which can be found at *catherinefaherty.com*. Look on the menu under "Publications" and then "Articles."

Chapter 10

A final word on social development

Ponder this quote by Linda Kreger Silverman, PhD, who founded the Institute for the Study of Advanced Development. She writes that,

> **"According to the dictionary, *socialization* is the ability to adapt to the needs of the group. Social development, on the other hand, is not the pressure to adapt, but a deep, comfortable level of self-acceptance that leads to true friendship with others."**

Animal friends

Everyone who has had the experience of living with a beloved dog or cat understands the deep ties that may develop between humans and animals. Some children may not be interested in animals, or they may be frightened or allergic. But for other children and teenagers, having a relationship with a dog, cat, or other animal offers a positively life-changing and long-lasting friendship.

In addition to the traditional idea of having a "pet," some animals may be trained to meet specific purposes, such as service animals and emotional support animals. There are now several national organizations that train service dogs for autistic children and adults; however, I wish to acknowledge Jim Sinclair as the initiator and early pioneer of this movement. Jim Sinclair has an extensive personal and professional background in living and working with animals, advocating for disabled people and animals, and assessing and serving autistic people's individual needs. Jim has been involved in animal rescue and animal rights advocacy for more than 30 years. In the late 1980s, Jim pioneered the concept of service dogs for autistic people, and, more recently, has been training and becoming qualified to work with disabled people in identifying their strengths, interests, and support needs and in helping them pursue their personal goals. Jim Sinclair is an autism rights activist and was one of the founders of Autistic Network International, an autistic-run self-help advocacy organization, along with Autreat (*autreat.com*), an annual retreat organized by and for the autistic community.

Internet safety: a plea

I have included a large section of workbook pages titled "Especially for Older Readers" that deal exclusively with online friends and Internet safety. These pages are only a beginning; I am providing you with a place to start communicating with your young person about these complex issues, but the discussion and education must continue. I strongly urge all parents to educate themselves about Internet safety basics through the many online informational programs. Educate yourself and take advantage of Internet controls for unwanted content. Prevention is essential.

Staying safe on the Internet may be even more complicated for some children, teens, and adults on the autism spectrum than it is for most typically developing individuals. Education is essential for safety and prevention of serious, life-altering problems. I cannot state this with greater seriousness and urgency. I know of several good-hearted young people—autistic teenagers and adults—who, in the course of exploring their natural sexual curiosity, unknowingly and naively became involved in illegal Internet activities, owing to ignorance about file sharing. Now, their lives have been changed forever because of getting involved with the court system, going to prison, and eventually being released with a serious record that radically and negatively

Friends

affects their vocational prospects—for a lifetime. Please educate yourselves as parents and as therapists, and do what it takes to control Internet access when necessary. Educate your young person honestly, clearly, and concretely about his or her responsibilities. Do not assume that young people know what they are doing while interacting on the Internet, even if they are intelligent, gifted, and talented.

Drawing by Thomas Johnson, 1996
"The Ruby Slippers"

Chapter 11
Feeling Upset

Workbook

Feeling Emotions

People feel emotions inside of them. *My emotions are feelings I have inside of me.* Examples of words to describe emotions are *happy, joyful, sad, angry, frustrated, scared, worried,* and _____ .

Many people automatically show how their emotions through their facial expressions. Changes on the face happen automatically and without thinking. For example, when a person is happy, often a smile will form on his face. When a person is scared, her face will change in a different way. Her eyes might open wide, and her eyebrows might rise up.

Sometimes, it is different for autistic children and adults.

- My face **might not show** how I feel inside.

- My face might show what others think is a **different emotion** than what I feel inside.

For example, an autistic girl might be feeling happy, but her face might not show a smile. She might have a serious look on her face. Even though she is feeling happy, other people might think she is bored or upset. But the truth is that she is happy.

Even if my face doesn't always show it, I do feel emotions. My face might not always communicate the feelings I have inside.

Naming Emotions

There are words that give names for different emotions. Some examples are:

Happy	**Delighted**
Joyful	**Sad**
Angry	**Worried**
Scared	**Depressed**
Anxious	**Frustrated**

As children grow up, most of them learn the words to describe how they are feeling inside.

Autistic children have emotions just like everybody else, but they might not be able to explain how they are feeling. They might have difficulty finding the words for how they feel. Or, they might know the words but don't know which words match how they are feeling in the moment. Or, they may not know it is possible to communicate how they feel in words.

Answering questions like, "How do you feel about this?" can be puzzling or confusing. There may be better ways to get information from an autistic child.

Feeling Anxious

Everyone feels anxious sometimes. *Anxious* means that a child or adult feels worried, uneasy, and restless. The person's hands might tremble, or he may cry, or he might get a stomachache or a headache. Sometimes he might want to run or hide. Sometimes feeling anxious turns into anger, and a person might want to yell or lash out. Or, a person might get very quiet when feeling anxious.

Children and adults with autism might feel anxious frequently.

I will mark what is true for me. ✏

I feel anxious when:

▶ There is too much happening at the same time. Something is just not the way it's supposed to be.

▶ I don't want to do something different.

▶ There is too much noise or bright light.

▶ I feel sick.

▶ I don't understand something. Someone is talking too much.

▶ There are too many people around.

▶ I don't know what I am supposed to do.

▶ I can't find the words to explain.

▶ I make a mistake.

▶ I am confused.

▶ I am too tired.

▶ I want to be alone.

▶ Other: _____

_____ .

What Happens When I Feel Anxious

When I feel anxious, my body does certain things.

I will mark what happens to me when I am anxious. ✏

- ▶ I get a stomachache.
- ▶ I get a headache.
- ▶ My hands tremble or shake.
- ▶ I get a ringing or buzzing in my ears.
- ▶ I just don't feel right.
- ▶ Parts of my body may twitch (motor tics).
- ▶ I say words or sounds, not on purpose (vocal tics).
- ▶ Other: _____ .

Sometimes, children who feel anxious might do some of these things.

I will mark the things I do. ✏

- ▶ Have a tantrum, yell, or scream
- ▶ Throw something or hit something
- ▶ Say, "I don't want to"
- ▶ Hit, bite, pinch, or scratch someone
- ▶ Run away
- ▶ Hide
- ▶ Get very, very, quiet
- ▶ Bite my hand or hit my head
- ▶ Scratch or pick my skin until it bleeds
- ▶ Rock back and forth or move my body in other ways
- ▶ Look for someone to help
- ▶ Other: _____

Being Oppositional

Being *oppositional* means that someone refuses to do what their parent or teacher or someone else wants them to do. It is called *oppositional* because the person does or says the opposite of what someone wants them to do.

Children and teenagers who are like this often are described as being *oppositional*. Many children with autism are not oppositional, but some children with autism can be very oppositional.

Some children become oppositional when they are anxious or upset. Sometimes it becomes a habit.

I will circle or highlight what is true for me. 🖉

▶ I can be oppositional, a lot. Often, I want to do things differently than what my parent or teacher says.

▶ People say I am "easygoing." Usually, I do what I am supposed to do.

▶ Sometimes I am oppositional, but sometimes I do what my parent or teacher tells me to do.

▶ I get oppositional when I am anxious or upset. Being oppositional gets people to leave me alone.

▶ Other: _____ .

When children are oppositional, it is difficult for other adults and children to play with them. Other people may become angry when a child is oppositional. They usually do not like to be with a child who is often being oppositional.

Hurting Myself

Once in a while, some children with autism may try to hurt themselves. Parents and teachers and other people feel very worried when children hurt themselves. This is called *self-injurious behavior*, or SIB. Some children with autism might try to hurt themselves when they are overwhelmed by sensory input or when they are feeling scared, angry, worried, frustrated, anxious, sad, or confused. There is more information about SIB in chapter 2.

If I never try to hurt myself, then I do not have to read more on this page. I can turn to the next page. →

I will circle or highlight what is true for me. ✎

Sometimes I hurt myself when:

▶ There is too much noise or too much happening. I am not sure what is going to happen.

▶ I am overwhelmed. People keep talking to me. I want to be left alone.

▶ I am frustrated or angry or worried.

▶ I want to say something, but I'm not able to say it. I don't know or understand what to do.

▶ Something else hurts, and it makes me feel better.

▶ Other: _____.

Hurting Other People

Once in a while, children may hit, kick, or scratch other people. They may throw things. This is called *aggression* or *being aggressive*, and it hurts other people or other things. Parents and teachers are very worried when children are aggressive. Usually, most autistic people do not want to hurt anyone on purpose. They probably didn't plan to hurt someone. But, sometimes, a child with autism may be very upset or angry and may hurt someone who is nearby.

I will circle or highlight what is true for me. 🖋

- ▶ I don't hurt, hit, kick, scratch, or pinch other people.
- ▶ Sometimes I have hurt other people, because I wanted to.
- ▶ Sometimes I have hurt other people, NOT on purpose.

If I become aggressive and hurt someone, it might be because:

- ▶ I am anxious, scared, frustrated, or angry.
- ▶ Someone is standing near me when I am upset.
- ▶ I am confused and I can't think of what to do.
- ▶ I want to get away, I but can't. I feel trapped.
- ▶ I am so upset that I can't communicate.
- ▶ I am angry with someone.
- ▶ I have too much energy in my body, and it comes out.
- ▶ I get angry about _____
  _____ .
- ▶ Other: _____
  _____ .

Reading Other People's Emotions

There are many ways that children and adults express their emotions.

- Some people are very expressive with their emotions. They may laugh or cry or yell.

- Some people are very quiet with their emotions. They may talk quietly, even if they have big feelings inside. They're not very expressive.

- Most people do some of both.

Many children with autism find it difficult to understand all the different ways that other people express their emotions. An autistic child might not know if another person is happy or sad or angry or worried. Or, she might think a person is very angry, when that person may really not be angry. This means that child got "the wrong message."

On the next page is an emotion-meter. It might help me "read" other people's emotions, so I get the "right message." It is like a thermometer for emotions.

My parent or teacher can make copies of the emotion-meter. They can fill it in to show me how they are feeling about something.

Emotion-Meter for My Parent

To the parent or teacher or other significant adult:

This is for you to fill out about yourself, to communicate to your child more accurately what you are feeling about an incident or situation. Fill in the information to describe what you are feeling. In the bottom box, indicate the level or degree that most accurately describes the intensity of your emotion in this particular situation. Color it in like a thermometer. Show it to your child to help him accurately get the right message, to read how and what you are feeling about the situation. For more ideas, see the section for parents, teachers, and therapists at the end of this chapter.

Person's name *(name of parent, teacher, or other person)*

The situation *(with whom, about what, where, and when)*

The emotion *(circle the word or write on the lines)* _____

Happy   Sad   Worried   Angry   Scared   Frustrated

or _____ and _____

The emotion-meter reading

(color the bar like a thermometer to indicate the appropriate level)

The biggest, most intense feeling

In the middle—some feeling, but not too much

Just a tiny bit of feeling

Emotion-Meter for Me

I will mark what is true for me. ✐

1. Describe the situation and the emotion, in boxes below.

The situation *(with whom, about what, where, and when)*

The emotion *(circle the word or write on the lines)* _____

Happy   Sad   Worried   Angry   Scared   Frustrated

or _____ and _____

2. The emotion-meter reading

(color the bar like a thermometer to indicate the appropriate level)

The biggest, most intense feeling ⌐3

In the middle—some feeling, but not too much ⌐2

Just a tiny bit of feeling ⌐1

3. What I can do when I am feeling _____ :

Counseling

Counseling is when a person goes to an office to talk or type computer conversations with a counselor or therapist. Sometimes counseling can help a person learn how to feel less anxious and how to feel better.

I will circle or highlight what is true for me. ✎

▶ Sometimes I talk with a counselor or a therapist. My therapist's name is _____ .

▶ I do not have a counselor or a therapist. I want to talk with a counselor or a therapist.

▶ My parent says I might go to a counselor or therapist sometime in the future.

▶ I like to go to my therapist's office.

▶ I don't like to go to my therapist's office.

I do these things with a counselor or therapist:

  ▶ Read this book
  ▶ Write lists about certain topics
  ▶ Mind map
  ▶ Draw pictures or comics
  ▶ Write stories or poems
  ▶ Play games
  ▶ Have computer conversations, without talking
  ▶ Read Social Stories
  ▶ Role-play
  ▶ Watch or make videos
  ▶ Other: _____ .

Feeling Better

Most children will be calmer and happier, and they will not try to hurt themselves or others, when they:

✓ Know what is going to happen and when it will be finished.

✓ Are comfortable in the sensory environment: sounds, sights, etc.

✓ Have physical exercise every day.

✓ Have time to enjoy their talents and focused interests.

✓ Can easily communicate what they need and want and share ideas.

✓ Play with peers in ways that are truly fun for them.

✓ Can have frequent breaks.

✓ Get good sleep.

✓ Experience that things make sense.

My parent and teacher can do things to help me feel good. They can try the ideas in this book. This list is for them. They can try:

☑ Adding structure (schedules, work systems, lists, etc).

☑ Reducing the sensory stimulation.

☑ Helping me exercise every day.

☑ Helping me get enough sleep every night.

☑ Teaching ways to communicate easily.

☑ Providing paper, pens, and keyboard for communication.

☑ Providing me with opportunities to enjoy my focused interests.

☑ Giving me frequent breaks and quiet times.

☑ Changing their expectations for me socially.

☑ Allowing social situations to be adapted.

☑ Helping me become familiar with new things gradually.

☑ Using strategies for well-being, from chapter 12.

Chapter 11

Especially for Older Readers

Many of the previous topics in this chapter are relevant when individually selected for older children, teenagers, and—in some cases—adults. Supplementary information *specifically* for older readers is provided on the following pages.

Make sure to read topics in chapter 2 about overwhelming stimulation, such as emotional pain and emotional empathy, and self-injurious behavior.

The first three pages in this section provide information on and opportunities for self-awareness and subsequent communication related to emotional expression. They also address statements made in frustration, such as "I want to die," what statements like this one mean, and what to do if such things are said.

The last four pages help the reader and support person assess whether saying "I want to die" is due to serious depression, rather than frustration. These pages provide introductory information about depression and the importance of getting help. Further, this section includes specific and concrete guidance for teens and adults, suggesting exactly what to say and how to initiate communication about this serious need.

The author's intent of the pages concerning suicidal thoughts is to make it as easy as possible for the person experiencing depression to initiate asking for help when he or she may not have any energy, desire, or clear, organized thinking to do so. And, the intent is to support important people in his or her life by providing a way to bring up this difficult subject.

Expressing Emotions

Children, teenagers, and adults feel emotions inside of them. No one else can see the feelings that are inside of a person.

People often show their emotions on the outside. This is called expressing emotions, or showing how you feel. Emotion is often shown on the face (with facial expressions) or with the body (through body language). Emotions are often expressed through the way a person talks (the loudness or softness of the voice, speed of talking, etc). These expressions happen automatically. Eventually, children learn to use words to express how they feel, to describe the emotions they feel inside.

Some people may not express their emotions in those typical ways—the ways other people expect. Sometimes people do not understand the emotional expressions of children, teenagers, and adults with autism.

This is why it is important to schedule times during which I can think about and express my inner feelings, through writing. I can write or draw comics or fill out a Communication Form. If I go to school or have a job, it is important to be able to fill out a Communication Form so I can express "How I am doing today."

An example of this type of Communication Form is found in chapter 12 on page 440.

Feeling Upset

What Does It Mean If Someone Says ...

"I want to die" or "I want to kill myself." Sometimes children, teenagers, and adults become very upset. They may say things quickly and automatically when they are upset. Another word for this is that they say things "impulsively."

Impulsive means to do or say something before thinking carefully and intelligently. Impulsive reactions are more likely to happen when people feel strong emotions. These statements are extreme examples of what some people may say impulsively when they are very anxious, upset, or angry:

- "I want to die."

- "I want to kill myself."

- "Why don't you just kill me?"

- "I wish I were dead."

After calming down, the person who said these statements may realize that the words are not really true. The person may not literally mean that they want to die.

(Or, the statements above may be true for the person. He or she may be very depressed. More information about these statements can be found on the following pages. Keep reading.)

I will circle or highlight and write what is true for me. 🖉

▶ This information is not relevant to me. I am not interested.

▶ I am interested in this topic.

▶ This information is important to me.

▶ I have said those statements about dying.

▶ I have questions or something to say about this topic: _____

_____

_____ .

These Statements May Become a Routine

Sometimes a person says, "I want to die" or "I want to kill myself" or "Why don't you kill me?" or other similar statements, when he or she is very anxious or feeling emotions such as sadness, misery, depression, anger, hostility, or other emotional pain.

These statements, repeated over and over, may become attached to the feeling of a strong emotion. So, when the person feels that strong emotion, he or she may repeat the same statement automatically.

If it happens frequently, the statement becomes a routine.

I will circle or highlight and write what is true for me. 🖉

▶ This information is not meaningful to me. I am not interested in reading more.

▶ I am interested in this topic.

▶ Sometimes I have talked about dying, but I don't remember exactly when.

▶ Sometimes I say these things: _____

_____

_____ .

▶ I have questions or something to say about this topic: _____

_____

_____ .

What Routine Statements May Really Mean

Routine statements such as "I want to die" are usually attached to emotions such as frustration, anger, fear, worry, hostility, depression, or other emotional pain.

It may be that the person who says these things is very unhappy about something. He or she may want something to stop. He or she may need to get away from something. It probably means that something needs to change in the person's life.

With help, the person can learn to identify what is needed or wanted. He or she can learn to use other words that communicate more accurately what is wanted or needed.

For example, when something is needed or wanted, instead of repeating the routine statement about wanting to die, the person tries to remember to begin the statement with these words, followed by accurate information that is true. It is recommended to try typing these statements, rather than talking.

- I need …

- I don't need …

- I want …

- I don't want …

- Help me to …

- Help me figure out what needs to happen …

- Help me with: _____ .
  Other trusted people may be able to help the person make changes for the better when they understand more about the person's needs.

Depression

If a person says, "I want to kill myself" or "I want to die" or other related statements, it is important to figure out if the person is saying these things impulsively (read the previous pages) or if it is really true that he or she wants to die. If the person truly feels like wanting to die, then he or she is depressed.

Being depressed is serious. It is an illness. The name of the illness is *depression*. Some symptoms of depression are feeling sad every day—for many weeks or months. There may be lots of crying and deep despair. Or, the person may not feel anything at all. The person may be tired all the time and sleep too much or not at all. The person may eat too much or not want to eat anything.

People who are depressed don't enjoy the things that used to make them happy. They may not be interested in their usual interests. They may not be able to concentrate on anything. They may not want to do anything at all.

If these things describe how a person is for many days, weeks, or months, he or she may be depressed. People who are depressed sometimes think about ways to die.

Very Important: A person who is depressed should tell someone his or her thoughts about dying. If the person can't or doesn't want to talk, then he can write or type his thoughts or show this page to someone he trusts. The person doesn't have to talk or say anything aloud. But he needs to communicate.

> **It is important for the person who is depressed to communicate with someone. It is important that other people get help for a person who is depressed and thinking about dying.**

Feeling Upset

Why Tell Someone If I Am Depressed?

Having the illness called *depression* is similar to having another illness, like pneumonia, influenza, strep throat, ear infections, or other illnesses. When people are sick for more than a week, they should get help from a doctor or nurse.

Doctors and/or therapists can help people who are sick with depression. There are medications and other therapies to help a person who has the illness called *depression*.

It is important and intelligent to get help if a person has questions or thinks about depression. Talking is not necessary to get help. Read the next page for what to do and how to do it.

I will circle or highlight and write what is true for me. 🖉

▶ The topic of depression may apply to me.

▶ Sometimes I think about wanting to die, but I don't say it aloud.

▶ I have thought about and planned ways to die.

▶ I think I may be depressed.

▶ I have at least one trusted person. His or her name is:

_____

▶ It is time to contact my trusted person.

The next page gives information about what to do and how to do it.

What to Do

I will choose either ① or ② .

Then I will do ③ .

① There is one person or more than person in my life with whom I usually communicate. This may include family members, teachers, therapists, friends, or someone else. His, her, or their names are:

_____

_____ .

I will circle the names of one or more of these people to communicate with about depression. OR …

② There is no one in my life with whom I usually communicate. I should contact a doctor, therapist, school counselor, or the local hospital. Or, if I cannot find a person, I should call a local "hotline" and ask to talk with someone about feeling depressed and thinking about dying. *It is important to tell the person that I am autistic (or that I have autism or Asperger's syndrome). If it's in person, I can bring this book and show the person this page. He or she may want to look at other pages, too.*

③ Say, write, or type this sentence:

I need to talk with you about depression and my thoughts of wanting to die.

If in person, I'll bring this book and show the person this page.

Choose one or more ways to communicate from this list:

 Make a phone call, saying the entire sentence: **"I need to talk with you about depression and my thoughts of wanting to die."**

 Type an e-mail and write the entire sentence: **"I need to talk with you about depression and my thoughts of wanting to die."**

 Show this book and point to page 403 on depression.

 Talk in person, saying the entire sentence: **"I need to talk with you about depression and my thoughts of wanting to die."**

 Bring my laptop or tablet and type the entire sentence: **"I need to type with you about depression and my thoughts of wanting to die."**

For Parents, Teachers, and Therapists

"Stress alters everything for me, including sensory stuff, my ability to think, to function, to analyze things ... There can be so much happening beneath the surface that a single event that seems from the outside like one little thing, no big deal, is a trigger for losing everything."

—Dave Spicer, on stress, anxiety, and falling apart

Ideas in This Chapter:

☑ Prevention

☑ Self-acceptance

☑ During an outburst

☑ After recovering from the outburst

☑ Mind the gap

☑ Using emotion-meters

☑ Reevaluate and reassess

☑ Reduce sensory stimulation

☑ Frequent breaks

☑ The quiet area

☑ Counseling

☑ Medication

☑ A special note about adolescence

☑ Depression and anxiety

Prevention

It is not surprising that visually structured strategies, when adapted for an individual child, can dramatically affect behavior in a positive way. Uncertainty leads to anxiety, which leads to behavioral problems. Reread the ideas in previous chapters and implement the suggestions that meet your child's needs. Adapt, modify, and individualize the strategies until they fit. Provide meaning for your child in ways he can see and understand. The more things that make sense to your child, the less anxious he will be.

Children with autism are less likely to have tantrums or become upset when:

1. **They know what is going to happen and when it will be finished.**

2. **People, activities, and things in the environment are familiar.**

3. **Sensory stimulation in the environment is reduced.**

4. **They engage in regular, daily physical activity.**

5. **They can enjoy their strengths, talents, and special interests.**

6. **They communicate their needs and wants effectively.**

7. **They can get help when they need it.**

8. **Social situations fit their desires and abilities.**

9. **They have frequent "breaks."**

10. **They are rested and get enough sleep regularly.**

11. **Things make sense.**

Almost all of the strategies that have been introduced in previous chapters are significant and often necessary as preventative behavioral management strategies. Review previous chapters and implement the strategies that are indicated for your child in an individualized manner.

Self-acceptance

Your child's anxiety may decrease as he gains better understanding of himself. Make this book, especially the personally meaningful pages, available to him often. When appropriate for your child, talk and/or write about autism and other related personal issues.  Emphasize the positive qualities and acknowledge the challenges. Help him see that he is not alone and that there are other people, with and without autism, who experience similar things.

During an outburst

In the midst of a child's outburst, remember to inhibit your natural inclination to talk, explain, or otherwise verbally process what is happening. In other words, don't talk! Usually, the most important things you can do during a behavioral crisis are *(1)* keep your child safe from injury, *(2)* keep others safe from injury, and *(3)* be quiet.

This means that after making sure your child is safe from injury, probably the single most important thing you can do at the time of the outburst is to not do or say anything. Of course, there may be individual children for whom a specific verbal routine is calming; however, in most cases, it is best not to add to the confusion and extreme anxiety by filling the airwaves with auditory stimulation (your talking!).

If something must be communicated during an outburst, you may write it down in a note. Keep the message simple and clear. Quietly hand the written note to your child, or place it somewhere where he can see it. If it is more convenient and your child can see it easily, you may even want to post the note onto a wall, a door, or a nearby piece of furniture. If your child is lying on the floor, you can place the note next to him, close to his face, so he can see it. In some cases, you might hold the note up in front of his eyes so he can read it. Do not say anything while you are doing this, and try not to make eye contact, which many children experience as additional, confusing visual stimulation.

If your child's outburst is loud and disruptive to others, he may need to go to a more secluded area during the disruption, if possible. You can remind him of this with a written note. You might write something like, "It's time to go to the dark and quiet back room." **Remember, it is better if you DO NOT talk to him at this time.**

After the outburst

Well after your child recovers from the outburst and has calmed down, you may want to communicate about what happened. Keep in mind that it may take much longer than you expect for your child to feel calm internally. It may be best if you continue to communicate in writing or by typing and agree to a time to communicate more, later. Write this time or date on the schedule or on another day on the calendar. Reread the workbook chapters and ideas about understanding and communication. Use a strategy you are both comfortable with that meets your child's needs. If you have already been practicing written communication, you will be a step ahead! This is when your proactive and consistent use of these strategies on a daily basis really pays off!

The more familiar your child is with using visual strategies, the easier it will be for him to communicate and learn, and the easier it will be for both of you to handle and prevent periods of upset.

Try writing notes by hand; using a computer to write and talk; drawing pictures and diagrams, Comic Strip Conversations, and Social Stories; and/or clarifying something by using a schedule or list. Remember, do these things when calm. In some cases, wait for another day to do them. Do NOT introduce a Social Story when your child is upset or is still recovering from an outburst. This is NOT the time to teach new skills or introduce new information that would require your child to think hard and process.

Reading the relevant workbook pages in this book together with your child may help you and your child identify the issue and decide on a preventative plan for the future. A preventative learning strategy that may work for your child is called "Mind the gap."

Mind the gap

Many children are surprised and confused at their own reactions to stress and anxiety. It may seem to your child that his emotional response has come out of the blue—unexpectedly—and suddenly, he is in the midst of a meltdown and out of control. "Mind the gap" is a strategy that has been used to help children and teenagers learn to be aware of their internal state, to give them control over their response to an event, and to teach alternative behavior. Readers from London will be familiar with this term; it is the recorded message that is heard upon disembarking the Underground, or the subway, as it is referred to in the United States. The verbal announcement "Mind the gap!" reminds travelers to be careful of the gap between the train and the platform. The American equivalent is, "Watch your step!"

Several years ago, Jack Wall, the former director of the Charlotte TEACCH Center, decided that this concept could be used to describe the period between anxiety-building incidents and the individual's reaction. Dr Wall, who was traveling in England at the time, found himself thinking about a particular child's outbursts when he noticed t-shirts with the phrase "Mind the Gap!" being sold at the Underground station. This strategy resulted.

By borrowing the phrase "Mind the Gap!", the emphasis is placed on helping the child become aware of the "zone" or the "gap" during which time a choice can be made as to what actions to take. Teresa Johnson, a former parent advocate for the Autism Society of North Carolina (and mother of Thomas, one of this book's illustrators), widely promoted its use by teaching parents in our area. The goal is for children and teenagers to become more aware of the buildup of anxiety within, the eternal events that may be the cause, and, finally, what to do about it. Teresa emphasizes that all children are different;

for your child to be successful, adaptations must be made in how you develop and use "Mind the gap." You may want to change the name to something more meaningful to your child. For one teenager, it was called the "Decision Zone." It could be used in coordination with behavioral management point systems, but, more often, it is used simply as a visual reminder about the process of stress buildup and what to do to avoid negative consequences. Social Stories can be written to show how "Mind the gap" fits into daily life. Here you see a sample of "Mind the gap," and general guidelines to help you individualize this strategy for your child.

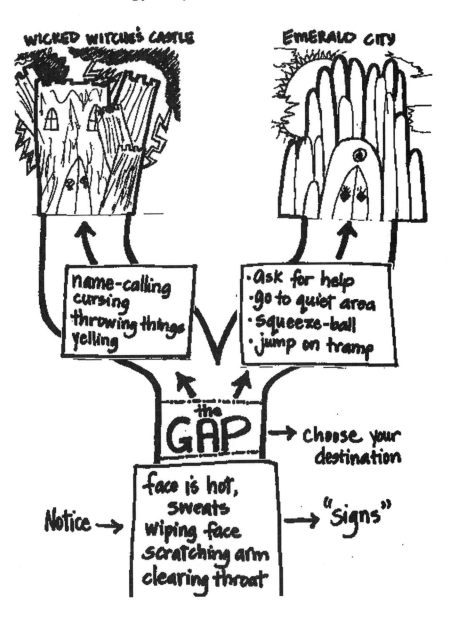

413

1. *Identify the behaviors to target*

First, before sitting down with the child, the adult must prepare by identifying which behaviors to target. Examples here are name-calling, cursing, engaging in self-injury, or throwing things.

2. *Identify his "signs"*

After identifying the targeted behaviors, make a mental list, noting the observable "signs" that the child exhibits sometime before the behavioral outburst. For example, his face might get red; he might sweat profusely and wipe his face; his body might get stiff; he might repeat certain phrases or words; he might scratch his arm … Try to note things your child will be able to learn to identify—feel or observe—about himself.

3. *Sit down with your child and make three lists*

Now, sit down with your child at a time when you are both calm and explain that, together, you are going to make a map that will help him feel better and make good choices. Write the list of the targeted behaviors on a piece of paper or a large index card. Point out this list in a matter-of-fact, calm manner.

Next, introduce your child to the idea of how his body has specific sensations or feelings or shows certain behaviors before he gets outwardly upset.

You can use previous pages from the workbook to help with this. Make a list with your child of the outwardly observable and internal signals your child can feel and see. This may be difficult for your child, so you can say something like, "I noticed that before you yelled yesterday, you had been scratching your arm a lot." The list can be written by hand or on the computer, by using fonts and styles of your child's design. Your child can help make this list, but it is not necessary if he hasn't yet learned to notice his body's signals.

Now make a list of the (positive) behavioral alternatives. Come up with a few simple strategies your child can use effectively in different situations. Be specific. For example, make a list of alternative words to say (instead of cursing), how to ask for help, how to take a break (how to leave and where to go), and other practices, like squeezing a squishy ball, counting to 50, breathing deeply, punching a beanbag, or jumping on a mini-trampoline. You may want to brainstorm ideas ahead of time with other teachers and parents. And, don't forget to ask your child for ideas! (Remember, you can ask by typing or writing!)

4. *Draw a map with two destinations*

    Draw a "map" with your child, by using a high-interest theme or topic. In the diagram on the previous page, the adult drew the roads and Thomas drew the two destinations on the top, at the end of the roads. Thomas has chosen "The Emerald City" to represent the positive outcomes and "The Wicked Witch's Castle" to represent the undesirable outcomes. Attach the three lists at the appropriate places on the map, as shown in the diagram.

    It is important that your child participate in creating the pictures of the two destinations. Help him by asking, "What would be the BEST thing that could ever happen?" and "What could be the WORST thing that could ever happen?" If he likes to draw, supply him with paper and pens. If he is not an artist,

415

then he can find pictures from magazines to represent his positive and negative images. He can even use photographs or postcards. One child used Pokemon cards for the two locations: a "good Pokemon" and a "bad Pokemon." Another child told me to draw two different scoreboards that showed two different final scores for his favorite football team and its rival. You can guess how the scores went! The idea is to encourage your child to use what is most meaningful to him.

Connect the "good behavior" with the positive outcome. For some children, points are earned or taken away. Special treats, videos, time with a video game, a trip to the art supply store, or other personally motivating activities may also be effective. For many children, however, the visual images of the positive and negative destinations are powerful and meaningful enough!

5. *Things to keep in mind*

Keys to this strategy are that it is visual and personally meaningful to the child in a concrete way. Teresa emphasizes that it must be interactive; refer to it, and change and adapt the lists as the child changes. Try to help him identify his body's reaction to stress, keeping in mind that he might not be able to recognize it yet. Until he learns his body's "signals," you can help him by calmly pointing them out when they occur. Say, "You are scratching your arm," and then point to the "Mind the gap" picture, drawing his attention to the lists and the behaviors that lead to the different destinations. You can literally point (without talking) to the positive behavioral alternatives that will propel him down the road to his positive destination.

Posters can be made and displayed in particular locations (different rooms of the house and places at school). Teresa suggests that parents make copies that are reduced to index-card size to post in the car and carry in a purse or pocket, so the visual cue is always available. She discovered that after Thomas became used to seeing the posters, she just had to remind him (when he was approaching "the gap") about making a choice between "The Emerald City" or "The Witch's Castle."

Using emotion-meters

Usually, adults assume that a child knows when adults are feeling angry or happy or sad, but many children with autism have trouble "reading" their parent's or teacher's expressions of emotional content. Some children assume that the adult may be angry, when it may not really be the case, or vice versa. Some children have difficulty detecting subtle differences in types of emotions or degrees of emotion. Some children may overreact or respond in seemingly inappropriate ways, simply because they misinterpret the adult's reaction. If this causes problems for you and your child, you might try experimenting with the emotion-meter for parents (page 394) to clarify how you are feeling.

Duplicate the workbook page and keep extras on hand, so it is easily available when you need it. First, practice using the emotion-meter to illustrate your feelings when everyone is feeling okay. Use it to illustrate happy feelings, as well as troubled ones. The more frequently you use it in daily life, the more familiar it will become. As with all visually structured strategies, once it becomes a familiar routine for your child, it will be more effective during a crisis, when you really need the help.

You can also try to teach him to use an emotion-meter to describe his own emotions (page 395). The emotion-meter may become a tool to help your child notice, identify, and communicate his internal emotional state. He might also begin to understand that there are different degrees of feelings and how to be aware of these internal feelings. At the bottom of page 395, there is a space in which to write a positive, preventative behavioral course of action. Depending on your child, possibilities could be going to the quiet area, jumping on the trampoline, writing on the computer, or other activities.

Reevaluate and reassess

If tantrums, aggression, or self-injurious behavior persist on a regular basis, even though you have added more structure to your child's life, you will need to step back, reevaluate, and reassess. Further simplify and increase the visually structured strategies and make sure he is getting regular physical activity. Look more closely at sensory issues, and make more accommodations in the environment. Try to see your child's daily life through his eyes and imagine it through his senses. Review the list under the previous heading, "Prevention," on page 408. What might be causing anxiety? What needs to be modified?

Does he need to communicate something more effectively? Give him Communication Forms (multiple-choice lists) for him to indicate what is true for him. Add more structure and exercise, use his special interests, give him breaks, write Social Stories, and simplify demands.

Reduce and moderate sensory stimulation

Respect sensory differences and take them seriously. Acknowledge that it may be impossible to really understand the extent of the differences in sensory experiences your child has to deal with every day. It is invisible to you—but huge to your child. Read what autistic adults write in their blogs about sensory overload and daily life. Review chapter 2 and your child's personal responses. Adapt and modify the environment. Incorporate regular physical activity and frequent breaks into his daily schedule. There are many resources, books, and Web sites devoted to helping people deal with the onslaught of sensory stimulation. As stated in chapter 2, you may want to have an experienced occupational therapist provide a sensory-integration assessment and a treatment program.

Frequent breaks

Allow your child to take frequent breaks. Show him on his schedule when the breaks will happen. Include a break time for his favorite activity on his work system for "what will happen next." Schedule breaks in the quiet area. Consider individually designed breaks to help each student with particular sensory needs. For example, for a student who needs to "get away," a break could consist of walking in the quiet hallways to run an errand, like delivering a message to the office. For a student who needs more sensory stimulation, the job of stacking library books or pushing them in a heavy cart would be beneficial.

Give him quiet breaks after new or unfamiliar activities and before and after dealing with new or unfamiliar people. Give him breaks after unexpected events and surprises. Frequent breaks will help him recover from possible confusion and overstimulation, regain an inner calm, pace himself for the day's demands, prevent the buildup of anxiety, and summon the much-needed energy and stamina with which to handle the world and its surprises. For information on schedules and work systems with examples of scheduled breaks, see pages 109-114.

The quiet area

The quiet area is a place of respite—a "getaway" for your child. He probably already has something like this on his own … his own retreat. One child "hid" in his father's closet. A middle-school child discovered how to slip into the custodian's storage area. By creating an "official" quiet area, you are acknowledging and supporting his need to have time to be alone and to get calm and centered. You are also structuring a way to teach him an important adaptive skill he can use to prevent a buildup of anxiety. The quiet area has been mentioned and discussed in previous chapters. See pages 56, 111, 113, 280, 322, 429, and 444 for more information about the quiet area.

Counseling

Some children may benefit from counseling, but "talk therapies" that require examining one's feelings and emotional processing are often not very effective with most autistic children. Find a therapist who is familiar with (or who wants to learn about) autism and the particular ways in which children with autism think and learn. Cognitive behavioral therapy is currently felt to be most helpful, with modifications consisting of visual cues and structure. Call your local chapter of the Autism Society

Feeling Upset

to get referrals for experienced therapists. Many of the ideas in this book, as well as the workbook itself, may be a useful tool to use in counseling sessions.

Medication

If aggression and self-injurious behavior continue, even after using the recommended strategies indicated for your child in this book, you may want to talk with your physician about medication that may decrease anxiety. If your physician is not experienced with the types of medications currently used with children who have autism, ask for a referral to a psychiatrist who is familiar with autism.

A special note about adolescence

Your child may be entering adolescence or may already be well into this stage of life. Gary Mesibov, former director of division TEACCH at the University of North Carolina at Chapel Hill, reminds us that just like any child upon reaching adolescence, the child with autism has some very specific and basic needs. They are:

- The need for privacy—time by himself or herself.

- The need to be more independent—to make more choices for himself or herself.

It is not surprising that, if these basic needs are not met, your older child may become anxious or angry. The same thing happens for any adolescent, whether autistic or typically developing. Remember and plan for these needs as your child grows.

It is more complicated for families with autistic teenagers. They often still require help with basic needs: hair washing, bathing, teeth brushing, choosing clothing, and other self-care skills that typical teens take care of on their own. Problems with sequencing, sensory confusion, and being dependent on external prompts often result in parents having to do so much more than they or the child really want. It is frustrating for all involved.

If you and your child's teachers have already taught him how to follow schedules and use work systems and checklists, and if he has practiced and mastered these visual organization skills, you are a step ahead of the game! You have built in a way to help your child be more independent, while still providing the guidance and support that may be necessary. Options and choices can be structured into the schedule. Providing checklists for chores, assignments, and especially self-care skills will help you give him the privacy he needs and the independence he craves.

Depression and anxiety

Depression and anxiety are not uncommon among teenagers and adults on the autism spectrum.

Evaluation by a psychiatrist who is familiar with autism and is flexible in his or her methods of communicating and commitment to listening to his or her autistic patients is imperative. It is a necessity that the physician receives accurate information; autistic patients may make assumptions as to what the doctor knows about their inner life and what details they need to communicate. The differences in an autistic style of understanding and communicating are often subtle and remain undetected on the part of the doctor (especially with highly verbal intelligent autistic people), who is making his or her own assumptions about the patient based on what is or is not communicated. And don't forget about body language and facial expressions—the doctor is usually interpreting these through lenses of typical development (see pages 173 and 404), which may be inaccurate. For these reasons and more, the communicative relationship between a physician and the autistic patient can be complicated—and potentially detrimental to successful treatment. Look for a physician with an open attitude—one with a willingness to engage in methods of communication that may be different from expected protocol and who listens without making assumptions.

The proper medication (sometimes requiring multiple trials to get it right) may provide sufficient relief so the person is able to take advantage of appropriate support and therapy. Participation during appropriate therapy in the development of self-awareness, self-knowledge, self-advocacy, and ways to organize one's thoughts and one's daily events may contribute to a greater sense of well-being. Exploring some of the recommendations in chapter 12 may also provide long-term benefit.

Chapter 12
Happiness—
A Feeling of
Well-Being

Workbook

Happiness

What Is Happiness?

Happiness is not something that can be physically touched ... it is invisible. It is a feeling inside of a person. Some people describe it as a soft or light feeling. It could be described as a calm, peaceful, and satisfied feeling. It could be a feeling that is joyful or cheerful. (More words for feelings related to happiness are listed on page 443.)

Happiness is a feeling of well-being. Most people like feeling happiness. When they feel sadness or another uncomfortable feeling, they usually want to know how to feel better and happier.

This chapter will describe the things scientists have discovered help people feel better and happier and have a feeling of well-being.

I will (circle) or highlight what is true for me. 🖉

▶ Sometimes I feel happy.

▶ I feel happy most of the time.

▶ I don't feel happy very much.

▶ I wish I could feel happy more often.

▶ I wonder what happiness is.

▶ Sometimes people tell me I need to be happy.

▶ Sometimes I am happy, but other people don't know I am happy.

▶ "Happy" is a funny word.

▶ What are other words related to happiness?

Exercise the Heart Muscle

Cardiovascular exercise keeps my body strong and helps me stay healthy. It is good to exercise once (or twice) each day, for about 20-30 minutes or more, with a good, fast heartbeat. This kind of exercise is called *cardiovascular* (or "cardio," for short) and may help me stay calmer throughout the day. Exercise is one of the things that helps create well-being or happiness.

I will circle or highlight what is true for me. 🖊

I would like to do this kind of cardio exercise:
- ▶ Walking fast or running or jogging
- ▶ Running up a hill and rolling down
- ▶ Jumping on a trampoline
- ▶ Swimming
- ▶ Dancing to music
- ▶ Riding a bicycle or a stationary bike
- ▶ Jumping rope or a pogo stick
- ▶ Rollerskating
- ▶ Horseback riding
- ▶ Walking up a snowy hill and sledding down
- ▶ Snowshoeing or cross-country skiing
- ▶ Other: _____ .

The times for doing exercise can be written on my schedule.

Stretching

Stretching keeps my body flexible and helps me stay healthy. Stretching is when I slowly and carefully move a part of my body and hold it for a count of 12 seconds or more. It feels good for my muscles, and it may help me feel calmer.

My parent, teacher, or therapist can help me find pictures of stretches I can do at school and at home. I should take a stretch break a few times each day. Stretching should feel good and not hurt. (*If it hurts, I should stop and tell my parent, teacher, or therapist.*) Stretching is one of the things that helps generate a feeling of calmness and well-being.

Check with a physical therapist or other health professional to learn about these:

- Using rubber resistance bands
- Doing specific stretches while sitting at a desk or on a chair
- Doing specific stretches while standing
- Doing specific stretches while lying on the floor
- Stretching upper-body muscles and lower-body muscles
- Taking stretch breaks during school
- Taking stretch breaks at home
- Doing yoga postures
- Other: _____

My schedule may show me when it's time to take a stretch break.

Relaxation

Relaxation is the word to describe when my body and my mind are calm. Most people have to learn how to relax.

With the help of my parent, teacher, or therapist, I may find out what helps me relax and practice it every day. Relaxation is one of the most valuable ways to help a person feel happiness or a sense of well-being.

We can mark some things to try. ✎

▶ Go to my quiet area. (See page 280.)

▶ Listen to my favorite calming music.

▶ Practice slow, deep breathing.

▶ Practice a tensing-and-relaxing muscle routine.

▶ Listen to music and guided visualizations.

▶ Watch a video that shows me a relaxation routine.

▶ Watch a video with my favorite things.

▶ Sit quietly and do nothing at all.

▶ Relax while stretching.

▶ Get (or give) a massage.

▶ Swing (in the basement, the yard, or a park).

▶ Stim in my favorite ways: _____ .

▶ Other: _____

My schedule shows me when it is time to practice relaxation.

Sleep

Getting enough sleep helps me feel rested. Sleep gives me more energy when I am awake. Getting enough sleep helps me feel better and get through the day.

With the help of my parent, teacher, or therapist, I can find out what helps me get enough sleep. Having a regular sleep pattern is one of the things that helps me to have a feeling of well-being or happiness.

For better sleep, we can try these ideas.

- Follow an evening routine.

- Take a warm bath in the evening.

- Wake up at the same time each day.

- Use heavy curtains to keep out light/noise.

- Open the curtains at sunrise to let the light come in.

- Use a white-noise machine.

- Use a weighted blanket.

- Sleep in a sleeping bag in a little tent.

- Bedtime routine includes calming music.

- Finish watching TV or using electronic devices an hour before bedtime.

- Avoid food with caffeine, sugar, and additives 2 hours before bed.

- Get enough exercise during the day.

- Other: _____ .

A Good Diet

When people are healthy, they usually feel good. They are more able to handle stress and anxiety when their bodies are healthy. Good nutrition is one of the ways of supporting a greater sense of well-being.

- Having a good diet means eating foods that contain a variety of vitamins and minerals, in the right amounts, at the right times, for each individual person.

- Some autistic children and adults might want to only eat certain foods and refuse most other foods. Depending on what they prefer, it might be difficult for children with autism to eat a good diet.

- One way to help have a good diet is by getting extra nutrition that comes in pills or liquids. These are called *vitamins and minerals*, or *nutritional supplements*.

- Some people follow the rules of a special diet. Some foods are allowed, and others are not. I may follow a special diet. The name of my diet is: _____

_____ .

My schedule shows me when it is time to eat meals and snacks and when it's time for nutritional supplements.

Happiness

Being Kind

Being kind helps people feel happy. The person who does a kind thing feels happier. The person who receives a kind thing feels happier, too. Here are some examples of being kind:

- Saying good morning to someone

- Spending time petting or playing with an animal friend

- Smiling

- Holding the door open for someone

- Sending someone a friendly card or note

- Sending a "get well" card to a sick person

- Helping someone if they ask for help

- Saying, "Can I help you?" if a person is carrying things

- Using good manners: Saying "please" and "thank you"

- Thanking someone for something they did for me

- Other examples from my life _____

_____ .

I will circle or highlight what is true for me. ✎

▶ I'd like some more ideas of ways I can be kind.

▶ I'd like some ideas of whom to be kind to.

▶ Other: _____ .

What Is Respect?

Respect describes how all people should treat one another. Respect is like a circle with two halves.

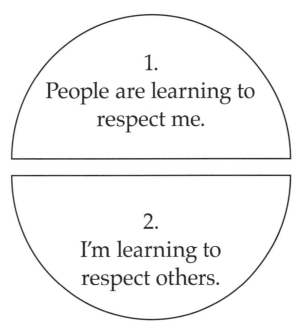

1.
People are learning to respect me.

2.
I'm learning to respect others.

1. People are learning to respect me. When people try to understand me, they respect me. When people know that autism is not bad or wrong—but that it is a way of being—they respect me. When they think I am okay the way I am, they respect me. Reading this book may help people understand and respect me.

2. I am learning to respect other people. I can try to remember that each person has his or her own thoughts. Each person has unique strengths, likes, dreams, and fears. Even if I don't understand why people are the way they are, they deserve respect. When someone is different from me, it does not mean he or she is wrong.

I show respect by trying to be polite and not making fun of or saying bad things about my brothers, sisters, friends, teachers, parents, and other children and adults.

All people deserve respect.

One Way People Are the Same

Even though everyone is unique, there is one way most people are the same: Most children and adults appreciate having understanding and respect. All people deserve respect, no matter whom they are.

I will circle or highlight what is true for me. 🖉

▶ I want other people to understand me.

▶ I like it when other children understand me.

▶ Even if I am different from someone else, I am OK.

▶ I want other children to know that autism is not wrong.

▶ I like it when my parent understands me.

▶ I like it when my teacher understands me.

▶ I try to remember that other children have their own thoughts. They might be different from my thoughts and opinions. That is OK.

▶ Even if someone else is different from me, he or she is OK.

▶ I can respect a person, even when we don't agree.

▶ I want to understand other children better.

▶ I want to understand other adults better.

▶ I want to learn more about respect and understanding.

▶ I want to understand _____ (name) better.

▶ I want _____ (name) to understand me.

▶ Other: _____ .

Are There Other Autistic People in the World?

- For every 88 people in the world, there is one person who is on the autism spectrum. That is a ratio of one per 88.

- There are autistic people of every age: children, teenagers, and adults.

- There are autistic adults and children of all races and ethnic groups who live in every country in the world.

- In North Carolina, where this book was written, there are approximately 60,000 people* on the autism spectrum. To estimate the number of autistic residents in your state or country, follow the directions on the next page.

Drawing by Maria White, 1999

* A recent estimate from the Autism Society of North Carolina can be found at *autismsociety-nc.org*.

How Many People with Autism Live in My State or Country?

- The name of my state (or country) is _____ _____ .

- The population of my state (or country) is _____ _____ (Find the population by searching on the Internet.)

- Follow these instructions to estimate the number of autistic people in your state or country.

- Write the population number in the box.

- Divide by 88.

There are approximately _____ people on the autism spectrum in _____ _____ (state or country), where I live.

$$88 \overline{\smash{\big)}\hspace{3cm}}$$

Fitting in or Being My Unique Self

No one is exactly the same. Every person is different from one another. Everyone is unique.

Every person has unique ways of being themselves.

But many people, especially children from about the age of 10 years all the way through the teenage years, until the ages of 20 or even older, try to look and act and talk the same as each other. They think it is better to be the same as each other, even if it is not their natural way of being. This is called "fitting in." Many children try to "fit in" instead of feeling comfortable being their unique selves.

There are some children who do not care if they "fit in." Sometimes children try to "fit in," but they may not know what to do or how to "fit in." Autistic children often find it difficult or impossible to "fit in."

Trying to "fit in" is not very fun. It is better to be yourself … and to grow into being your best self!

I am unique.

It is perfectly OK to be me, just the way I am.

 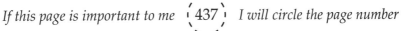

Appreciation and Gratitude

Appreciation means to cherish or value something. *Gratitude* means being thankful. People may appreciate and be grateful for items they have, ideas they think about, people they know, activities they do, and the little things that are a part of daily life.

Feeling appreciation and gratitude helps people feel happier. One way to do this is to notice and be grateful for things like having clean air to breathe, a warm house when it is cold outside, food to eat, a functional laptop or tablet, a parent who takes care of them, and other things.

Children, teenagers, and adults can learn to appreciate something every day. Feeling grateful and saying "thank you" helps everyone feel happier.

One way to learn to appreciate and feel grateful is to keep a gratitude journal. It is a special book (or document on my tablet or laptop) where I can list things I appreciate. Once or twice each week I may write one or more things on the list in my gratitude journal.

My schedule or calendar can remind me when to add something in my gratitude journal.

Expressing How I Am

All people have feelings inside of them. No one else can see the inside feelings. Most children usually show their inside feelings on the outside, on their face or with their body. This may happen automatically.

Emotions shown on the face are called *facial expressions*. Emotions shown with the body are called *body language*. Emotions can also be expressed by the way a person talks (loudly, softly, quickly, slowly, etc). This happens without people thinking about it. Children also learn to use words to express how they feel inside.

Sometimes other people have trouble understanding how an autistic child is feeling. **Autistic children may not show their feelings on their faces in ways other people can understand. Other people may not be able to tell how the child is feeling by looking at the child's face or body.**

This is why it is important to think about and express my inner feelings in other ways. I may write, type, draw comics, or fill out a form. If I go to school or have a job, it is especially important to fill out a Communication Form with a checklist showing "How I am doing today."

One example of a Communication Form for school can be found on the next page.

How I Am Today (Example of a Daily Communication Form for School)

When Ms Jarvis reads this finished form, she may understand me better. She'll know how I am doing today. If there is a problem, she may have ideas about how to fix it or how to make things better. If there isn't a problem, she will appreciate knowing that everything is okay for me right now.

I will circle and write what is true for me. ✏

▶ Some work is easy today. The easy work is: _____
_____ .

▶ Some work is hard today. It hard work is: _____
_____ .

▶ Today, my favorite thing is: _____ .

▶ I feel calm right now.

▶ I feel excited right now.

▶ I feel worried right now.

▶ I feel angry right now.

▶ I feel happy right now.

▶ I feel something else right now. It is: _____ .

▶ The reason for my feelings: _____
_____ .

▶ I don't know how I feel right now, but I'm doing okay.

▶ I don't know how I feel right now, but I'm NOT doing okay.

▶ Something else I want to say is: _____
_____ .

More about Happiness

The last part of this chapter was written for older children, teenagers, and adults. My parent, teacher, or therapist can look through the following pages and decide if any of the pages may be interesting or helpful for me.

Chapter 12

Especially for Older Readers

Research* about happiness shows that about 50% of a person's happiness seems to be genetic. This means that a certain level of happiness you may have—a tendency toward cheerfulness or grumpiness, peacefulness or worry, contentment or unease, may be similar to how some of your relatives (parents, grandparents, siblings, or others) experience levels of happiness.

Only about 10% (a very small amount) of happiness depends on "life circumstance." This includes things like how much money you have, where you live, your appearance, how much education you have, and so on. This is surprising to many people who think that winning the lottery or having more money will make them happy, or that moving to a new house will make them happy, or that being in other life situations will make them happy.

However, about 40% (almost half) of a person's happiness is determined by how he thinks, what he does, and how he behaves. This means there are certain things that people can do to become happier.

Much of the rationale in this chapter is based on the research in positive psychology and happiness. Several pages in this chapter are adapted from previous published writings by Catherine Faherty— in particular, sections from the chapter about life lessons from the book *Understanding Death and Illness and What They Teach about Life.*

* Statistics are as cited in the book *The How of Happiness: A Scientific Approach to Getting the Life You Want* by Sonja Lyubomirsky, Penguin Press, 2007.

Happiness Words

If I look up the word "happiness" in a dictionary or thesaurus, I will find that there are many words to describe feelings of happiness. The words toward the top of this list describe strong feelings of happiness. The words toward the bottom of the list describe mild or gentle feelings of happiness. All of these usually feel good to a person.

- Blissful
- Ecstatic
- Gleeful
- Joyful
- Elated
- Delighted
- Happy
- Cheerful
- Pleasurable
- Glad
- Peaceful
- Safe and secure
- Content
- Well
- Satisfied

Some figures of speech related to being happy are:

- In high spirits
- On cloud nine
- Happy as a lark
- Tickled pink
- Snug as a bug in a rug

More about Relaxation

Earlier in this chapter, the practice of relaxation was introduced. Most people have to learn how to relax. It is something that gets better and better the more a person practices. It is recommended that a person practice relaxation every day, as part of his regular daily schedule. It is one of the things that help increase a sense of well-being or happiness.

Relaxation helps the mind and the body slow down. There are ideas that may help with relaxation on page 429, but a person doesn't have to do anything at all. While relaxing, a person doesn't have to think about anything. It may be a time to do nothing at all. Relaxing can be considered one form of meditation.

It is helpful to practice relaxing while sitting or lying down in a quiet room. But as a person becomes better and better at relaxing, it is possible to relax in other situations, too, even if it is not totally quiet around them.

The more someone practices relaxing, the calmer he may become in his daily life. He may not get upset as often, and, if he is upset, he may be able to calm down more easily. It takes practice, but it is worth it.

I will circle or highlight what is true for me. ✐

▶ I am interested in learning more about relaxation.

▶ I'd like to practice relaxing.

▶ I'd like to learn about relaxing and about meditation.

▶ I'm not interested in this now, but maybe I will be in the future.

▶ Other: _____.

More about Exercise

As discussed earlier in this chapter, researchers have found that one of the things a person can do to lead to a greater sense of well-being and happiness is exercise.

Physical exercise is often effective in relieving depression. It reduces anxiety and stress. It reduces the risk of many diseases, such as diabetes, colon cancer, hypertension, and heart disease. It elevates serotonin levels, which help people feel more content and satisfied.

Exercise helps build bones, muscles, and joints. It improves sleep and helps control weight gain. It improves the quality of life.

Why Does Exercise Help So Much?

It increases feelings of self-esteem and helps people feel more control in their lives. While exercising, people may be distracted from things they worry about and negative thoughts that make them feel bad. Depending on the exercise, it can sometimes be an opportunity for social contact, as in cases of walking or going to the gym with a partner.

Researchers have found that exercise may be the most effective instant happiness booster, as compared with all other activities.

Make an Exercise Plan

Here is a worksheet to help make a plan for exercise.

I will (circle) the types of cardio exercises I will try to get my heart beating fast and my muscles moving:

▶ Walking briskly

▶ Running or jogging

▶ Cycling outside or on a stationary bike

▶ Walking up and down stairs

▶ Something else: _____
   (See page 445 for more ideas.)

I will try to exercise _____ (circle how many) days per week:

2	3	4	5

I will try to exercise on these days: (circle which days)

Mondays   Tuesdays   Wednesdays   Thursdays   Fridays   Saturdays   Sundays

I will try to exercise (how many) minutes each time:

20	30	40	50

My goal(s) of this exercise plan is to (circle which of these are true):

▶ Get physically fit

▶ Feel happier

▶ Lose weight

▶ Develop an exercise routine

▶ Another goal: _____

Acceptance

Acceptance is acknowledging that something has happened. It is knowing that something is the way it is and choosing to feel okay about it. Acceptance is often the first step in helping us deal positively with things that have happened or that are happening—things that are causing emotional pain, such as anger, sadness, disappointment, frustration, worry, or another emotion.

Accepting ourselves the way we are, called *self-acceptance*, is a big part of becoming happier.

Acceptance is an intelligent and wise action. Researchers have discovered that acceptance (and then forgiveness) is something that increases a person's sense of well-being—a feeling of happiness.

I will circle or highlight what is true for me. 🖉

▶ There is something I need to accept. It is _____

_____ .

▶ Right now, I can't think of anything I need to accept.

▶ I accept myself as I am.

▶ I am not sure if I really accept myself as I am.

▶ I want to accept myself as I am.

▶ I want to understand more about acceptance.

▶ Other: _____ .

Chapter 12

Forgiveness

To forgive means to accept that something has happened, and then to let go of the emotional pain associated with it.

People may think about their lives and choose to forgive other people for certain things they did or said. We may forgive other people, but the act of forgiving actually benefits us—the people who do the forgiving—by helping us let go of the emotional pain. This means we don't have to feel the emotional pain anymore. (See chapter 2 for information about emotional pain.)

People may forgive others, but they may also choose to forgive themselves for things they have done, thought, or felt. Forgiveness is quiet and personal, but it is powerful. Forgiveness requires courage and love. Researchers have found that that people who forgive are among those who obtain a greater a sense of well-being and more happiness.

I will circle or highlight what is true for me. ✏️

▶ I have bad feelings about something or someone. The bad feelings are because _____ .

▶ There are people whom I want to forgive. I want to forgive (names):

_____

_____

▶ There is something I did, said, or felt that I now regret. I want to forgive myself for _____ .

▶ I have questions or something to say about forgiveness:

_____

_____

_____ .

Gratitude

Scientific studies have shown that expressing gratitude can have a significant effect on many aspects of our lives, including increasing our happiness and emotional and physical well-being.

Gratitude includes:

- Appreciating things, events, experiences, or people
- Remembering the good things that have happened
- Thanking someone for something they have done or given
- Thanking a higher source (for example, God)
- Appreciating nature

People who are grateful have some of these characteristics:

- More energy
- More happiness, more hope and positive feelings
- More likely to feel connected to others and to life around them
- More forgiving with others
- Less depressed, lonely, anxious, or envious

It's best to focus on gratitude once or twice per week. It can be done by keeping a gratitude journal in a book or on my laptop or tablet.

I will circle or highlight what is true for me. 🖉

▶ I am interested in feeling more gratitude.

▶ I am interested in expressing gratitude on a regular basis.

▶ I'd like to write in a gratitude journal.

▶ I'm not interested now, but maybe I will be sometime in the future.

▶ I'd like some help in feeling gratitude in my life.

▶ Other: _____.

Why Feel and Express Gratitude?

People often "take things for granted." This means they may not notice some of the good things in their lives. Sometimes people only pay attention to the things they do not like. They may think too much about the people who bother them. They may spend their time thinking about what they do not like, what they lack, or what is missing from their lives. If they do this, their days and nights will be filled with feelings about things that make them feel bad.

Wise people know that paying attention to what is good, and being grateful for the good things, is a good way to live. These people will feel that their lives are full of good and positive experiences.

Saying "thank you" to others and keeping a gratitude journal are wise things to do. Paying attention to what to be grateful for increases the chances of feeling that life is full of more good things than bad things.

I will circle, highlight, and write what is true for me. 🖉

▶ I mostly notice things I don't like in my life.

▶ I sometimes notice good things—things I like in my life.

▶ I'd like to keep a gratitude journal.

▶ Some good things in my life are: _____ .

▶ I usually don't thank people.

▶ If I were going to thank someone, I would thank (name)

_____

for this: _____ .

▶ I usually thank people when they have done something for me.

▶ Other: _____ .

Courage

Courage is the quality of mind and spirit that helps a person face fear or uncertainty with confidence. Courage helps a person do what may seem too difficult or what feels impossible to accomplish. Instead of giving up, a person can choose to have courage.

Courage is the antidote to fear. Every person needs courage to live in the world. It takes courage to do things that feel too difficult. Sometimes it takes courage to talk to people. Sometimes it takes courage to get up in the morning and face the day. It takes courage to learn about oneself, to accept some things, and to communicate with others.

Anyone can choose to have courage. With courage, a person can feel confident when trying new things. Choosing courage and trying what seems difficult help a person become stronger, wiser, and happier.

I will (circle), highlight, and write what is true for me. 🖉

▶ I understand what courage is.

▶ I have had to be brave many times.

▶ Sometimes I am afraid or worried about: _____ .

▶ I need courage to do these things: _____ .

▶ I have something to say or questions about courage:

_____

_____

_____ .

Kindness

Scientific studies have shown that doing small acts of kindness, beyond what we normally do, and varying the types of things we do (not always the same kind deeds), lead to a greater sense of happiness. Kind deeds involve helping others. Being kind may …

- Help me think of others more positively

- Increase a feeling of being connected to others

- Distract me from my own problems

- Improve my self-image

- Help me become a compassionate person

- Improve my self-confidence

- Lead others to like and appreciate who I am

- Decrease depression

- Increase a sense of well-being and a feeling of happiness

I will circle or highlight what is true for me. 🖉

▶ I am interested in experimenting with doing more kind deeds.

▶ I'm interested in doing more kind deeds, but I'm not sure what to do.

▶ I'd like to help other people sometimes.

▶ I am not interested in doing kind deeds.

▶ I'm not interested now, but maybe I will be sometime in the future.

▶ I'd like some help in figuring out how to be more kind.

▶ Other: _____

_____ .

Relationships

Research shows that close relationships increase a feeling of well-being and happiness in a person's life. Relationships do not have to be romantic relationships. Having a friend increases feelings of happiness. Here is a list of how to nurture all kinds of relationships, be they friends or romantic relationships.

- Agree on a specific time to be together or a time to IM. If each person has different needs related to how much time to share, be honest about your needs and come to an agreement that is healthy for both of you. Use a calendar to schedule agreed upon times.

- Express what you admire about the other person—what you appreciate. Express the positive things when you notice them.

- Pay attention when the person tells you about good things that have happened; celebrate his or her personal successes.

- When there are disagreements, try to discuss them calmly. It may help to ask for a break from talking and schedule a time later to continue. Remember to add it to the schedule or calendar. You may want to suggest typing instead of talking.

- Pay attention to a person when she is telling you what she is feeling or thinking about—her inner life. Listen to her. If it is hard to concentrate or understand while she is talking, tell her you want to hear what she has to say, but you'd rather have the conversation by typing.

- Communicate your own thoughts and feelings—your inner life. This can also be done by typing in person or through e-mail.

Review the three categories of communication that are discussed in the workbook pages called "Especially for Older Readers" in chapter 8.

Remember that communication can happen through talking or typing. If your friend is unfamiliar with communicating through typing, you can suggest experimenting with this method. Read chapter 8 either alone or together with your friend or romantic partner.

Chapter 12

More about Relationships

Often, when people think about relationships, they think of typical friendships or romantic relationships. They think of seeing and doing things together in person. However, there are other types of relationships with others that may add to a person's feeling of well-being and happiness. For example, a person may have a good relationship with an animal friend. Sometimes the animal friend may be the person's best friend. It is vitally important that the person take good care of the animal friend, making sure that the animal is fed healthy food, kept clean, and taken care of by a vet when necessary. It is important to spend time with the animal friend and to treat the animal friend kindly and with love. Animal friendships are sometimes among the closest and deepest relationships a person has.

Another type of relationship may be with an online friend. Safety has been discussed in detail in the last section of chapter 10. In cases where an online acquaintance truly becomes a good friend, most of the suggestions listed on the previous page hold true.

I will (circle) or highlight what is true for me. 🖉

▶ I have an animal friend (or more than one animal friend). His or her name(s) is: _____.

▶ My animal friend is my closest relationship.

▶ I treasure my animal friend(s).

▶ I have an online friend. His or her name is: _____.

▶ I have read the information on page 346 in chapter 10.

▶ Other comment about this topic:_____

_____.

Love

People use the word *love* for different reasons. There are different meanings for the word *love*.

Sometimes people say they love a thing, like a toy or game. Or, they may say they love a certain book, TV show, video, or DVD. Sometimes people say they love *doing something*, like playing a sport or drawing pictures, or using their laptop. Most of these "loves" have to do with enjoying something in the physical or material world.

Sometimes people say they love *an idea* or love thinking about *something important* to them. Sometimes they say they love a *person*. Sometimes people say they love *nature*, or they love *God*.

A special kind of love is described as "unconditional love" or "true compassion." This type of love stays strong, even when a person is upset, worried, sad, or angry. "Agape" (pronounced "ah-GHA-pee") is the Greek word for this special kind of love. A Christian practice is for people to love others, even others that do not love them back.

"Loving kindness" is another way of understanding what true love is. A Buddhist practice teaches people to feel loving kindness for the earth and all living things.

Teaching about love is an important part of most religions and spiritual traditions worldwide.

Researchers have discovered that people who feel this type of special love in their lives have a greater sense of well-being and happiness.

Chapter 12

Faith

Faith is feeling confident that things happen the way they do for a reason. Having faith is knowing that things are and will be okay.

We may not know the reason why things happen the way they do, but we can try to accept and trust in the process of life. When people have faith, they are able to more easily accept what happens in life.

People may have faith in another person. People may have faith in themselves. People may have faith in an idea or a belief. People may have faith in God or a higher power. People may have faith in many things or in one big thing.

Having faith that there is a reason for living, even when we don't know what it is, helps people deal with the ups and downs of life. Researchers have discovered that people who have faith also have a greater sense of well-being and happiness.

I will circle , highlight, and write what is true for me. 🖉

▶ I usually feel confident that things are and will be okay.

▶ I believe that things will work out okay in the end.

▶ Sometimes I am not sure if things are okay.

▶ I have faith in certain people. The person or people whom I trust are (names): _____ .

▶ I have faith in certain ideas or beliefs.

▶ I have faith in God.

▶ I have faith in _____ .

▶ I don't know if I have faith.

▶ I don't have much faith in anything.

▶ I would like to talk with someone about faith.

▶ Other: _____

_____ .

Live One Day at a Time

To "live one day at a time" suggests that a person thinks about the present moment, with his or her full attention on what's happening right now. Another way to say this is to "be here now." It is also called "being present."

It is good to have future goals to work toward; however, it is also important to experience the present moment each day and to live one day at a time.

Living one day at a time can be compared to walking up stairs. When walking up stairs, people take one step at a time, eventually getting to the top. But, on the way up, they must keep their attention on each single step, one by one, or they may fall.

Each single step can be compared to living each single day, one day at a time. Step by step. Day by day.

The idea of living one day at a time is to keep our attention on what is happening right now and doing our best (page 73) in this moment, this day. It reminds us to experience life in the present moment. Researchers have found that "living one day at a time" helps increase a feeling of well-being and happiness.

I will (circle), highlight, and write what is true for me. 🖉

▶ I am interested in understanding more about what it means to live one day at a time.

▶ Sometimes I think about what is going to happen in the future.

▶ Sometimes I wonder what is going to happen.

There is more information about this topic on the next page.

More about Living One Day at a Time

I will circle **, highlight, and write what is true for me.** 🖊

I worry about the future, and it is hard for me to live one day at a time. If this is true, I can try to do the following:

▶ Have someone help me write my schedule each day.

▶ Check my schedule when I am not sure what is going to happen.

▶ Write any changes on the schedule.

▶ Have someone help me add information to a weekly or monthly calendar.

▶ Check with the other people in my life about events or other things that need to be included on the daily schedule and the calendar.

▶ After updating my schedule and calendar, try to remember to "be present" and do my best today, moment by moment.

▶ Write my worries on a piece of paper that I keep in a "worry box," so I don't have to keep thinking about them.

▶ Sometimes I worry or wonder about something in particular—something very specific in the future. I sometimes worry about this: _____

_____

_____ .

▶ I want to learn more about "living one day at a time."

▶ I have something to say or questions to ask: _____

_____

_____ .

"Ups and Downs"

"Ups" are considered the things people enjoy. "Ups" are the things that help make a person feel happy or joyful or content or satisfied or another nice feeling.

"Downs" are considered the things that make a person feel sad or angry or afraid or another uncomfortable feeling.

Life is made up of both ups and downs. Some wise people say that experiencing the "downs" helps us notice and appreciate the "ups." For many of us, it may not be possible to know "up" without contrasting it with "down."

Life is full of "ups and downs." I will circle, highlight, and write what is true for me.

I am interested in understanding more about what it means for life to be "full of ups and downs."

Some of the "ups" in my life are: _____ ,

_____ ,

_____ .

Some of the "downs" in my life are: _____ ,

_____ ,

_____ .

A Positive Attitude

Attitude refers to a way people think. Attitude affects how people act. It affects how they grow into adults. It is the energy that "feeds" thoughts and behavior. A positive attitude is a way of thinking that is healthy and helpful.

The results of some experiments show that plants grow strong and healthy when subjected to music that creates a positive feeling. The experiments also showed that plants grow weak and sickly when subjected to music that creates negative feelings. Some doctors have noticed that sick people who have a positive attitude often get well sooner than sick people who have a negative attitude.

Laboratory results of controlled experiments with water and freezing conditions have shown that beautiful snowflake crystals are formed when water is surrounded by a positive attitude. A negative attitude results in no snowflake crystals, or badly formed crystals, as explained in the book, *The Secret of Water*, by Masaru Emoto.

Researchers who study happiness have found that having a positive attitude is one of the ways to increase a person's sense of well-being and happiness.

I will circle or highlight what is true for me. 🖉

▶ I usually have a positive attitude.

▶ I try to have a positive attitude, but it's hard for me.

▶ Usually, I do not try to have a positive attitude.

▶ I'd like to see the book, *The Secret of Water*, by Masaru Emoto.

▶ Other comment: _____

_____ .

Developing a Positive Attitude

It is natural for people to experience happiness, sadness, anger, frustration, fear, worry, and other emotions at different times, on different days. But, people can learn to practice thoughts and behaviors that are healthy and helpful, even when feeling unhappy or anxious. Try this when feeling unhappy:

Notice how you are feeling. You may want to write or draw while doing this. Take a few deep breaths and let your body relax. Let go of tension in your body until you feel calmer. Use your favorite relaxation strategies. (See pages 429 and 444.)

Continue relaxing and/or do some stretching (page 428) and/or cardio exercise (pages 427 and 445). Afterward, be willing to let go of the uncomfortable emotions you felt earlier. Forgive others and yourself. (See page 448.) Be willing to believe that something positive may be learned or gained from the current situation. Read through the pages in this chapter and reflect on one or more of the following ideas: courage, acceptance, forgiveness, faith, gratitude, kindness, and love. Learning from mistakes and following the Seven-Step Plan (pages 87-88) is an example of keeping a positive attitude after making a mistake.

Communicate by talking or typing, in person or by e-mail, with a trusted person about wanting to find something positive in the current situation. Read pages of this book together.

A positive attitude is a healthy way of being. Researchers have found that having a positive attitude is one of the factors in feeling a sense of well-being and happiness.

Live Life to the Fullest

"Doing your best" (page 73), "learning from mistakes" (pages 87-88), and "having a positive attitude" (page 459) help people live life to the fullest.

Experiencing life, with all its "ups and downs" (page 460), is another part of living life to the fullest.

Living a life to the fullest means accepting (page 447) and being grateful (page 449) for the ups and downs. Celebrating the "ups" and learning from the "downs" is living a full life.

I will circle, highlight, and write what is true for me. 🖉

▶ I am interested in understanding more about what it means to live life to the fullest.

▶ I want to learn more about some of the things mentioned on this page.

▶ I want to learn more about: _____ ,
_____ ,
_____ .

▶ I don't want to learn more about any of these things.

▶ Other comment or question: _____ ,
_____ ,
_____ .

Making the World a Better Place

What does this really mean?

The place refers to planet Earth. *A better place* means a better environment for people and other living things. It may mean improvements in physical health, safety and security, emotional experiences, mental development, and spiritual awareness. It may mean a healthier environment for all of nature, including plants, animals, and the Earth in general.

Every person, young and old, can do things to make something better in the world. Sharing your talents, skills, and interests with others may make the world a better place. A piece of artwork, a smoothly working piece of machinery, a fiddle tune that makes someone tap their foot, sending a holiday card, making an interesting photograph, organizing an event, writing an essay, sharing an idea, explaining how something works to someone, giving someone a ride, taking out the trash, and on and on … little and big things may make moments in this world better. Offering an act of kindness toward someone makes the world a better place—for that moment, it is better. Working for something that you believe in makes the world a better place.

Researchers have found that people who do things that make the world a better place typically enjoy a greater feeling of well-being and happiness.

For an extensive list of autism-friendly ideas that can help make the world a better place, see chapter 16, pages 282-289, from *Understanding Death and Illness and What They Teach about Life* (Future Horizons, 2009).

For Parents, Teachers, and Therapists

"If we can keep working to gain self-awareness, then, as time goes on, it becomes possible to do more than merely survive. It becomes possible to take an active part in charting the course of one's life. It becomes possible to find fulfillment."

—Dave Spicer

Ideas in This Chapter:

☑ Exercise

☑ Relaxation

☑ Diet

☑ Sleep

☑ Research on happiness

Exercise

Develop an exercise program for your child and include it in her daily schedule. Running and doing other cardio exercise helps reduce the buildup of anxiety and often results in a marked decrease in self-injurious and aggressive behaviors. For some children, two exercise periods each day may be helpful.

Help your teenager find exercise that is enjoyable so it becomes something he or she looks forward to. For many teens, using weight machines at the YMCA or the local health club is the perfect structure. Using the computerized program for each machine, following a prescribed circuit, recording progress, and generally having the same routine each time may keep him or her interested in working out. Outdoors, you may find a workout circuit at a park or trail. Inviting a friend or relative to be a workout partner for your child will add a social element, at the level of parallel play, which may make it enjoyable for both.

See workbook pages 427-428 and 445-446 for exercise ideas and page 110 for an example of exercise time included on a child's schedule.

Relaxation

Explore a variety of supportive strategies for relaxation until you find one that works for your child or teen. Teach relaxation routines and visual imagery through the use of written or picture directions. Try listening to recordings of instructions and/or music. Try watching videos that visually teach a relaxation routine or ones that show pictures your child enjoys that are relaxing for him. You might want to find a therapist who is experienced with relaxation strategies to help you locate resources and/or create your own (music and/or videos).

Your town or city may have yoga instructors or meditation instructors who work with children. Observe one of the sessions without your child present, so you will know whether or not it would be appropriate for him or her. If you ask, an instructor may provide private sessions and/or be willing for you to make a video of him or her for your child's practice at home.

As with other strategies, the key may be to link the relaxation routine to your child's focused interest. (See the entry on Ty's schedule for "Train Trip" with Ms Cramer on page 110.) For children whose stimming serves to help them feel relaxed and centered, using or modifying a favorite way to stim may work beautifully. Examples could be having your child toss a soft or squishy ball from one hand to another, rock in a rocking chair, or fidget with something in his hand, while relaxing on a beanbag. Make sure that the particular stimming routine is one that is relaxing for him and not stimulating.

And, as with other strategies, it is best to build a positive, preventative routine by having your child learn and practice the relaxation routine on a regular, daily basis. Do not introduce these types of strategies for the first time when he is upset. Crisis moments are NOT the time to try to teach something new. The more familiar he is with a certain strategy, the more effective it will be when he needs to use it in times of real need. See pages 429 and 444 for more ideas and pages 110-113 for an example of relaxation time included on a schedule.

Diet

There is an abundance of nutritional advice available in bookstores and natural food stores and of course on the Internet. Specific diets for children with autism are recommended by some professionals and parents. Many autistic children have very strict food preferences. The combination of these two factors can make "diet and nutrition" an overwhelming and confusing subject for parents.

Some dietary regimes, such as gluten-free, casein-free diets, have been found have positive effects for some children and adults with autism. High costs can be involved, as well as a change in lifestyle and food restrictions. Choosing a specialized diet is a personal decision on the part of the family and their healthcare practitioner. Especially when contemplating expensive, time-consuming, and dramatic changes in diet, educate yourself as much as possible.

Look for research and talk with other parents who have tried the diet with their child. Consult with your doctor. *What are the pros and cons? Is this something you will be able to follow through with every day? Will your child cooperate?* If you decide to try a particular diet with your child, use his schedule and other visual strategies to prepare him for the changes in his meal routines and food choices. Above all, be sure to allow a realistic trial period, after which you can evaluate the effectiveness of the diet. It is not my intent here to evaluate or recommend any particular diet.

Most of us realize that the health of our bodies is directly affected by the type and quality of the food we ingest, along with other lifestyle factors. It is common sense that the better we feel, the better we are able to handle the demands and stressors in daily life. This is true for your child, as well. It is important to help him eat in a healthy manner, as much as possible. This may be extremely difficult if your child is a picky eater. There may be particular vitamins or supplements that will support his overall health. (See page 111 for an example of a schedule that indicates a time to take vitamins.) It is comforting to know that most parents of older children and adults with autism will say that as their children grew up, they were more willing to try new foods. If you have questions or concerns about your child's nutrition, you should consult an experienced physician or nutritionist, especially those who are familiar with a broad range of children.

Sleep

It is not unusual for autistic children, teenagers, and adults to experience differences and/or disturbances in their sleep cycles and sleep habits. Many autistic individuals simply enjoy the dark and quiet of night—it may be easier and more rewarding to be awake when everyone else is quietly sleeping and the noise of the world is at a minimum. Family members with children who do not fall asleep easily or those who wake up in the middle of the night and stay awake most of the night are often sleep deprived. Experiment with the list of suggestions on page 430 and research ideas online and by talking with physicians, sensory-integration therapists, or sleep experts. Do your best to create a bedtime routine and pay attention to the sensory aspects that may be affecting your child's ability to relax. Some have found help by taking melatonin, which is available over the counter in the U.S. Make sure you check with your doctor prior to trying over-the-counter medications.

Research on happiness

This chapter is devoted to introducing your child or teenager to aspects of life and specific practices to include in daily life that contribute to feeling a sense of well-being and happiness. Most of the topics in this chapter have been studied by various researchers in the field of positive psychology and have been found to be part of the equation that appear to affect the 40% of happiness we can influence. Apart from the scientific feature, these themes represent solid and positive cultural truths that nourish the seeker of an emotionally, mentally, spiritually, and physically healthy life—as well as being just plain old good ideas to help a person feel better!

Pick and choose the pages that may be most relevant for your child at any given point in time. Use this chapter as a starting point for exploring important lifelong practices, and return to it as your child grows. These pages are meant for adults, as well as older children and teens. In addition to matters dealing with taking care of the body, such as *exercise* and *relaxation*, the author has strived to offer concrete, clear, and practical information for abstract qualities such as *kindness, respect, acceptance, gratitude, forgiveness, love, faith,* and a *positive attitude.*

The pages that feature facts about how many people on the spectrum there are in the world and figuring out how many there are in your town are included to help your child begin to feel and know that he or she isn't alone in being autistic.

Advice such as *not worrying about fitting in, living life to the fullest,* and *making the world a better place* can be complex but important concepts— life lessons—to grow into. It has been a wonderful exploration for me to attempt to break down such a collection of beautiful qualities and describe them in ways that make them understandable to a wide range of individuals. It is my sincere prayer that they will help readers develop a sense of understanding and contribute to a fulfilling life experience.

What I feel strongly to be a basic, essential, and fundamental need— making self-expression as accessible as possible—has been repeated throughout this book on several of the workbook pages and in the sections for parents, teachers, and therapists. In this chapter, you will find it again on the pages called "Expressing How I Am Today," followed by the sample Communication Form, "How I Am Today."

The material on nurturing relationships is more advanced but contains real-world, concrete suggestions and support for maturing individuals who understand that they must participate in caring for their relationships with friends and romantic partners—and while doing so, respect and take care of themselves.

Illustrators and Other Contributors

Jade McWilliams

Jade McWilliams drew the stunning and astute illustrations found on the title pages of all 12 chapters in this book. She enthusiastically and immediately agreed to take on the project and sincerely hopes that her drawings visually and easily convey the topics of each chapter, without the viewer having to read or listen to words.

Jade is an autistic self-advocate who wants autistic people to be able to live in ways that make them feel happy, comfortable, and satisfied. She is especially interested in activism that focuses on alternative communication, play, art, storytelling, mentoring, and visual accessibility. Jade considers herself a "maker." She loves to draw, sew, color, and create beautiful things with her hands. You can see some of her creations by visiting her Etsy shop (*www.zfjade.etsy.com*).

To learn more about Jade and her thoughts and experiences with neurodiversity, autism, and being an augmented and alternative communication user, visit her blog at *www.astronautsarecool.com*.

Jade loves monkeys; her favorite is the white-faced capuchin monkey from Costa Rica. She also loves science fiction and is a big fan of Star Trek, Planet of the Apes, and Frank Herbert's *Dune* books.

If you would like to purchase prints of her illustrations from this book, you can order them by e-mailing Jade at *astronautzfjade@gmail.com*.

Thomas Johnson

The 70 small pencil sketches throughout the book were drawn by Thomas Johnson at age 10. To see samples of his talent at age 18, view his beautiful illustrations in my book, *Understanding Death and Illness and What They Teach About Life,* or visit my Web site at *catherinefaherty.com.*

Maria White

The pencil sketch of the boy with blocks (page 435) was drawn by Maria White in 1999. Maria was a major illustrator in the initial publication of this book in 2000.

Kelly Davis

Kelly's enthusiasm for editing the parent and teacher sections of the first edition of this book comes from both personal and professional experience. Kelly was educated as a historian and worked in advertising and publishing. Kelly's two children, now young adults, are on the autism spectrum. Her assistance and perspective came as a refreshing boost in the completion of the first edition of this book. Kelly is currently the creator and owner of a successful small business, Lusty Monk Mustard, a delicious, Asheville-made product. Visit *lustymonk.com* to "get a taste" of Kelly's mischievous and light-hearted spirit.

Teresa Johnson

Teresa's encouragement and support were evident during all the phases of creating the first edition of this book. Early on, she suggested that her son Thomas contribute the small sketches for the parent and teacher sections. She helped structure his "assignments," keeping him on track. At the time, Teresa worked for the Autism Society of North Carolina as a parent advocate. Today, Teresa owns and runs a delightfully unique coffee shop in downtown Asheville. Stop in when you are in town! Visit her Web site at *wallstreetcoffeehouse.web.com*.

John Engle

When I write (and talk), I have a tendency to repeat myself. John Engle, who is known to keep a clear, orderly, and uncluttered environment, did an amazing job of editing the wording in the original workbook pages. He located every inconsistency, disagreeing pronoun, unnecessary repetition, and redundancy … all of my verbal clutter! However, some pages were written after John returned his edits to me, along with the additions for this edition. If there are grammatical faults, I take full responsibility for them. John would never have let them pass!

John is a gifted old-time musician, fiddle teacher, and philosopher. His beautiful prose poem is featured on page 337 at the conclusion of my book, *Understanding Death and Illness and What They Teach About Life*. More recently, John was interviewed and featured in the film documentary "Neurotypical," by Adam Larsen.

Dave Spicer

Dave is quoted at the beginning of many of the sections for parents and teachers, and his thoughts about creativity are featured in the parent and teacher section at the end of chapter 4. As an autistic self-advocate and activist, Dave has contributed to the autism community in myriad ways. Dave once stated that his "peak skill is being able

to use words to describe what it is like to have autism." Dave's gentle and thoughtful manner, articulate explanations, and enlightening visual images have a powerful effect on all who hear him speak.

Dave's contributions touch people locally, nationally, and internationally. Years ago, Dave began presenting at professional events, such as TEACCH Winter In-service and the 1998 Swedish Autism Society Asperger Syndrome Conference, near Stockholm. One of his essays has been published in *High-Functioning Autism or Asperger Syndrome?*, in the series *Current Issues in Autism*, edited by Eric Schopler, Gary Mesibov, and Linda Kunce.

Dave has attended and presented at Autreat (*autreat.com*), an annual retreat sponsored by Autism Network International, an organization by and for autistic people. He was the first autistic person to serve on the board of the Autism Society of North Carolina. Most recently, Dave gave a presentation on the opening day of Autism Pride Week, held in Asheville, NC, in June 2013. To read Dave's collections of essays, poems, and conference presentations, go to *davespicer.org*.

Irene Vassos

Irene Vassos is a talented fabric artist, a delightful musician and singer, and, before her retirement, a gifted technology coordinator

for Pittsfield public schools in the Berkshire mountains of western Massachusetts. She is particularly inspired when creating databases and training people to use her beloved Macs in creative ways. Irene's encouragement and technology consultation helped keep me on track from the very beginning to the end of the original edition of this book. She breathes life into her many projects, and I was fortunate to have Irene's help with this one. Her computer skills and eye for design are at the core of this book's visual appeal. My favorite thing about Irene is that she is my cousin.

Acknowledgments

I am grateful for the immense support I received during the initial writing of the first edition of this book and when I worked on this revised and updated version.

I first want to thank my former colleagues, the staff of the Asheville TEACCH Center, for their support during the writing of the first edition back in 1999. This multitalented group of people cheerfully took over my responsibilities when I took time off to write. I am grateful to the late Eric Schopler, PhD, founder and first TEACCH director, for his humanity and genius. And much gratitude to Gary Mesibov, PhD, former director of TEACCH, for helping us understand autism as a culture, and for his insight, mentorship, and generous advice whenever I ask. Thank you to Jack Wall, PhD, former director of the Charlotte TEACCH Center, for permission to include "Mind the Gap," and to Teresa Johnson for her help in describing the details of its use.

Thank you to the talented artists, Thomas Johnson and Maria White, whose drawings were selected from the first edition of this book. A very special thank you to Jade McWilliams, whose illustrations grace the title pages of all 12 chapters in this new edition. I am in awe of Jade's commitment and devotion to visual communication in such beautiful ways.

Thank you to Dave Spicer for his commitment to education about autism and for writing his thoughts about artistic talent; to John Engle for editing the first edition of the workbook pages and sharing his thoughts so candidly; to Kelly Davis for her enthusiasm and clarity in editing the sections for parents and teachers in the first edition; to our photographer, Marilyn Ferikes; and to Adela Allen for permission to begin the book with her quote. Thank you to my cousin, Irene Vassos, for welcoming innumerable marathon weeks in front of the computer, and to Kemper Brown and the late Ken Jones of the Electronic Office, who patiently picked me up from the depths of despair during a computer crisis in the initial writing of this book. Thank you to Wayne Gilpin and Kelly Gilpin of Future Horizons, who agreed to my proposal of this updated and revised edition. Thank you to Emoke B'Racz (owner of Malaprop's, Asheville's very best independent bookstore in the world) and Gail Addis for providing me with my very own writing retreat—a sacred space in which to work on this newly updated book.

Thank you to the many children, families, and autistic adults whom I have the privilege of knowing. You truly enrich my life. I humbly thank you for giving me an intimate view of the fascinating culture of autism.

And, finally, thank you to my friends, who always cheer me on, and to the following members of my family for their unconditional support, without which this project would not have happened. To my mother, who gave me creativity, stamina, and drive; to my late father, who taught me about empathy and the importance of service; to both of them, for the belief they instilled in me that "For every problem, there is a solution;" to my husband, who teaches me every day about selflessness; to my son, who is a model of serving people with dedication, an open heart, and an intelligent mind; and to my grandson, who gives me joy. I am forever grateful to the Source of all good things!

About the Author

Catherine Faherty taught a variety of students with diverse learning styles before creating a model classroom for elementary-aged students with ASD in the Buncombe County schools in 1985. From 1990 to 2012, she worked as an autism specialist with the internationally recognized TEACCH program in Asheville, North Carolina, as a parent consultant; child and adult therapist; consultant to school programs; trainer of teachers and other professionals locally, nationally, and internationally; and facilitator of social groups for adults on the spectrum, along with support and education groups for parents and family members. She has written manuals used in TEACCH trainings and co-developed a multitude of training models. Catherine is the author of three books, one of which was recognized as the Autism Society of America's 2009 Outstanding Literary Work. She is also one of the few Social Stories instructors authorized by Carol Gray. Her mentoring and consultation (via long-distance technology) are sought after by therapists, teachers, and parents in the United States and abroad. She speaks at conferences and provides training worldwide. Catherine is a devoted ally to autistic self-advocates. For more information, visit *catherinefaherty.com.*

31690 022605 57

Carmel Clay Public Library
Renewal Line: 317-814-3936
carmelclaylibrary.org

Withdrawn From
Carmel Clay Public Library

CHECKED FOR WRITING

New 4/2/21 BW		
10/27/22 KB		